Learning Angular

Second Edition

A no-nonsense guide to building real-world apps
with Angular 5

Christoffer Noring

Pablo Deeleman

BIRMINGHAM - MUMBAI

Learning Angular

Second Edition

First published: May 2016

Second edition: December 2017

Production reference: 1051217

Published by Packt Publishing Ltd.
Livery Place
35 Livery Street
Birmingham
B3 2PB, UK.
ISBN 978-1-78712-492-9

www.packtpub.com

Credits

Authors
Christoffer Noring
Pablo Deeleman

Copy Editor
Safis Editing

Reviewer
Pablo Deeleman

Project Coordinator
Ulhas Kambali

Commissioning Editor
Ashwin Nair

Proofreader
Safis Editing

Acquisition Editor
Reshma Raman

Indexer
Pratik Shirodkar

Content Development Editor
Nikhil Borkar

Graphics
Jason Monteiro

Technical Editor
Subhalaxmi Nadar

Production Coordinator
Arvindkumar Gupta

About the Authors

Christoffer Noring is a software developer with more than 10 years of experience. He has successfully delivered software for different industries, ranging from telecom to aviation. Throughout his career, he has worked on everything, right from databases to frontends. He is very passionate about community and sharing knowledge, which is why he frequently speaks on topics ranging from TDD, React, and NativeScript to Angular. He also writes books and blogs frequently. He holds the title of Google Developer Expert in web technologies and AngularJS/Angular. He is also a Telerik Developer Expert in the mobile framework, NativeScript.

Christoffer currently works for McKinsey as a fullstack developer. He is the author and maintainer of the book, *RxJS Ultimate*, which aims to be a free resource to help the community.

I would like to thank Reshma for reaching out and ensuring that this book happened in the first place. Also, thank you Nikhil for all your comments and words of support. A big thank you to Pablo for ensuring this book lives up to the quality our readers deserve.
Sara my wife, my life partner, my team mate. Thank you for your ideas and, most of all, your encouragement and patience, and for pushing me towards my true potential.
I would also like to direct a big thank you to my brother, Magnus, for your support and showing me that hard work pays off. To my nephew, Vilgot, thank you for the light, love, and joy you have brought and are bringing to our family, and for reminding me what is important in life.
Lastly, a big big thank you to my parents Berith and Oystein for your love and support and turning me into the person I am.

Pablo Deeleman is a former UI/UX designer who fell in love with JavaScript and CSS back in 1998, during the good old days of Netscape Navigator and Microsoft Internet Explorer 3. The discovery of Node.js back in 2011 became a turning point in his career, from where he decided to embrace full-time JavaScript-driven development, carving out a career as a JavaScript full stack engineer with special focus on single-page application development.

With sound expertise in libraries and frameworks, such as Backbone.js, Knockout.js, Polymer, React, AngularJs, and Angular, Pablo Deeleman built his career in a wide range of companies encompassing internationally acclaimed tube sites, fintech start-ups, and award-winning gaming and gambling sites. He currently works as a senior frontend engineer and Angular specialist for Red Hat, the multinational company providing open source software products to the enterprise community.

Pablo has also authored *Learning Angular 2* (Packt, 2016) and currently lives in sunny and bustling Barcelona, where he fulfills his other great passion: playing piano.

Producing a book is always a daunting task, and its success is not only due to the hard work achieved by its authors but also due to the team that makes it possible behind the scenes. In that sense, Reshma Raman, Nikhil Borkar, and the awesome people at Packt have all my respect and appreciation. Thank you very much indeed to Christoffer Noring; you have turned this project into an unparalleled reference guide in the Angular arena, which will help countless people to build big things and become great developers in the years to come. Your contribution to the Angular community is priceless.
I'd also like to thank Gemma, my partner in crime and my accomplice for her patience and understanding. Kudos to my team at Red Hat and to my very own personal frontend squad: Pere, David, and Eric. I only have words of appreciation to my IT family in Barcelona who always support and encourage me to keep challenging myself: Andreia, Marc, Gabriel, and Rafael. Also, a big thank you goes to Gerard and Antonio Jesus, my favorite backend engineers ever.
Last but not least, thanks to my parents, Paul and Pepa, and my late brother, Raul, for allowing me to sit at the computer for so many hours when I was a child. That sacrifice finally paid off.

www.PacktPub.com

For support files and downloads related to your book, please visit www.PacktPub.com.

Did you know that Packt offers eBook versions of every book published, with PDF and ePub files available? You can upgrade to the eBook version at www.PacktPub.com and as a print book customer, you are entitled to a discount on the eBook copy. Get in touch with us at service@packtpub.com for more details.

At www.PacktPub.com, you can also read a collection of free technical articles, sign up for a range of free newsletters and receive exclusive discounts and offers on Packt books and eBooks.

https://www.packtpub.com/mapt

Get the most in-demand software skills with Mapt. Mapt gives you full access to all Packt books and video courses, as well as industry-leading tools to help you plan your personal development and advance your career.

Why subscribe?

- Fully searchable across every book published by Packt
- Copy and paste, print, and bookmark content
- On demand and accessible via a web browser

Customer Feedback

Thanks for purchasing this Packt book. At Packt, quality is at the heart of our editorial process. To help us improve, please leave us an honest review on this book's Amazon page at `https://www.amazon.com/dp/1787124924`.

If you'd like to join our team of regular reviewers, you can email us at `customerreviews@packtpub.com`. We award our regular reviewers with free eBooks and videos in exchange for their valuable feedback. Help us be relentless in improving our products!

Table of Contents

Preface

We have come a long way since 2010, when AngularJS was first released. Internet wasn't really made to be an application platform but one for rendering static pages. This has, of course, changed as developers have started treating it more and more as their main application platform. The promise of reaching billions of people has been too enticing. This meant that the web had to grow up. Different approaches have been tried during the years, such as JSP, GWT, Web Forms for .NET, and so on—approaches that have been more or less successful. What is clear is that when AngularJS showed up, it was greeted as a savior. It made it super easy for everyone to quickly create an application with JavaScript, CSS, HTML, and even use AJAX. It's still a valid choice for building small to medium applications.

The easier something is to use, the more likely it is that people will treat it like ketchup and start adding more and more to it to and use it everywhere. AngularJS was never meant for large enterprise applications. The Internet progressed and more and more features became available in the browser. There was an idea of wanting to incorporate all these new features but also to ensure that AngularJS could be used for really large applications. A decision was taken that it would be easier to start over from scratch and create Angular, the successor of AngularJS. And so, on 14 September 2016, the release version of Angular saw the light of day. Since then major versions of Angular have been produced at a furious pace.

We are now on version 5. This does not mean that Angular core concepts have changed, they have been retained. Certain breaking changes have been introduced along the way, but every major version has firstly corrected bugs, introduced new features, and really aimed at making Angular apps as fast as possible and their footprint as small as possible. This is a worthy goal to have in today's mobile-first world.

This book aims to introduce the reader to all the major facets of Angular, and show you how to build small, medium, and, even, large applications. You don't need much knowledge to get started with Angular applications, but there are many layers to it. As your app grows in size, you will want to care about making it prettier, faster, easier to maintain, and so on. This book is written with that in mind. Take your time reading this book. If you want to read a few chapters and build some apps, do it. If you want to jump straight into the more advanced features, then that is your prerogative.

We hope you will enjoy reading this book as much as we enjoyed writing it

What this book covers

Chapter 1, *Creating our First Component in Angular*, covers Semantic versioning. This is an important concept to grasp, so you know whether to adopt new releases based on your needs. This chapter also introduces the reader to the Angular CLI and the reader will be taking their first steps into writing an Angular application.

Chapter 2, *IDEs and Plugins*, introduces you to the most popular IDEs. The most common Angular plugins and snippets are also described to further boost developer productivity.

Chapter 3, *Introducing TypeScript*, introduces TypeScript, which is the chosen language for coding Angular apps. There is more to TypeScript than just adding types. Your code can be made elegant and more secure, and using the right features will save you from typing quite a lot.

Chapter 4, *Implementing Properties and Events in our Components*, covers how to send data to components and how to bind methods to them so that the components have the ability to communicate upstream.

Chapter 5, *Enhancing our Component with Pipes and Directives*, shows how you can make your component more consistent and reusable with the help of pipes and directives.

Chapter 6, *Building an Application with Angular Components*, dives right into our goal of building a real application. We address how to think and how to use the most common structural directives in order to control how the data should be displayed and act when being manipulated by UI elements.

Chapter 7, *Asynchronous Data Services with Angular*, introduces the RxJS library, which not only helps us with AJAX but also facilitates reactive application patterns. All things async become one concept under RxJS, the possibilities that this introduces are endless.

Chapter 8, *Firebase*, explains Firebase, which is a product by Google that allows you to have backend as a service. Firebase lets you focus on building Angular apps while it takes care of almost everything else. The best part is Firebase's reactive nature, which makes chat-like applications as well as collaboration apps a breeze to create.

Chapter 9, *Routing*, explains the concept of routing, so you can scale your application seamlessly.

Chapter 10, *Forms in Angular*, covers the two main ways of dealing with forms and user input: template-driven and the reactive approach.

Chapter 11, *Angular Material*, takes you through Angular Material, which not only offers a beautiful interface but also comes with a bunch of components that will make it a piece of cake to quickly assemble an impressive application.

Chapter 12, *Animating Components with Angular*, covers how well Angular supports the developer in leveraging and controlling quite advanced animations.

Chapter 13, *Unit Testing in Angular*, explains unit testing in Angular. The Angular team has really added first-class support for testing, so you, with a very few lines of code, are able to test all the possible constructs your mind can dream up. Everything from component, service, and directives to E2E testing.

Appendix A, *SystemJS*, covers SystemJS, which is a module loader and used to be the only way to set up an Angular application. It's still a valid way to set up your project. This Appendix will cover the core parts of SystemJS and zoom in on the Angular set up bit in particular.

Appendix B, *Webpack with Angular*, aims at showing the developer how to set up your Angular project with Webpack. There definitely exists a user base that wants complete control of every aspect of a web project. If that is you, then this appendix is for you.

What you need for this book

To really appreciate this book, we assume that you are familiar with HTML, CSS, and JavaScript, to a certain degree, as well as calling services with AJAX. We also assume that you have a fair understanding of REST. Modern web application development has become quite a daunting task, but it is our hope that you will, after having read this book, feel that you understand more about what's going on, and that you will also feel more than able to take on your next web development project using Angular.

As you will spend most of your time writing JavaScript, HTML, or CSS code, we only assume that you have access to a decent text editor. The more accomplished editor you use, the more help you will get, which is why we introduce some plugins and best practices in this book to make your everyday work less painful.

Who this book is for

This book is intended for web developers with no prior knowledge of Angular but who are experienced in JavaScript, Node.js, HTML, and CSS and are reasonably familiar with the idea of Single Page Applications.

Conventions

In this book, you will find a number of text styles that distinguish between different kinds of information. Here are some examples of these styles and an explanation of their meaning. Code words in text, database table names, folder names, filenames, file extensions, pathnames, dummy URLs, user input, and Twitter handles are shown as follows: "Import the reactive `Forms` module."

A block of code is set as follows:

```
class AppComponent {
  title:string = 'hello app';
}
```

Any command-line input or output is written as follows:

```
npm install -g @angular/cli
```

New terms and **important words** are shown in bold. Words that you see on the screen, for example, in menus or dialog boxes, appear in the text like this: "We go to the **Database** menu option on our left."

Warnings or important notes appear like this.

Tips and tricks appear like this.

Reader feedback

Feedback from our readers is always welcome. Let us know what you think about this book-what you liked or disliked. Reader feedback is important for us as it helps us develop titles that you will really get the most out of. To send us general feedback, simply email feedback@packtpub.com, and mention the book's title in the subject of your message. If there is a topic that you have expertise in and you are interested in either writing or contributing to a book, see our author guide at www.packtpub.com/authors.

Customer support

Now that you are the proud owner of a Packt book, we have a number of things to help you to get the most from your purchase.

Downloading the example code

You can download the example code files for this book from your account at http://www.packtpub.com. If you purchased this book elsewhere, you can visit http://www.packtpub.com/support and register to have the files emailed directly to you. You can download the code files by following these steps:

1. Log in or register to our website using your email address and password.
2. Hover the mouse pointer on the **SUPPORT** tab at the top.
3. Click on **Code Downloads & Errata**.
4. Enter the name of the book in the **Search** box.
5. Select the book for which you're looking to download the code files.
6. Choose from the drop-down menu where you purchased this book from.
7. Click on **Code Download**.

Once the file is downloaded, please make sure that you unzip or extract the folder using the latest version of:

- WinRAR / 7-Zip for Windows
- Zipeg / iZip / UnRarX for Mac
- 7-Zip / PeaZip for Linux

The code bundle for the book is also hosted on GitHub at https://github.com/PacktPublishing/Learning-Angular-Second-Edition. We also have other code bundles from our rich catalog of books and videos available at https://github.com/PacktPublishing/. Check them out!

Downloading the color images of this book

We also provide you with a PDF file that has color images of the screenshots/diagrams used in this book. The color images will help you better understand the changes in the output. You can download this file from http://www.packtpub.com/sites/default/files/downloads/LearningAngularSecondEdition_ColorImages.pdf.

Errata

Although we have taken every care to ensure the accuracy of our content, mistakes do happen. If you find a mistake in one of our books-maybe a mistake in the text or the code-we would be grateful if you could report this to us. By doing so, you can save other readers from frustration and help us improve subsequent versions of this book. If you find any errata, please report them by visiting http://www.packtpub.com/submit-errata, selecting your book, clicking on the **Errata Submission Form** link, and entering the details of your errata. Once your errata are verified, your submission will be accepted and the errata will be uploaded to our website or added to any list of existing errata under the Errata section of that title. To view the previously submitted errata, go to https://www.packtpub.com/books/content/support and enter the name of the book in the search field. The required information will appear under the **Errata** section.

Piracy

Piracy of copyrighted material on the internet is an ongoing problem across all media. At Packt, we take the protection of our copyright and licenses very seriously. If you come across any illegal copies of our works in any form on the internet, please provide us with the location address or website name immediately so that we can pursue a remedy. Please contact us at copyright@packtpub.com with a link to the suspected pirated material. We appreciate your help in protecting our authors and our ability to bring you valuable content.

Questions

If you have a problem with any aspect of this book, you can contact us at questions@packtpub.com, and we will do our best to address the problem.

1

Creating Our First Component in Angular

When it comes to Angular development, there are some things that are good to know and some things that we need to know to embark on our great journey. One of the things that is good to know is **semantic versioning**. This is good to know because it is the way the Angular team has chosen to deal with changes. This will hopefully make it easier to find the right solutions to future app development challenges when you go to `https://angular.io/` or Stack Overflow and other sites to search for solutions.

Another important, but sometimes painful, topic is that of project setup. It is a necessary evil that needs to be done in the beginning of a project, but getting this right early on can reduce a lot of friction as your application grows with you. Therefore, a large part of this chapter is dedicated to demystifying and enabling you as a developer to save you from future frustrations and migraines.

We will also be able to create our first application at the end of this chapter and get a feel for the anatomy of an Angular application. To sum up, here are the main themes that we will explore in this chapter.

In this chapter, we will:

- Learn about semantic versioning, why it matters, and Angular's take on it
- Discover how we set up our project using Angular CLI
- Create our first application and begin to understand the core concepts in Angular

It's just Angular – introducing semantic versioning

Using semantic versioning is about managing expectations. It's about managing how the user of your application, or library, will react when a change happens to it. Changes will happen for various reasons, either to fix something broken in the code or add/alter/remove a feature. The way authors of frameworks or libraries use to convey what impact a certain change has is by incrementing the version number of the software.

A production-ready software usually has version 1.0 or 1.0.0 if you want to be more specific.

There are three different levels of change that can happen when updating your software. Either you patch it and effectively correct something. Or you make a minor change, which essentially means you add functionality. Or lastly you make a major change, which might completely change how your software works. Let's describe these changes in more detail in the following sections.

Patch change

A patch change means we increment the right most digit by one. Changing the said software from 1.0.0 to 1.0.1 is a small change, usually a bug fix. As a user of that software you don't really have to worry; if anything, you should be happy that something is suddenly working better. The point is, you can safely start using 1.0.1.

Minor change

This means the software is increased from 1.0.0 to 1.1.0. We are dealing with a more severe change as we increase the middle digit by one. This number should be increased when functionality is added to the software and it should still be backwards compatible. Also in this case it should be safe adapting the 1.1.0 version of the software.

Major change

At this stage, the version number increases from 1.0.0 to 2.0.0. Now this is where you need to look out. At this stage, things might have changed so much that constructs have been renamed or removed. It might not be compatible to earlier versions. I'm saying *it might* because a lot of software authors still ensure that there is a decent backwards compatibility, but the main point here is that there is no warranty, no contract, guaranteeing that it will still work.

What about Angular?

The first version of Angular was known by most people as Angular 1; it later became known as AngularJS. It did not use semantic versioning. Most people actually still refer to it as Angular 1.

Then Angular came along and in 2016 it reached production readiness. Angular decided to adopt semantic versioning and this caused a bit of confusion in the developer community, especially when it was announced that there would be an Angular 4 and 5, and so on. Google, as well as the Google Developer Experts, started to explain to people that it wanted people to call the latest version of the framework Angular - just Angular. You can always argue on the wisdom of that decision, but the fact remains, the new Angular is using semantic versioning. This means Angular is the same platform as Angular 4, as well as Angular 11, and so on, if that ever comes out. Adopting semantic versioning means that you as a user of Angular can rely on things working the same way until Google decides to increase the major version. Even then it's up to you if you want to remain on the latest major version or want to upgrade your existing apps.

A fresh start

As mentioned before, Angular represents a full rewrite of the AngularJS framework, introducing a brand new application architecture completely built from scratch in TypeScript, a strict superset of JavaScript that adds optional static typing and support for interfaces and decorators.

In a nutshell, Angular applications are based on an architecture design that comprises of trees of web components interconnected by their own particular I/O interface. Each component takes advantage under the covers of a completely revamped dependency injection mechanism.

To be fair, this is a simplistic description of what Angular really is. However, the simplest project ever made in Angular is cut out by these definition traits. We will focus on learning how to build interoperable components and manage dependency injection in the next chapters, before moving on to routing, web forms, and HTTP communication. This also explains why we will not make explicit references to AngularJS throughout the book. Obviously, it makes no sense to waste time and pages referring to something that will not provide any useful insights on the topic, besides the fact we assume that you might not know about Angular 1.x, so such knowledge does not have any value here.

Web components

Web components is a concept that encompasses four technologies designed to be used together to build feature elements with a higher level of visual expressivity and reusability, thereby leading to a more modular, consistent, and maintainable web. These four technologies are as follows:

- **Templates**: These are pieces of HTML that structure the content we aim to render
- **Custom elements**: These templates not only contain traditional HTML elements, but also the custom wrapper items that provide further presentation elements or API functionalities
- **Shadow DOM**: This provides a sandbox to encapsulate the CSS layout rules and JavaScript behaviors of each custom element
- **HTML imports**: HTML is no longer constrained to host HTML elements, but to other HTML documents as well

In theory, an Angular component is indeed a custom element that contains a template to host the HTML structure of its layout, the latter being governed by a scoped CSS style sheet encapsulated within a shadow DOM container. Let's try to rephrase this in plain English. Think of the range input control type in HTML5. It is a handy way to give our users a convenient input control for entering a value ranging between two predefined boundaries. If you have not used it before, insert the following piece of markup in a blank HTML template and load it in your browser:

```
<input id="mySlider" type="range" min="0" max="100" step="10">
```

You will see a nice input control featuring a horizontal slider in your browser. Inspecting such control with the browser developer tools will unveil a concealed set of HTML tags that were not present at the time you edited your HTML template. There you have an example of shadow DOM in action, with an actual HTML template governed by its own encapsulated CSS with advanced dragging functionality. You will probably agree that it would be cool to do that yourself. Well, the good news is that Angular gives you the toolset required for delivering this very same functionality, so we can build our own custom elements (input controls, personalized tags, and self-contained widgets) featuring the inner HTML markup of our choice and our very own style sheet that does not affect (nor is impacted) by the CSS of the page hosting our component.

Why TypeScript over other syntaxes?

Angular applications can be coded in a wide variety of languages and syntaxes: ECMAScript 5, Dart, ECMAScript 6, TypeScript, or ECMAScript 7.

TypeScript is a typed superset of ECMAScript 6 (also known as ECMAScript 2015) that compiles to plain JavaScript and is widely supported by modern OSes. It features a sound object-oriented design and supports annotations, decorators, and type checking.

The reason why we picked (and obviously recommend) TypeScript as the syntax of choice for instructing how to develop Angular applications in this book is based on the fact that Angular itself is written in this language. Being proficient in TypeScript will give the developer an enormous advantage when it comes to understanding the guts of the framework.

On the other hand, it is worth remarking that TypeScript's support for annotations and type introspection turns out to be paramount when it comes to managing dependency injection and type binding between components with a minimum code footprint, as we will see further down the line in this book.

Ultimately, you can carry out your Angular projects in plain ECMAScript 6 syntax if that is your preference. Even the examples provided in this book can be easily ported to ES6 by removing type annotations and interfaces, or replacing the way dependency injection is handled in TypeScript with the most verbose ES6 way.

For the sake of brevity, we will only cover examples written in TypeScript and actually recommend its use because of its higher expressivity thanks to type annotations, and its neat way of approaching dependency injection based on type introspection out of such type annotations.

Setting up our workspace with Angular CLI

There are different ways to get started, either using the Angular quickstart repository on the `https://angular.io/` site, or installing the scaffolding tool Angular CLI, or lastly, you could use Webpack to set up your project. It is worth pointing out that the standard way of creating a new Angular project is through using *Angular CLI* and scaffold your project. Systemjs, used by the quickstart repository, is something that used to be the default way of building Angular projects. It is now rapidly diminishing, but it is still a valid way of setting up an Angular project. The interested reader is therefore recommended to check the `Appendix A`, *SystemJS* for more information on it.

Setting up a frontend project today is more cumbersome than ever. We used to just include the necessary script with our JavaScript code and a `link` tag for our CSS and `img` tag for our assets and so on. Life used to be simple. Then frontend development became more ambitious and we started splitting up our code in modules, we started using preprocessors for both our code and CSS. All in all, our projects became more complicated and we started to rely on build systems such as Grunt, Gulp, Webpack, and so on. Most developers out there are not huge fans of configuration, they just want to focus on building apps. Modern browsers, however, do more to support the latest ECMAScript standard and some browsers have even started to support modules, which are resolved at runtime. This is far from being widely supported though. In the meantime, we still have to rely on tools for bundling and module support.

Setting up a project with leading frameworks such as React or Angular can be quite difficult. You need to know what libraries to import and ensure that files are processed in the correct order, which leads us into the topic of scaffolding tools. For AngularJS, it was quite popular to use Yeoman to scaffold up a new application quickly and get a lot of nice things preconfigured. React has a scaffolder tool called *create-react-app*, which you probably have saved and it saves countless hours for React developers. Scaffolder tools becomes almost a necessity as complexity grows, but also where every hour counts towards producing business value rather than fighting configuration problems.

The main motivation behind creating the Angular CLI tool was to help developers focus on app building and not so much on configuration. Essentially, with a simple command, you should be able to scaffold an application, add a new construct to it, run tests, or create a production grade bundle. Angular CLI supports all that.

Prerequisites

What you need to get started is to have Git and Node.js installed. Node.js will also install something called NPM, a node package manager that you will use later to install files you need for your project. After this is done, you are ready to set up your Angular application. You can find installation files to Node.js at `https://nodejs.org`.

The easiest way to have it installed is to go to the site:

```
https://nodejs.org/en/download/
```

Installing Node.js will also install something called NPM, Node Package Manager, which you will need to install dependencies and more. The Angular CLI requires Node 6.9.0 and NPM 3 or higher. Currently on the site, you can choose between an LTS version and the current version. The LTS version should be enough.

Installation

Installing the Angular CLI is as easy as running the following command in your Terminal:

```
npm install -g @angular/cli
```

On some systems, you may need to have elevated permissions to do so; in that case, run your Terminal window as an administrator and on Linux/macOS instead run the command like this:

```
sudo npm install -g @angular/cli
```

First app

Once the Angular CLI is in place the time has come to create your first project. To do so place yourself in a directory of your choice and type the following:

```
ng new <give it a name here>
```

Type the following:

```
ng new TodoApp
```

This will create a directory called `TodoApp`. After you have run the preceding command, there are two things you need to do to see your app in a browser:

- Navigate to the just created directory
- Serve up the application

This will be accomplished by the following commands:

```
cd TodoApp
npm start
```

At this point, open up your browser on `http://localhost:4200` and you should see the following:

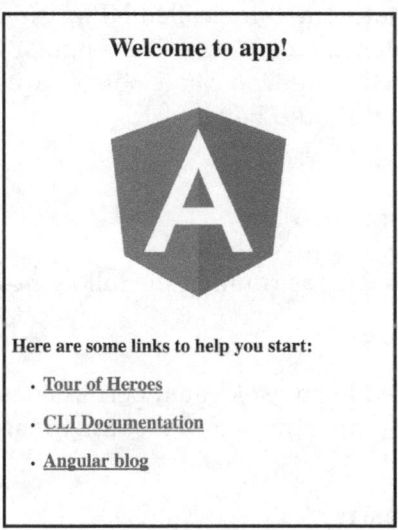

Testing

The Angular CLI doesn't just come with code that makes your app work. It also comes with code that sets up testing and includes a test. Running the said test is as easy as typing the following in the Terminal:

```
npm test
```

You should see the following:

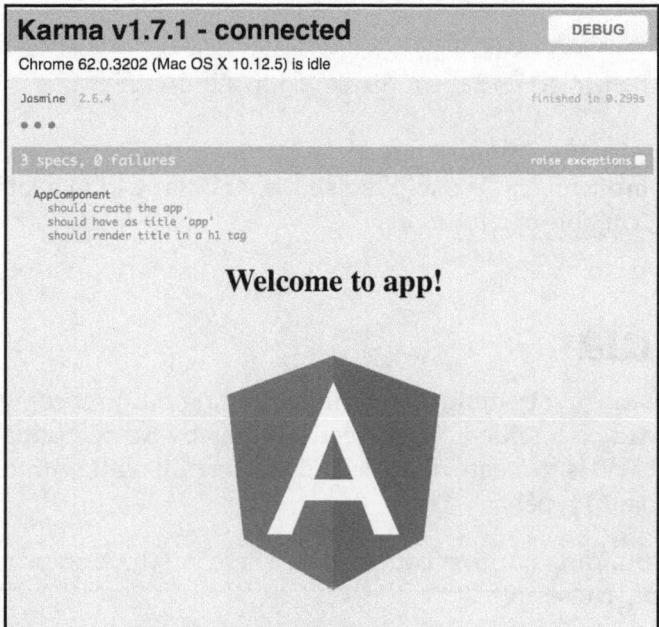

How come this works? Let's have a look at the `package.json` file that was just created and the `scripts` tag. Everything specified here can be run using the following syntax:

```
npm run <key>
```

In some cases, it is not necessary to type `run` and it will be enough to just type:

```
npm <key>
```

This is the case with the `start` and `test` commands.

The following listing makes it clear that it is possible to run more commands than `start` and `test` that we just learned about:

```
"scripts": {
  "ng": "ng",
  "start": "ng serve",
  "build": "ng build",
  "test": "ng test",
  "lint": "ng lint",
  "e2e": "ng e2e"
}
```

So far we have learned how to install the Angular CLI. Using the Angular CLI we have learned to:

1. Scaffold a new project.
2. Serve up the project and see it displayed in a browser.
3. Run tests.

That is quite an accomplishment. We will revisit the Angular CLI in a later chapter as it is a very competent tool, capable of a lot more.

Hello Angular

We are about to take the first trembling steps into building our first component. The Angular CLI has already scaffolded our project and thereby carried out a lot of heavy lifting. All we need to do is to create new file and starting filling it with content. The million dollar question is what to type?

So let's venture into building our first component. There are three steps you need to take in creating a component. Those are:

1. Import the component decorator construct.
2. Decorate a class with a component decorator.
3. Add a component to its module (this might be in two different places).

Creating the component

First off, let's import the component decorator:

```
import { Component } from '@angular/core';
```

Then create the class for your component:

```
class AppComponent {
  title:string = 'hello app';
}
```

Then decorate your class using the `Component` decorator:

```
@Component({
  selector: 'app',
  template: `<h1>{{ title }}</h1>`
})
export class AppComponent {
  title: string = 'hello app';
}
```

We give the `Component` decorator, which is function, an object literal as an input parameter. The object literal consists at this point of the `selector` and `template` keys, so let's explain what those are.

Selector

A `selector` is what it should be referred to if used in a template somewhere else. As we call it `app`, we would refer to it as:

```
<app></app>
```

Template/templateUrl

The `template` or `templateUrl` is your view. Here you can write HTML markup. Using the `template` keyword, in our object literal, means we get to define the HTML markup in the same file as the component class. Were we to use `templateUrl`, we would then place our HTML markup in a separate file.

The preceding example also lists the following double curly braces, in the markup:

```
<h1>{{ title }}</h1>
```

This will be treated as an interpolation and the expression will be replaced with the value of `AppComponent`'s `title` field. The component, when rendered, will therefore look like this:

```
hello app
```

Telling the module

Now we need to introduce a completely new concept, an Angular module. All types of constructs that you create in Angular should be registered with a module. An Angular module serves as a facade to the outside world and it is nothing more than a class that is decorated by the decorate `@NgModule`. Just like the `@Component` decorator, the `@NgModule` decorator takes an object literal as an input parameter. To register our component with our Angular module, we need to give the object literal the property `declarations`. The `declarations` property is of a type array and by adding our component to that array we are registering it with the Angular module.

The following code shows the creation of an Angular module and the component being registered with it by being added to `declarations` keyword array:

```
import { AppComponent } from './app.component';

@NgModule({
  declarations: [AppComponent]
})
export class AppModule {}
```

At this point, our Angular module knows about the component. We need to add one more property to our module, `bootstrap`. The `bootstrap` keyword states that whatever is placed in here serves as the entry component for the entire application. Because we only have one component, so far, it makes sense to register our component with this `bootstrap` keyword:

```
@NgModule({
  declarations: [AppComponent],
  bootstrap: [AppComponent]
})
export class AppModule {}
```

It's definitely possible to have more than one entry component, but the usual scenario is that there is only one.

For any future components, however, we will only need to add them to the `declarations` property, to ensure the module knows about them.

So far we have created a component and an Angular module and registered the component with said the module. We don't really have a working application yet, as there is one more step we need to take. We need to set up the bootstrapping.

Setting up a bootstrap file

The `main.ts` file is your bootstrap file and it should have the following content:

```
import { platformBrowserDynamic } from '@angular/platform-browser-dynamic';
import { AppModule } from './app/app.module';

platformBrowserDynamic().bootstrapModule(AppModule);
```

What we do in the preceding code snippet is to provide the recently created module as an input parameter to the method call `bootstrapModule()`. This will effectively make the said module, the entry module of the application. This is all we need to create a working application. Let's summarize the steps we took to accomplish that:

1. Create a component.
2. Create a module and register our created component in its declaration property.
3. Also register our component in the modules bootstrap property to make it serve as an application entry point. Future components we create just need to be added to the `declarations` property.
4. Bootstrap our created module by using the said module as an input parameter to the `bootstrapModule()` method.

You as a reader have had to swallow a lot of information at this point and take our word for it. Don't worry, you will get a chance to get more acquainted with components in this chapter as well as Angular modules in upcoming chapters. For now, the focus was just to get you up and running by giving you a powerful tool in the form of the Angular CLI and show you how few steps are actually needed to have an app rendered to the screen.

Diving deeper into Angular components

We have come a long way now, from tapping on TypeScript for the first time to learning how to code the basic scripting schema of an Angular component. However, before jumping into more abstract topics, let's try to build another component so we really get the hang of how creating it really works.

Component methods and data updates

Create a new `timer.component.ts` file in the same folder and populate it with the following basic implementation of a very simple component. Don't worry about the added complexity, as we will review each and every change made after the code block:

```
import { Component } from '@angular/core';

@Component({
  selector: 'timer',
  template: `<h1>{{ minutes }}:{{ seconds }} </h1>>`
})
export class TimerComponent {
  minutes: number;
  seconds: number;

  constructor(){
    this.minutes = 24;
    this.seconds = 59;
  }
}
```

At this point, we have created a whole new component by creating the `TimerComponent` class and decorated it with `@Component`, just as we learned how to do in a previous section. We learned in the previous section that there is more to be done, namely to tell an Angular module that this new component exists. The Angular module is already created so you just need to add our fresh new component to its `declarations` property, like so:

```
@NgModule({
  declarations: [
    AppComponent, TimerComponent
  ],
  bootstrap: [AppComponent]
})
```

As long as we only had the `AppComponent` we didn't really see the point of having an Angular module. With two components registered with our module, this changes. When a component is registered with an Angular module it becomes available to other constructs in the module. It becomes available to their `template/templateUrl`. This means that we can have `TimerComponent` rendered inside of our `AppComponent`.

Let's therefore go back to our `AppComponent` file and update its template to show just that:

```
@Component({
  selector: 'app',
  template: `<h1>{{ title }}</h1> <timer></timer>`
})
export class AppComponent {
  title: string = 'hello app';
}
```

In the preceding code, we highlight in bold how we add the `TimerComponent` to the `AppComponent`s template. Or rather we refer to the `TimerComponent` by its `selector` property name, which is `timer`.

Let's show the `TimerComponent` again, in it's entirety, and highlight the `selector` property because this is a really important thing to understand; that is, how to place a component in another component:

```
import { Component } from '@angular/core';

@Component({
  selector: 'timer',
  template: `<h1>{{ minutes }}:{{ seconds }} </h1>>`
})
export class TimerComponent {
  minutes: number;
  seconds: number;

  constructor(){
    this.minutes = 24;
    this.seconds = 59;
  }
}
```

We want to do more than just display a handful of numbers, right? We actually want them to represent a time countdown, and we can achieve that by introducing these changes. Let's first introduce a function we can iterate on in order to update the countdown. Add this function after the constructor function:

```
tick() {
  if(--this.seconds < 0) {
    this.seconds = 59;
    if(--this.minutes < 0) {
      this.minutes = 24;
      this.seconds = 59;
    }
  }
}
```

Selectors in Angular are case sensitive. As we will see later in this book, components are a subset of directives that can support a wide range of selectors. When creating components, we are supposed to set a custom tag name in the `selector` property by enforcing a dash-casing naming convention. When rendering that tag in our view, we should always close the tag as a non-void element. So `<custom-element></custom-element>` is correct, while `<custom-element />` will trigger an exception. Last but not least, certain common camel case names might conflict with the Angular implementation, so avoid them.

Going from static to actual data

As you can see here, functions in TypeScript need to be annotated with the type of the value they return, or just void if none. Our function assesses the current value of both minutes and seconds, and then either decreases their value or just resets it to the initial value. Then this function is called every second by triggering a time interval from the class constructor:

```
constructor() {
  this.minutes = 24;
  this.seconds = 59;
  setInterval(() => this.tick(), 1000);
}
```

Here, we spot for the first time in our code an arrow function (also known as a lambda function, fat arrow, and so on), a new syntax for functions brought by ECMAScript 6, which we will cover in more detail in `Chapter 3`, *Introducing TypeScript*. The `tick` function is also marked as private, so it cannot be inspected or executed outside a `PomodoroTimerComponent` object instance.

So far so good! We have a working Pomodoro timer that countdowns from 25 minutes to 0, and then starts all over again. The problem is that we are replicating code here and there. So, let's refactor everything a little bit to prevent code duplication:

```
constructor() {
  this.reset();
  setInterval(() => this.tick(), 1000);
}

reset() {
  this.minutes = 24;
  this.seconds = 59;
}

private tick() {
  if(--this.seconds < 0) {
    this.seconds = 59;
    if(--this.minutes < 0) {
      this.reset();
    }
  }
}
```

We have wrapped the initialization (and reset) of minutes and seconds inside our function `resetPomodoro`, which is called upon instantiating the component or reaching the end of the countdown. Wait a moment though! According to the Pomodoro technique, Pomodoro practitioners are allowed to rest in between Pomodoros or even pause them should an unexpected circumstance get in the way. We need to provide some sort of interactivity so the user can start, pause, and resume the current Pomodoro timer.

Adding interactivity to the component

Angular provides top-notch support for events through a declarative interface. This means it is easy to hook up events and have the point to method. It's also easy to bind data to different HTML attributes, as you are about to learn.

Let's first modify our template definition:

```
@Component({
  selector: 'timer',
  template: `
    <h1>{{ minutes }}: {{ seconds }} </h1>
    <p>
      <button (click)="togglePause()"> {{ buttonLabel }}</button>
    </p>

  `
})
```

We used a multiline text string! ECMAScript 6 introduced the concept of template strings, which are string literals with support for embedded expressions, interpolated text bindings, and multiline content. We will look into them in more detail in Chapter 3, *Introducing TypeScript*.

In the meantime, just focus on the fact that we introduced a new chunk of HTML that contains a button with an event handler that listens to click events and executes the togglePause() method upon clicking. This (click) attribute is something you might not have seen before, even though it is fully compliant with the W3C standards. Again, we will cover this in more detail in Chapter 4, *Implementing Properties and Events in Our Components*. Let's focus on the togglePause() method and the new buttonLabel binding. First, let's modify our class properties so that they look like this:

```
export class TimerComponent {
  minutes: number;
  seconds: number;
  isPaused: boolean;
  buttonLabel: string;
  // rest of the code will remain as it is below this point
}
```

We introduced two new fields. The first is buttonLabel, which contains the text that will later on be displayed on our newly-created button. isPaused is a newly-created variable that will assume a true/false value, depending on the state of our timer. So, we might need a place to toggle the value of such a field. Let's create the togglePause() method we mentioned earlier:

```
togglePause() {
  this.isPaused = !this.isPaused;
  // if countdown has started
  if(this.minutes < 24 || this.seconds < 59) {
    this.buttonLabel = this.isPaused ? 'Resume' : 'Pause';
  }
}
```

In a nutshell, the `togglePause()` method just switches the value of `isPaused` to its opposite and then, depending on such a new value and whether the timer has started (which would entail that any of the time variables has a value lower than the initialisation value) or not, we assign a different label to our button.

Now, we need to initialize these values, and it seems there is no better place for it. So, the `reset()` function is the place where variables affecting the state of our class are initialized:

```
reset() {
  this.minutes = 24;
  this.seconds = 59;
  this.buttonLabel = 'Start';
  this.togglePause();
}
```

By executing `togglePause()` every time, we reset it the to make sure that whenever it reaches a state where it requires to be reset, the countdown behavior will switch to the opposite state it had previously. There is only one tweak left in the controller method that handles the countdown:

```
private tick() {
  if(!this.isPaused) {
    this.buttonLabel = 'Pause';
    if(--this.seconds < 0) {
      this.seconds = 59;
      if(--this.minutes < 0) {
        this.reset();
      }
    }
  }
}
```

Obviously, we do not want the countdown to continue when the timer is supposed to be paused, so we wrap the whole script in a conditional. In addition to this, we will want to display a different text on our button whenever the countdown is not paused and once again when the countdown reaches its end; stopping and then resetting the Pomodoro to its initial values will be the expected behavior. This reinforces the need of invoking the `togglePause` function within `resetPomodoro`.

Improving the data output

So far, we have reloaded the browser and played around with the newly created toggle feature. However, there is apparently something that still requires some polishing: when the seconds counter is less than 10, it displays a single-digit number instead of the usual two-digit numbers we are used to seeing in digital clocks and watches. Luckily, Angular implements a set of declarative helpers that format the data output in our templates. We call them pipes, and we will cover them in detail later in Chapter 4, *Implementing Properties and Events in Our Components*. For the time being, let's just introduce the number pipe in our component template and configure it to format the seconds output to display two digits all the time. Update our template so that it looks like this:

```
@Component({
  selector: 'timer',
  template: `
    <h1>{{ minutes }}: {{ seconds | number: '2.0' }}</h1>
    <p>
      <button (click)="togglePause()">{{ buttonLabel }}</button>
    </p>
  `
})
```

Basically, we appended the pipe name to the interpolated binding in our template separated by a pipe (|) symbol, hence the name. Reload the template and you will see how the seconds figure always displays two digits, regardless of the value it assumes.

We have created a fully functional Pomodoro timer widget that we can reuse or embed in more complex applications. Chapter 6, *Building an Application with Angular Components*, will guide us through the process of embedding and nesting our components in the context of larger component trees.

In the meantime, let's add some UI beautification to make our component more appealing. We already introduced a class attribute in our button tag as an anticipation of the implementation of the Bootstrap CSS framework in our project. Let's import the actual style sheet we downloaded through npm when installing the project dependencies. Open `timer.html` and add this snippet at the end of the `<head>` element:

```
<link
href="http://maxcdn.bootstrapcdn.com/bootstrap/3.3.6/CSS/bootstrap.min.CSS"
rel="stylesheet"
integrity="sha384-1q8mTJOASx8j1Au+a5WDVnPi2lkFfwwEAa8hDDdjZlpLegxhjVME1fgjW
PGmkzs7" crossorigin="anonymous">
```

Now, let's beautify our UI by inserting a nice page header right before our component:

```
<body>
  <nav class="navbar navbar-default navbar-static-top">
    <div class="container">
      <div class="navbar-header">
        <strong class="navbar-brand">My Timer</strong>
      </div>
    </div>
  </nav>
</body>
```

Tweaking the component button with a Bootstrap button class will give it more personality and wrapping the whole template in a centering container will definitely compound up the UI. So let's update the template in our template to look like this:

```
<div class="text-center">
  <img src="assets/img/timer.png" alt="Timer">
  <h1> {{ minutes }}:{{ seconds | number:'2.0' }}</h1>
  <p>
    <button class="btn btn-danger" (click)="togglePause()">{{ buttonLabel
}}</button>
  </p>
</div>
```

Summary

We looked at web components according to modern web standards and how Angular components provide an easy and straightforward API to build our own components. We covered TypeScript and some basic traits of its syntax as a preparation for Chapter 3, *Introducing TypeScript*. We saw how to set up our working space and where to go to find the dependencies we need to bring TypeScript into the game and use the Angular library in our projects, going through the role of each dependency in our application.

Our first component taught us the basics of creating a component and also allowed us to get more familiar with another important concept, Angular modules, and also how to bootstrap the application. Our second component gave us the opportunity to discuss the form of a controller class containing property fields, constructors, and utility functions, and why metadata annotations are so important in the context of Angular applications to define how our component will integrate itself in the HTML environment where it will live. Our first web component features its own template and such templates host property bindings declaratively in the form of variable interpolations, conveniently formatted by pipes. Binding event listeners is now easier than ever and its syntax is standards-compliant.

The next chapter will cover, in detail, all the TypeScript features we need to know to get up to speed with Angular in no time.

2
IDEs and Plugins

Before moving on with our journey through Angular, it's time to take a look at IDEs. Our favorite code editor can become an unparalleled ally when it comes to undertaking an agile workflow entailing TypeScript compilation at runtime, static type checking and introspection, and code completion and visual assistance for debugging and building our app. That being said, let's highlight some major code editors and take a bird's eye view of how each one of them can assist us when developing Angular applications. If you're just happy with triggering the compilation of your TypeScript files from the command line and do not want to have visual code assistance, feel free to skip to the next section. Otherwise, jump straight to the following section that covers the IDE of your choice.

In this chapter, you will learn about:

- The most common editors
- Installing and configuring plugins that will boost your productivity
- Learning about snippets that will make you an ever faster coder by providing you with ready-made code for the most common scenarios

IDEs

An **Integrated Development Environment** (**IDE**) is the term we use for something that is more powerful than Notepad or a simple editor. Writing code means we have different requirements than if we were to write an essay. The editor needs to be able to indicate when we type something wrong, provide us with insights about our code, or preferably give us a so called auto completion that will give us a list of methods once we start typing its beginning letter. A coding editor can and should be your best friend. For frontend development, there are a lot of great choices out there and no environment is really better than the other; it depends on what works best for you. Let's embark on a journey of discovery and we will let you be the judge on what environment will best suit you.

Atom

Developed by GitHub, the highly customization environment and ease of installation of new packages has turned Atom into the IDE of choice for a lot of people.

In order to optimize your experience with TypeScript when coding Angular apps, you need to install the Atom TypeScript package. You can install via the APM CLI or just use the built-in package installer. The functionalities included are pretty much the same as we have in Sublime after installing the Microsoft package: automatic code hints, static type checking, code introspection, or automatic build upon save to name a few. On top of that, this package also includes a convenient built-in `tsconfig.json` generator.

Sublime Text 3

This is probably one of the most widespread code editors nowadays, although it has lost some momentum lately with users favoring other rising competitors such as GitHub's very own Atom. If this is your editor of choice, we will assume that it's already installed on your system and you also have Node (which is obvious, otherwise, you could have not installed TypeScript in the first place through NPM). In order to provide support for TypeScript code editing, you need to install Microsoft's TypeScript plugin, available at `https://github.com/Microsoft/TypeScript-Sublime-Plugin`. Please refer to this page to learn how to install the plugin and all the shortcuts and key mappings.

Once successfully installed, it only takes *Ctrl* + Space Bar to display code hints based on type introspection. On top of that, we can trigger the build process and compile the file to the JavaScript we are working on by hitting the *F7* function key. Real-time code error reporting is another fancy functionality you can enable from the command menu.

Webstorm

This excellent code editor supplied by IntelliJ is also a great pick for coding Angular apps based on TypeScript. The IDE comes with built-in support for TypeScript out of the box so that we can start developing Angular components from day one. WebStorm also implements a built-in transpiler with support for file watching, so we can compile our TypeScript code into pure vanilla JavaScript without relying on any third-party plugins.

Visual Studio Code

Visual Studio Code, a code editor backed by Microsoft, is gaining momentum as a serious contender in the Angular medium, mostly because of its great support for TypeScript out of the box. TypeScript has been, to a greater extent, a project driven by Microsoft, so it makes sense that one of its popular editors was conceived with built-in support for this language. This means that all the nice features we might want are already baked in, including syntax and error highlighting and automatic builds.

What really makes Visual Studio so great is not only its design and ease of use, but also the access to a ton of plugins and there are some great ones for Angular development, so let's look at the leading ones.

 Angular language service:

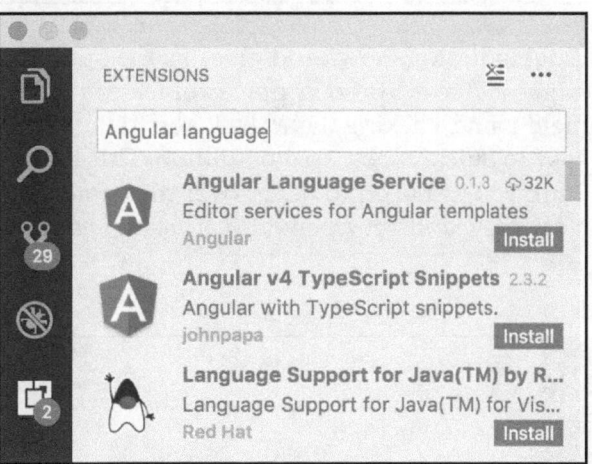

By looking for `Angular language`, you are able to get a list of plugins matching it. Install the one on top.

After having done so, you will have enriched Visual Studio Code with:

- Code completion
- Go to definition
- Quick info
- AOT diagnostic messages

Just to demo its ability, let's add a description field to our code like so:

```
 8    export class AppComponent {
 9      title = 'app works!';
10      description:string= 'some description';
11    }
12
```

Let's now edit our template and realize we have code completion in the template:

```
app.component.ts      app.component.html ●
1    <h1>
2      {{title}} {{d}}
3    </h1>          🔧 description                    property
4
```

As we start to type a visual indicator shows and gives us the option to complete the word for us, if we select the suggested text. Another powerful feature that is supported is the ability to hover over a field name, clicking it and be taken to the component class it belongs to. This makes it very easy to quickly look up a definition. This is known as a *go to definition* feature. To use said feature you just need to hover over the name and, on a Mac, hold down the command button. Very easy, and very powerful, as stated earlier.

Typescript Hero:

To use this plugin, simply start coding like this, and click the lightbulb icon to the left to have your imports automatically added to your file:

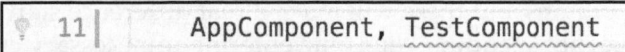

Having decent code completion and imports is a must unless you like to wear out your fingers. There are also snippets and pieces of code that will make your coding even faster.

Angular 5 Typescript snippets (Dan Wahlin, John Papa):

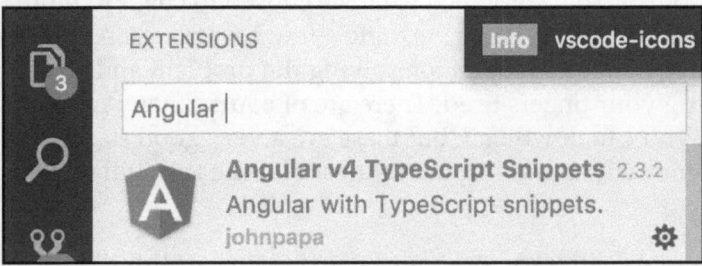

This is a really powerful plugin. It comes with three different types of snippets:

- Angular snippets
- RxJS snippets
- HTML snippets

It works the following way. Type a snippet shortcut, and press *Enter* when asked to and the code will be added:

```
a-component
```

Pressing *Enter* will result in the following code:

```
import { Component, OnInit } from '@Angular/core';

@Component({
  selector: 'selector-name',
  templateUrl: 'name.component.html'
})
export class NameComponent implements OnInit {
  constructor() {}

  ngOnInit(){}
}
```

As you can see, you get a ton of code for almost no effort. There are 42 snippets in total and they are all listed in the plugin description in Visual Studio.

There are a ton more plugins, but these will make a real difference starting out. It's all about being productive, not spending your time entering unnecessary characters.

Summary

The point of this chapter has been to try to empower you as a software developer. There are many choices for editors, some of which we have chosen to cover in more detail. There are also many plugins and snippets that save quite a few keystrokes. At the end of the day, your focus and energy should be spent on solving the problem and structuring your solution, not making your fingers tired. There are of course many more plugins, snippets, and shortcuts that you can download, but these are a very good start. We encourage you to learn more about your editor and its possibilities, because this will make you faster and more efficient.

In the next chapter, you will learn all about Typescript, everything from the basics to the professional level. The chapter will cover what problems are solved by introducing types, but also the language construct itself. Typescript, as a superset of JavaScript, contains a lot of powerful concepts and marries really well with the Angular Framework, as you are about to discover.

3
Introducing TypeScript

In the previous chapter, we built our very first component and we used TypeScript to shape the code scripts, which gave form to it. All the examples included in this book use its syntax. As we will see later in this book, writing our scripts in TypeScript and leveraging its static typing will give us a remarkable advantage over the other scripting languages.

This chapter is not a thorough overview of the TypeScript language. We will just focus on the core elements of the language and study them in detail on our journey through Angular. The good news is that TypeScript is not all that complex, and we will manage to cover most of its relevant parts.

In this chapter, we will:

- Look at the background and rationale behind TypeScript
- Discover online resources to practice while we learn
- Recap on the concept of typed values and how to represent them
- Build our own types, based on classes and interfaces
- Learn to better organize our application architecture with modules

Understanding the case for TypeScript

The natural evolution of the early JavaScript-driven small web applications into thick monolithic clients unveiled the shortcomings of the ECMAScript 5 JavaScript specification. In a nutshell, large-scale JavaScript applications suffered from serious maintainability and scalability problems as soon as they grew in size and complexity.

This issue became more relevant as new libraries and modules required seamless integration onto our applications. The lack of good mechanisms for interoperability led to really cumbersome solutions that never seemed to fit the bill.

As a response to these concerns, ECMAScript 6 (also called as ES6 or ES2015) promised to solve these maintainability and scalability issues by introducing better module loading functionalities, an improved language architecture for better handling of scope, and a wide variety of syntactic sugar to better manage types and objects. The introduction of class-based programming turned into an opportunity to embrace a more OOP approach when building large-scale applications.

Microsoft took on the challenge and spent nearly two years building a superset of the language, combining the conventions of ES6 and borrowing some proposals from ES7. The idea was to launch something that helped out with building enterprise applications with a lower error footprint by means of static type checking, better tooling, and code analysis.

After two years of development led by Anders Hejlsberg, lead architect of C# and creator of Delphi and Turbo Pascal, TypeScript 0.8 was finally introduced in 2012 and it reached Version 1.0 two years later. TypeScript was not only running ahead of ECMAScript 6, but it also implemented the same features and provided a solid environment for building large-scale applications by introducing, among other features, optional static typing through type annotations, thereby ensuring type checking at compile time. This contributes to catching errors in earlier stages of the development process. The support for declaration files also gives developers the opportunity to describe the interface of their modules, so other developers can better integrate them into their code workflow and tooling.

The benefits of TypeScript

The following infographic provides a bird's eye view of the different features that distinguish ECMAScript 6 from ECMAScript 5, and then differentiates TypeScript from the two.

As a superset of ECMAScript 6, one of the main advantages of embracing TypeScript in your next project is the low entry barrier. If you know ECMAScript 6, you are pretty much all set, since all the additional features in TypeScript are optional. You can pick and introduce in your practice the features that help you to achieve your goal. All in all, there is a long list of strong arguments for advocating for TypeScript in your next project and all of them obviously apply to Angular as well. Here is a short rundown of arguments, just to name a few:

- Annotating our code with types ensures a consistent integration of our different code units and improves code readability and comprehension.
- The TypeScript's built-in type-checker will analyze your code at runtime and help you prevent errors even before executing your code.

- The use of types ensures consistency across your applications. In combination with the previous two, the overall code errors footprint gets minimized in the long run.
- TypeScript extends classes with longtime demanded features such as class fields, private members, enums, and so on.
- The use of decorators opens the door to extend our classes and implementations in unparalleled ways.
- Creating interfaces and type definition files (which we will not cover in this book) ensures a smooth and seamless integration of our libraries in other systems and codebases.
- TypeScript support across the different IDEs on store is terrific, and we can benefit from code highlighting, real-time type checking, and automatic compilation at no cost.
- The TypeScript syntax will definitely please developers coming from other backgrounds such as Java, C#, C++, and so on.

Introducing TypeScript resources in the wild

Now, we are going to take a look at where we can get further support to learn and test-drive our new knowledge of TypeScript.

The TypeScript official site

Obviously, our first stop is the official site for the language: `http://www.typescriptlang.org`. There, we can find a more extensive introduction to the language and links to IDEs and corporate supporters of this project. Nevertheless, the most important sections that we will definitely revisit more often are the learn section and the play sandbox.

The learn section gives us access to a quick tutorial to get up to speed with the language in no time. It might be interesting as a recap on what we discussed in the previous chapter, but we would suggest you skip it in favor of the sample pages and the language spec, the latter being a direct link to the full extensive documentation of the language at GitHub. This is a priceless resource for both new and experienced users.

The play section offers a convenient sandbox, including some readymade code examples, covering some of the most common traits of the language. We encourage you to leverage this tool to test out the code examples we will see throughout this chapter.

The TypeScript official wiki

We made a reference to the TypeScript wiki in the previous chapter when speaking about the most basic parameters we need to know when executing commands with the TypeScript compiler API.

The code for TypeScript is fully open sourced at GitHub, and the Microsoft team has made a good effort at documenting the different facets of the code in the wiki available on the repository site. We encourage you to go take a look at it any time you have a question or want to delve deeper into any of the language features or form aspects of its syntax.

The wiki is located at: `https://github.com/Microsoft/TypeScript/wiki`.

Types in TypeScript

Working with TypeScript or any other coding language means basically working with data, and such data can represent different sorts of content. This is what we know as types, a noun used to represent the fact that such data can be a text string, an integer value, or an array of these value types, among others. This is nothing new to JavaScript, since we have always been working implicitly with types, but in a flexible manner. This means that any given variable could assume (or return, in the case of functions) any type of value. Sometimes, this leads to errors and exceptions in our code because of type collisions between what our code returned and what we expected it to return type-wise. While this flexibility can still be enforced by means of any type that we will see later on in this chapter, statically typing our variables gives us and our IDEs a good picture of what kind of data we are supposed to find on each instance of code. This becomes an invaluable way to help debug our applications at compile time before it's too late. To investigate how a language feature works, I suggest you use a playground for two reasons. The first reason is to learn how the feature works. The second reason is to know the corresponding ES5 code it produces. I suggest using the following playground for this: `https://www.typescriptlang.org/play/`.

String

Probably one of the most widely used primitive types in our code will be the string type, where we populate a variable with a piece of text:

```
var brand: string = 'Chevrolet';
```

Check out the type assignation next to the variable name, which is separated by a colon symbol. This is how we annotate types in TypeScript, as we already saw in the previous chapter.

Back to the string type, we can use either single or double quotes, and it is same as ECMAScript6. We can define multiline text strings with support for text interpolation with placeholder variables by using the same type:

```
var brand: string = 'Chevrolet';
var message: string = `Today it's a happy day! I just bought a new ${brand} car`;
```

Declaring our variables – the ECMAScript 6 way

TypeScript, as a superset of ECMAScript 6, supports expressive declaration nouns such as `let`, which informs us that the variable is scoped to the nearest enclosing block (either a function `for` loop or any enclosing statement). On the other hand, `const` is an indicator that the values declared this way are meant to always feature the same type or value once populated. For the rest of this chapter, we will enforce the traditional `var` notation for declaring variables, but do remember to use `let` and `const` where appropriate.

The let keyword

In a lot of cases in the code, I have been using `var` to declare objects, variables, and other constructs. It is really discouraged when starting with ES6 or TypeScript. There is a reason for that and it's because ES5 only have method scope. For most developers coming from another language and start using JavaScript, this comes as a bit of a shock. So firstly, what do we mean with function scope? We mean that a variable is unique within the context of a function, like so:

```
function test() {
  var a;
}
```

There can be no other variable `a` in that function. If you do declare more of it, then you will effectively redefine it. OK, so that's good, but when is the scoping not there? It is not there in `for`-loops, for example. In Java you would write:

```
for (int i = 0; i < arr.length; i++) {
}
```

In Java, you would know that the variable i would never leak outside of the for-loop and you could write:

```
int i = 3;
for (int i = 0; i < arr.length; i++) {
}
```

And know that the variable i outside of the for-loop would not affect the variable i inside the for-loop, they would be separated or scoped, as it is called. OK, so users of ES5 JavaScript have had this language flaw for a long time and recently a fix for this has been added to ES6 and Typescript respectively, namely the let keyword. Use it like this:

```
let i = 3;
for (let i = 0; i < arr.length; i++) {
}
```

The reason this works is that the TypeScript compiler translates this to the following ES5 code:

```
var i = 3;
for (var i_1 = 0; i_1 < arr.length; i_1++) {
}
```

The compiler essentially renames the variable within the for-loop, so that a name collision doesn't happen. So remember, no more var, just use the let keyword when in doubt.

Const

The const keyword is a way for you to convey that this data should never be changed. As a code base grows, it is easy that changes happen by mistake; such a mistake might be costly. To get compile time support for this, the const keyword is there to help you. Use it in the following way:

```
const PI = 3.14;
PI = 3 // not allowed
```

The compiler will even indicate that this is not allowed with the following message:

```
Cannot assign to PI because it is a constant or a read-only property
```

A word of caution here: this works only on the top level. You need to be aware of this if you declare objects as `const`, like so:

```
const obj = {
  a : 3
}
obj.a = 4; // actually allowed
```

Declaring the `obj` const does not freeze the entire object from being edited, but rather what `obj` points to. So, the following would not be allowed:

```
obj = {}
```

Here, we actively change what `obj` points to, not one of its child properties, therefore it is not allowed and you get the same compile error as earlier.

Number

Number is probably the other most widespread primitive data type along with string and boolean. The same as in JavaScript, number defines a floating point number. The number type also defines hexadecimal, decimal, binary, and octal literals:

```
var age: number = 7;
var height: number = 5.6;
```

Boolean

The Boolean type defines data that can be `True` or `False`, representing the fulfillment of a condition:

```
var isZeroGreaterThanOne: boolean = false;
```

Array

Assigning wrong member types to arrays and handling exceptions that arise by that can be now easily avoided with the `Array` type, where we describe an array containing certain types only. The syntax just requires the `postfix` `[]` in the type annotation, as follows:

```
var brand: string[] = ['Chevrolet', 'Ford', 'General Motors'];
var childrenAges: number[] = [8, 5, 12, 3, 1];
```

If we try to add a new member to the `childrenAges` array with a type other than number, the runtime type checker will complain, making sure our typed members remain consistent and our code is error-free.

Dynamic typing with the any type

Sometimes, it is hard to infer the data type out of the information we have at some point, especially when we are porting legacy code to TypeScript or integrating loosely typed third-party libraries and modules. Don't worry, TypeScript supplies us with a convenient type for these cases. The `any` type is compatible with all the other existing types, so we can type any data value with it and assign any value to it later on. This great power comes with a great responsibility, though. If we bypass the convenience of static type checking, we are opening the door to type errors when piping data through our modules, and it will be up to us to ensure type safety throughout our application:

```
var distance: any;
// Assigning different value types is perfectly fine
distance = '1000km':
distance = '1000'
// Allows us to seamlessly combine different types
var distance: any[] = ['1000km', '1000'];
```

The null and undefined JavaScript literals require special mention. In a nutshell, they are typed under the `any` type. This makes it possible later on to assign these literals to any other variable, regardless of its original type.

Custom type

In Typescript, you are able to come up with your own type if you need to, by using the `type` keyword in the following way:

```
type Animal = 'Cheetah' | 'Lion';
```

What we have created now is a type with x number of allowed values. Let's create a variable from this type:

```
var animal: Animal = 'Cheetah';
```

This is perfectly allowed as `Cheetah` is one of the allowed values, and works as intended. The interesting part happens when we give our variable a value it does not expect:

```
var animal: Animal = 'Turtle';
```

This results in the following compiler error:

```
error TS2322: Type '"Turtle"' is not assignable to type 'Animal'.
```

Enum

Enum is basically a set of unique numeric values that we can represent by assigning friendly names to each one of them. The use of enums goes beyond assigning an alias to a number. We can use them as a way to list, in a convenient and recognizable way, the different variations that a specific type can assume.

Enums are declared using the enum keyword, without var or any other variable declaration noun, and they begin numbering members starting at 0 unless explicit numeric values are assigned to them:

```
enum Brands { Chevrolet, Cadillac, Ford, Buick, Chrysler, Dodge };
var myCar: Brands = Brands.Cadillac;
```

Inspecting the value of myCar will return 1 (which is the index held by Cadillac in the enum). As we mentioned already, we can assign custom numeric values in the enum:

```
enum BrandsReduced { Tesla = 1, GMC, Jeep };
var myTruck: BrandsReduced = BrandsReduced.GMC;
```

Inspecting myTruck will yield 2, since the first enumerated value was set as 1 already. We can extend value assignation to all the enum members as long as such values are integers:

```
enum StackingIndex {
  None = 0,
  Dropdown = 1000,
  Overlay = 2000,
  Modal = 3000
};
var mySelectBoxStacking: StackingIndex = LayerStackingIndex.Dropdown;
```

One last trick worth mentioning is the possibility to look up the enum member mapped to a given numeric value:

```
enum Brands { Chevrolet, Cadillac, Ford, Buick, Chrysler, Dodge };
var MyCarBrandName: string = Brands[1];
```

It should be mentioned that from TypeScript 2.4 it is possible to assign string values to Enums.

Void

The `void` type definitely represents the absence of any type and its use is constrained to annotating functions that do not return an actual value. Therefore, there is no return type either. We already had the chance to see this with an actual example in the previous chapter:

```
resetPomodoro(): void {
  this.minutes = 24;
  this.seconds = 59;
}
```

Type inference

Typing our data is optional since TypeScript is smart enough to infer the data type of our variables and function return values out of context with a certain level of accuracy. When no type inference is possible, TypeScript will assign the dynamic any type to the loosely typed data at the cost of reducing type checking to a bare minimum.

An example of inferring at work can be seen in the following code:

```
var brand = 'Chevrolet';
```

This holds the same effect, that is, it will lead to a compilation error if you try to assign a non-compatible data type to it like so:

```
var brand: string = 'Chevrolet';
var brand2 = 'Chevrolet';
brand = false; // compilation error
brand = 114; // compilation error
```

Functions, lambdas, and execution flow

The same as in JavaScript, functions are the processing machines where we analyze input, digest information, and apply the necessary transformations to the data provided to either transform the state of our application or return an output that will be used to shape our application's business logic or user interactivity.

Functions in TypeScript are not that different from regular JavaScript, except for the fact that functions, just as everything else in TypeScript, can be annotated with static types and thus, they better inform the compiler of the information they expect in their signature and the data type they aim to return, if any.

Annotating types in our functions

The following example showcases how a regular function is annotated in TypeScript:

```
function sayHello(name: string): string {
    return 'Hello, ' + name;
}
```

We can clearly see two main differences from the usual function syntax in regular JavaScript. First, we annotate with type information the parameters declared in the function signature. This makes sense since the compiler will want to check whether the data provided when executing the function holds the correct type. In addition to this, we also annotate the type of the returning value by adding the postfix string to the function declaration. In these cases, where the given function does not return any value, the type annotation void will give the compiler the information it requires to provide a proper type checking.

As we mentioned in the previous section, the TypeScript compiler is smart enough to infer types when no annotation is provided. In this case, the compiler will look into the arguments provided and the return statements to infer a returning type from it.

Functions in TypeScript can also be represented as expressions of anonymous functions, where we bind the function declaration to a variable:

```
var sayHello = function(name: string): string {
    return 'Hello, ' + name;
}
```

However, there is a downside to this syntax. Although typing function expressions this way is allowed, thanks to type inference, the compiler is missing the type definition in the declared variable. We might assume that the inferred type of a variable that points to a function typed as a string is obviously a string. Well, it's not. A variable that points to an anonymous function ought to be annotated with a function type. Basically, the function type informs about both the types expected in the function payload and the type returned by the function execution, if any. This whole block, in the form of (arguments: type) => returned type, becomes the type annotation our compiler expects:

```
var sayHello: (name: string) => string = function(name: string): string {
    return 'Hello, ' + name;
}
```

Why such a cumbersome syntax, you might ask? Sometimes, we will declare variables that might depend on factories or function bindings. Then, it is always a good practice to provide as much information to the compiler as we can. This simple example might help you to understand better:

```
// Two functions with the same typing but different logic.
function sayHello(input: string): string {
  return 'Hello, ' + input;
}

function sayHi(input: string): string{
  return 'Hi, ' + input;
}

// Here we declare the variable with is own function type
var greetMe: (name: string) => string;
greetMe = sayHello;
```

This way, we also ensure that later function assignations conform to the type annotations set when declaring variables.

Function parameters in Typescript

Due to the type checking performed by the compiler, function parameters require special attention in TypeScript.

Optional parameters

Parameters are a core part of the type checking applied by the TypeScript compiler. TypeScript offers an optional functionality by adding the ? symbol as a postfix to the parameter name we want to make optional. This allows us to leave out the second parameter in the function call.

```
function greetMe(name: string, greeting?: string): string {
  console.log(greeting);
  if(!greeting) { greeting = 'Hello'; }
  return greeting + ', ' + name;
}

console.log( greetMe('Chris') );
```

This code will attempt to print out the greeting variable as well as produce a proper greeting. Running this code like this:

```
greetMe('Chris');
```

Will give us the following result:

```
undefined
Hello Chris
```

So, an optional parameter doesn't really get set unless you explicitly make it so. It is more of a construct so that you can get help with deciding what parameters are mandatory and which ones are optional. Let's exemplify that:

```
function add(mandatory: string, optional?: number) {}
```

You can invoke this function in the following ways:

```
add('some string');
add('some string', 3.14);
```

Both versions are allowed. Using optional parameters in your function signature forces you to place them last, like the previous example. The following example illustrates what not to do:

```
function add(optional?: number, mandatory: string) {}
```

This would create a situation where both parameters would be mandatory:

```
add(11); // error. mandatory parameter missing
```

Even the compiler would complain and say the following:

A required parameter cannot follow an optional parameter

Remember, optionals are great, but place them last.

Default parameters

TypeScript gives us another feature to cope with the scenario depicted earlier in the form of default parameters, where we can set a default value that the parameter will assume when not explicitly populated upon executing the function. The syntax is pretty straightforward, as we can see when we refactor the previous example here:

```
function greetMe(name: string, greeting: string = 'Hello'): string {
    return `${greeting}, ${name}`;
}
```

Just as with optional parameters, default parameters must be put right after the non-default parameters in the function signature. There is a very important difference, which is that default parameters are always safe to use. Why they are safe to use, is indicated by the ES5 code below. The ES5 code below is the resulting code from compiling the above TypeScript to ES5. The following code indicates that the compiler adds an IF clause that checks whether the variable `greeting` is undefined and if so gives it a starter value:

```
function greetMe(name, greeting){
  if (greeting === void 0) { greeting = 'Hello'; }
  return greeting + ', ' + name;
}
```

As you can see, the compiler adds an `if`-clause investigating your value and if it is not set, it adds the value you provided earlier.

> The type is inferred when you are dealing with default parameters as you assign a value to them. In the preceding code snippet, greeting is inferred to be a string by it being assigned the string value `'Hello'`.

Rest parameters

One of the big advantages of the flexibility of JavaScript when defining functions is the functionality to accept an unlimited non-declared array of parameters in the form of the arguments object. In a statically typed context such as TypeScript, this might not be possible, but it actually is by means of the REST parameter's object. Here, we can define, at the end of the arguments list, an additional parameter prefixed by ellipsis (. . .) and typed as an array:

```
function greetPeople(greeting: string, ...names: string[]): string{
  return greeting + ', ' + names.join(' and ') + '!';
}

alert(greetPeople('Hello', 'John', 'Ann', 'Fred'));
```

It's important to note that the Rest parameters must be put at the end of the arguments list and can be left out whenever not required. Let's have a look at the resulting ES5 code to understand what the TypeScript compiler produces:

```
function greetPeople(greeting) {
  var names = [];
  for (var _i = 1; _i < arguments.length; _i++) {
    names[_i - 1] = arguments[_i];
  }
```

```
    return greeting + ', ' + names.join(' and ') + '!';
}

    alert(greetPeople('Hello', 'John', 'Ann', 'Fred'));
```

What we can see here is that the built-in arguments array is being used. Also, that its content is copied over into the `names` array:

```
for (var _i = 1; _i < arguments.length; _i++) {
  names[_i -1] = arguments[_i];
}
```

It really makes perfect sense when you think about it. So, Rest parameters is your friend when you don't know the number of arguments.

Overloading the function signature

Method and function overloading is a common pattern in other languages such as C#. However, implementing this functionality in TypeScript clashes with the fact that JavaScript, which TypeScript is meant to compile to, does not implement any elegant way to integrate this functionality out of the box. So, the only workaround possibly requires writing function declarations for each of the overloads and then writing a general-purpose function that will wrap the actual implementation and whose list of typed arguments and returning types are compatible with all the others:

```
function hello(name: string): string {}
function hello(name: string[]): string {}
function hello(name: any, greeting?: string): string {
  var namesArray: string[];
  if (Array.isArray(names)) {
    namesArray = names;
  } else {
    namesArray = [names];
  }
  if (!greeting) {
    greeting = 'Hello';
  }
  return greeting + ', ' + namesArray.join(' and ') + '!';
}
```

In the preceding example, we are exposing three different function signatures and each of them feature different type annotations. We could even define different returning types if there was a case for that. For doing so, we should have just annotated the wrapping function with an any return type.

Better function syntax with and scope handing with lambdas

ECMAScript 6 introduced the concept of fat arrow functions (also called lambda functions in other languages such as Python, C#, Java, or C++) as a way to both simplify the general function syntax and also to provide a bulletproof way to handle the scope of the functions that are traditionally handled by the infamous scope issues of tackling with the `this` keyword.

The first impression is its minimalistic syntax, where, most of the time, we will see arrow functions as single-line, anonymous expressions:

```
var double = x => x * 2;
```

The function computes the double of a given number, x, and returns the result, although we do not see any function or return statements in the expression. If the function signature contains more than one argument, we just need to wrap them all between braces:

```
var add = (x, y) => x + y;
```

This makes this syntax extremely convenient when developing functional operations such as `map`, `reduce`, and others:

```
var reducedArray = [23, 5, 62, 16].reduce((a, b) => a + b, 0);
```

Arrow functions can also contain statements. In this case, we will want to wrap the whole implementation in curly braces:

```
var addAndDouble = (x, y) => {
  var sum = x + y;
  return sum * 2;
}
```

Still, what does this have to do with scope handling? Basically, the value of this can point to a different context, depending on where we execute the function. This is a big deal for a language that prides itself on an excellent flexibility for functional programming, where patterns such as callbacks are paramount. When referring to `this` inside a callback, we lose track of the upper context and that usually forces us to use conventions such as assigning the value of `this` to a variable named self or that, which will be used later on within the callback. Statements containing interval or timeout functions make a perfect example of this:

```
function delayedGreeting(name): void {
  this.name = name;
```

```
    this.greet = function(){
      setTimeout(function() {
        alert('Hello ' + this.name);
      }, 0);
    }
  }

  var greeting = new delayedGreeting('Peter');
  greeting.greet(); // alert 'Hello undefined'
```

When executing the preceding script, we won't get the expected `Hello Peter` alert, but an incomplete string highlighting a pesky greeting to `Mr. Undefined`! Basically, this construction screws the lexical scoping of this when evaluating the function inside the timeout call. Porting this script to arrow functions will do the trick, though:

```
function delayedGreeting(name): void {
  this.name = name;
  this.greet = function() {
    setTimeout(() => alert('Hello ' + this.name), 0);
  }
}
```

Even if we break down the statement contained in the arrow function into several lines of code wrapped by curly braces, the lexical scoping of this will keep pointing to the proper context outside the `setTimeout` call, allowing a more elegant and clean syntax.

General features

There are some general features in TypeScript that don't really apply specifically to either classes, functions, or parameters, but rather makes coding more efficient and fun. The idea is that the fewer lines of code you have to write, the better it is. It's not only about fewer lines, but also about making things clearer. There are a ton of such features in ES6 that TypeScript has also implemented, but here, I will just name a few that are likely to occur in your Angular project.

Spread parameter

A spread parameter is using the same syntax . . . ellipsis as the REST parameters, but it is used differently. It's not used as a parameter inside of a function, but rather inside the function body.

Let's illustrate what that means:

```
var newItem = 3;
var oldArray = [ 1, 2 ];
var newArray = [
  ...oldArray,
  newItem
];
console.log( newArray )
```

This would output:

```
1,2,3
```

What we do here is add an item to an existing array without changing the old array. The oldArray variable still contains 1, 2, but the newArray contains 1, 2, 3. This general principle is called *immutability*, which essentially means don't change, but rather create a new state from the old state. It's a principle used in functional programming both as a paradigm, but also for performance reasons.

You can also use a REST parameter on objects; yes, really. You would write it like this:

```
var oldPerson = { name : 'Chris' };
var newPerson = { ...oldPerson, age : 37 };
console.log( newPerson );
```

The result from running this code is:

```
{ name: 'Chris', age: 37 }
```

A merge between the two objects. Just like with the example of the list, we would not change the previous variable, oldPerson. A newPerson variable would take the information from oldPerson, but add its new values to it. Looking at the ES5 code you can see why:

```
var __assign = ( this && this.__assign ) || Object.assign || function(t) {
  for (var s, i = n, n = arguments.length; i < n; i++) {
    s = arguments[i];
    for (var p in s) if (Object.prototype.hasOwnProperty.call( s, p )) {
      t[ p ] = s[ p ];
    }
    return t;
  };
  var oldPerson = { name : 'Chris' };
  var newPerson = __assign({}, oldPerson, { age: 37 });
  console.log( newPerson );
}
```

What's happening here is that an `assign` function is being defined. Said function loops the keys of `oldPerson` variables and assigns those to a new object and lastly adds the content of the `newPerson` variable. If you look at the preceding function, it either defines a function that does this or it uses `Object.assign`, which is part of ES6 standard, if available.

Template strings

Template string is all about making your code clearer. Imagine the following scenario:

```
var url = 'http://path_to_domain' +
'path_to_resource' +
'?param=' + parameter +
'=' + 'param2=' +
parameter2;
```

So, what's wrong with this? The answer is readability. It's hard to imagine what the resulting string will look like, but it is also very easy for you to edit the previous code by mistake, and suddenly, the result will not be what you want. Most languages use a format function for this and that is exactly what template strings is, a format function. It is used in the following way:

```
var url = `${baseUrl}/${path_to_resource}?param=
           ${parameter}&param2={parameter2}`;
```

This is a much more condensed expression and so it is much easier to read, so use it, always.

Generics

Generics is an expression for saying that we have a general code behavior that we can employ regardless of data type. Generics are very often used to operate on collections as collections often have similar behavior regardless of types. Generics can however be used on constructs such as methods. The idea is also that Generics should indicate if you are about to mix types in a way that isn't allowed:

```
function method<T>(arg: T): T {
  return arg;
}
console.log(method<number>(1)); // works
console.log(method<string>(1)); // doesn't work
```

In the preceding example, the `T` is not decided until you actually use the method. As you can see, the type of `T` varies from number to `String` depending on how you call it. It also ensures that you are inputting the correct type of data. This can be seen in the following row:

```
console.log(method<string>(1)); // doesn't work
```

Here, we clearly specify that `T` should be a string, but we insist on feeding it a value of type number. The compiler clearly states that this is not OK.

You can, however, be more specific on what `T` should be. By typing the following, you ensure that `T` is of type `Array`, so any type of value you input must adhere to this:

```
function method<T>(arg: T[]): T[] {
  console.log(arg.length); // Array has a .length, so no more error
  return arg;
}

class A extends Array {
}

class Person {
}

var p = new Array<Person>();
var person = new Person();
var a = new A();

method<Person>(p);
method<A>(a);
method<Person>(person);
```

In this case, we decide that `T` should be either of type `Person` or `A` and we also see that the input needs to be of type array:

```
function method<T>(arg: T[]) {}
```

So, inputting a single object is not OK. So why do we do this? In this case, we want to ensure that certain methods are available such as `.length` and that we, in a given moment, don't care if we operate on something of type `A` or `Person`.

You can also decide that your type `T` should adhere to an interface like this:

```
interface Shape {
  area(): number;
}
```

```
class Square implements Shape {
  area() { return 1; }
}

class Circle implements Shape {
  area() { return 2; }
}

function allAreas<T extends Shape>(...args: T[]): number {
  let total = 0;
  args.forEach (x => {
    total += x.area();
  });
  return total;
}

allAreas(new Square(), new Circle());
```

The following line limits what T can be:

```
T extends Shape
```

As you can see, Generics is quite powerful to use if you have a common behavior that many different data types can relate to. You most likely won't be writing your own generic code, at least not initially, but it's good to know what is going on.

Classes, interfaces, and class inheritance

Now that we have overviewed the most relevant bits and pieces of TypeScript, it's time to see how everything falls into place to build TypeScript classes. These classes are the building blocks of TypeScript and Angular applications.

Although the noun class was a reserved word in JavaScript, the language itself never had an actual implementation for traditional POO-oriented classes as other languages such as Java or C# did. JavaScript developers used to mimic this kind of functionality, leveraging the function object as a constructor type, which would be later on instanced with the new operator. Other common practices such as extending our function objects were implemented by applying prototypal inheritance or by using composition.

Now, we have an actual class functionality, which is flexible and powerful enough to implement the functionality our applications require. We already had the chance to tap into classes in the previous chapter. Let's look at them in more detail now.

Anatomy of a class – constructors, properties, methods, getters, and setters

The following piece of code illustrates how a class could be. Please note that the class property members come first and then we include a constructor and several methods and property accessors. None of them features the reserved word function and all the members and methods are properly annotated with a type except constructor:

```
class Car {
  private distanceRun: number = 0;
  color: string;

  constructor(public isHybrid: boolean, color: string = 'red') {
    this.color = color;
  }

  getCasConsumsption(): string {
    return this.ishybrid ? 'Very low' : 'Too high!';
  }

  drive(distance: number): void {
    this.distanceRun += distance;
  }

  static honk(): string {
    return 'HOOONK!';
  }

  get distance(): number {
    return this.distanceRun;
  }
}
```

This class layout will probably remind us of the component class we built back in Chapter 1, *Creating Our Very First Component in Angular*. Basically, the class statement wraps several elements that we can break down into:

- **Members**: Any instance of the Car class will feature two properties - color typed as string, and distanceRun typed as a number and they will only be accessible from within the class itself. If we instance this class, distanceRun, or any other member or method marked as private, it won't be publicly exposed as part of the object API.

- **Constructor**: The constructor function is executed right away when an instance of the class is created. Usually, we want to initialize the class members here, with the data provided in the constructor signature. We can also leverage the constructor signature itself to declare class members, as we did with the isHybrid property. To do so, we just need to prefix the constructor parameter with an access modifier such as private or public. Same as we saw when analyzing functions in the previous sections, we can define rest, optional, or default parameters as depicted in the previous example with the color argument, which fallbacks to red when it is not explicitly defined.

- **Methods**: A method is a special kind of member that represents a function and therefore, can return, or not, a typed value. Basically, it is a function that becomes part of the object API. Methods can be private as well. In this case, they are basically used as helper functions within the internal scope of the class to achieve the functionalities required by other class members.

- **Static members**: Members marked as static are associated with the class and not with the object instances of that class. This means that we can consume static members directly, without having to instantiate an object first. In fact, static members are not accessible from the object instances and thus, they cannot access other class members using this. These members are usually included in the class definition as helper or factory methods in order to provide a generic functionality not related to any specific object instance.

- **Property accessors**: In ES5, we could define custom setters/getters in a very verbose way with Object.defineProperty. Now, things have become quite simpler. In order to create property accessors (usually pointing to internal private fields as in the example provided), we just need to prefix a typed method named as the property we want to expose with set (in order to make it writable) and get (in order to make it readable).

As a personal exercise, why don't you copy the preceding piece of code at the playground page (http://www.typescriptlang.org/Playground) and execute it? We can even see an instance object of the Car class in action by appending this snippet right after the class definition and running the code and inspecting the output in the browser's developer tools console:

```
var myCar = new Car(false);
console.log(myCar.color);  // 'red'
// Public accessor returns distanceRun:
console.log(myCar.distance)  // 0
myCar.drive(15);
console.log(myCar.distance);  // 15 (0 + 15)
myCar.drive(21);
console.log(myCar.distance);  // 36 (15 + 21)
```

```
// What's my carbon footprint according to my car type?
myCar.getGasConsumption();  // 'Too high!'
Car.honk();  // 'HOOONK!' no object instance required
```

We can even perform an additional test and append the following illegal statements to our code, where we attempt to access the private property distanceRun or even apply a value through the distance member, which does not have a getter.

```
console.log(myCar.distanceRun);
myCar.distance = 100;
```

Right after inserting these code statements in the playground text field, a red underline will remark that we are attempting to do something that is not correct. Nevertheless, we can carry on and transpile and run the code, since ES5 will honor these practices. All in all, if we attempt to run the tsc compiler on this file, the runtime will exit with the following error trace:

```
example_26.ts(21,7): error TS1056: Accessors are only available when
targeting ECMAScript 5 and higher
example_26.ts(29,13): error TS2341: Property 'distanceRun' is private and
only accessible within class 'Car'
```

Constructor parameters with accessors

Normally, when creating a class, you need to give it a name, define a constructor, and create one or more backing fields, like so:

```
class Car {
  make: string;
  model: string;
  constructor(make: string, model: string) {
    this.make = make;
    this.model = model;
  }
}
```

For every field you need to add to the class you normally need to:

- Add an entry to the constructor
- Add an assignment in the constructor
- Create the backing field

This is really boring and not very productive. TypeScript have made it so, so that you don't need to type the backing fields by us using accessors on the constructor parameters. We can now type:

```
constuctor( public make: string, private model: string ) {}
```

Giving a parameter a public accessor means it will create a public field and giving it a private accessor means it creates a private field for us like so:

```
class Car {
  public make: string;  // creating backing field
  private model: string;

  constructor(make: string, model: string) {
    this.make = make;  //doing assignment
    this.model = model;
  }
}
```

And trying to access said fields would be like so:

```
var car = new Car('Ferrari', 'F40');
car.make  // Ferrari
car.model  // not accessible as it is private
```

In ES5, we don't have the concept of fields so that disappears, but assignment in the constructor is still there:

```
function Car(make) {
  this.make = make;
  this.model = model;
}
```

But, you don't have to do any of it in TypeScript, ever again. So, the preceding code using the constructor accessor approach only becomes:

```
class Car {
  constructor(public make: string, public model: string) {}
}
```

As you can see, more than half of the code disappears; this is really a selling point for TypeScript, as it saves you from typing quite a lot of tedious code.

Interfaces in TypeScript

As applications scale and more classes and constructs are created, we need to find ways to ensure consistency and rules compliance in our code. One of the best ways to address the consistency and type validation issue is to create interfaces.

In a nutshell, an interface is a code blueprint defining a certain field's schema and any types (either classes, function signatures) implementing these interfaces are meant to comply with this schema. This becomes quite useful when we want to enforce strict typing on classes generated by factories, when we define function signatures to ensure that a certain typed property is found in the payload, or other situations.

Let's get down to business! Here, we define the `Vehicle` interface. `Vehicle` is not a class, but a contractual schema that any class that implements it must comply with:

```
interface Vehicle {
  make: string;
}
```

Any class implementing the `Vehicle` interface must feature a member named `make`, which must be typed as a string according to this example. Otherwise, the TypeScript compiler will complain:

```
class Car implements Vehicle {
  // Compiler will raise a warning if 'make' is not defined
  make: string;
}
```

Interfaces are therefore extremely useful to define the minimum set of members any type must fulfill, becoming an invaluable method for ensuring consistency throughout our codebase.

It is important to note that interfaces are not used just to define minimum class schemas, but any type out there. This way, we can harness the power of interfaces for enforcing the existence of certain fields and methods in classes and properties in objects used later on as function parameters, function types, types contained in specific arrays, and even variables. An interface may contain optional members as well and even members.

Let's create an example. To do so, we will prefix all our interface types with an I (uppercase). This way, it will be easier to find its type when referencing them with our IDE code autocompletion functionality.

First, we define an `Exception` interface that models a type with a mandatory message property member and an optional `id` member:

```
interface Exception {
  message: string;
  id?: number;
}
```

We can define interfaces for array elements as well. To do so, we must define an interface with a sole member, defining index as either a number or string (for dictionary collections) and then the type what we want that array to contain. In this case, we want to create an interface for arrays containing `Exception` types. This is a type comprising of a string message property and an optional ID number member, as we said in the previous example:

```
interface ExceptionArrayItem {
  [index: number]: IException;
}
```

Now, we define the blueprint for our future class, with a typed array and a method with its returning type defined as well:

```
interface ErrorHandler {
  exception: ExceptionArrayItem[];
  logException(message: string; id?: number: void;)
}
```

We can also define interfaces for standalone object types. This is quite useful when it comes to defining a templated constructor or method signatures, which we will see later in this example:

```
interface ExceptionHandlerSettings {
  logAllExceptions: boolean;
}
```

Last but not least, in the following class, we will implement all these interface types:

```
class ErrorHandler implements ErrorHandler {
  exceptions: ExceptionArrayItem[];
  logAllExceptions: boolean;
  constructor(settings: ExceptionHandlerSettings) {
    this.logAllExceptions = settings.logAllExceptions;
  }

  logException(message: string, id?: number): void {
    this.exception.push({ message, id });
  }
}
```

Basically, we are defining an error handler class here that will manage an internal array of exceptions and expose a method to log new exceptions by saving them into the aforementioned array. These two elements are defined by the `ErrorHandler` interface and are mandatory. The class constructor expects the parameters defined by the `ExceptionHandlerSettings` interface and uses them to populate the exception member with items typed as `Exception`. Instancing the `ErrorHandler` class without the `logAllExceptions` parameter in the payload will trigger an error.

So far, I've been explaining interfaces as we are used to seeing them in other high level languages, but interfaces in TypeScript are on steroids; let me exemplify that by using the following code:

```
interface A {
   a
}

var instance = <A>{ a: 3 };
instance.a = 5;
```

Here, we declare an interface, but we also create an instance from an interface here:

```
var instance = <A>{ a: 3 };
```

This is interesting because there are no classes involved here. That means writing a mocking library is a piece of cake. Let's explain a bit what we mean with a mock library. When you are developing code you might think in interfaces before your start thinking in concrete classes. This is because you know what methods needs to exist but you might not have decided exactly how the methods should carry out a task. Imagine that you are building an order module. You have logic in your order module and you know that you at some point need to talk to a database service that will help you persist your order. You come up with a contract for said database service, an interface. You defer implementation of said interface until later. At this point a mocking library come in and is able to create a mock instance from an interface. Your code at this point might looking something like this:

```
class OrderProcessor {
   constructor(private databaseService: DatabaseService) {}

   process(order) {
     this.databaseService.save(order);
   }
}

interface DatabaseService {
}
```

```
let orderProcessor = new
OrderProcessor(mockLibrary.mock<DatabaseService>());
orderProcessor.process(new Order());
```

So mocking at this point gives us the ability to defer implementation of DatabaseService until we are done writing the OrderProcessor. It also makes the test experience of OrderProcessor a whole lot better. Where we in other languages needed to bring in mock library as 3rd party dependency we can now utilize a built in construct in TypeScript by typing the following:

```
var databaseServiceInstance = <DatabaseService>{};
```

This will give us an instance of DatabaseService. A word of warning though, you are responsible for adding a process() method to your instance. Your instance starts out as an empty object.

This would not raise any problems with the compiler; this means that it is a powerful feature, but it leaves it to you to verify that what you create is correct.

Let's emphasize how powerful this TypeScript feature really is by looking at some more code cases, where it pays off to be able to mock away things. Let's reiterate that the reason for mocking anything in your code is to make it easier to test.

Assume your code looks something like this:

```
class Stuff {
  srv:AuthService = new AuthService();
  execute() {
    if (srv.isAuthenticated())  // do x
    else  // do y
  }
}
```

A better way to test this is to make sure that the Stuff class relies on abstractions, which means that the AuthService should be created elsewhere and that we talk to an interface of AuthService rather than the concrete implementation. So, we would modify our code to look like this:

```
interface AuthService {
  isAuthenticated(): boolean;
}

class Stuff {
  constructor(srv:AuthService) {}
  execute() {
    if (srv.isAuthenticated()) { /* do x */ }
```

```
        else { /* do y */ }
    }
}
```

To test this class, we would normally need to create a concrete implementation of `AuthService` and use that as a parameter in the `Stuff` instance, like this:

```
class MockAuthService implements AuthService {
    isAuthenticated() { return true; }
}
var srv = new AuthService();
var stuff = new Stuff(srv);
```

It would, however, become quite tedious to have to write a mock version of every dependency that you wanted to mock away. Therefore, mocking frameworks exist in most languages. The idea is to give the mocking framework an interface that it would create a concrete object from. You would never have to create a mock class, as we did previously, but that would be something that would be up to the mocking framework to do internally. Using said mock framework it would look something like this:

```
var instance = mock<Type>();
```

We have already stated so far how easy it is to create an instance from an interface, like so:

```
var instance = <A>{ a: 3 };
```

This means creating a mocking framework is then as easy as typing the following:

```
function mock<T>(startData) {
    return <T>Object.assign({}, startData);
}
```

And using it in the following way:

```
interface IPoint {
    x;
    y;
}

class Point implements IPoint {
    x;
    y;
}
var point = mock<IPoint>({ x: 3 });
console.log(point);
```

Let's wrap up this section about interfaces by highlighting that classes can implement more than one interface, but also that interfaces are supercharged and facilitates testing quite a lot.

Extending classes with class inheritance

Just like a class can be defined by an interface, it can also extend the members and functionality of other classes as if they were its own. We can make a class inherit from another by appending the keyword extends to the class name, including the name of the class we want to inherit its members from:

```
class Sedan extends Car {
  model: string;
  constructor(make: string, model: string) {
    super(maker);
    this.model = model;
  }
}
```

Here, we extend from a parent class, Car, which already exposed a make member. We can populate the members already defined by the parent class and even execute their own constructor by executing the super() method, which points to the parent constructor. We can also override methods from the parent class by appending a method with the same name. Nevertheless, we will still be able to execute the original parent's class methods as it will be still accessible from the super object. Coming back to the interface, they can also inherit definition from other interfaces. Simply put, an interface can inherit from another interface.

As a word of caution, ES6 and TypeScript do not provide support for multiple inheritance. So, you may want to use composition or middleman classes instead, in case you want to borrow functionalities from different sources.

Decorators in TypeScript

Decorators are a very cool functionality, originally proposed by Google in AtScript (a superset of TypeScript that finally got merged into TypeScript back in early 2015) and also a part of the current standard proposition for ECMAScript 7. In a nutshell, decorators are a way to add metadata to class declarations for use by dependency injection or compilation directives (`http://blogs.msdn.com/b/somasegar/archive/2015/03/05/typescript-lt-3-angular.aspx`). By creating decorators, we are defining special annotations that may have an impact on the way our classes, methods, or functions behave or just simply altering the data we define in fields or parameters. In that sense, decorators are a powerful way to augment our type's native functionalities without creating subclasses or inheriting from other types.

This is, by far, one of the most interesting features of TypeScript. In fact, it is extensively used in Angular when designing directives and components or managing dependency injection, as we will see from `Chapter 5`, *Enhancing our Components with Pipes and Directives*, onwards.

Decorators can be easily recognized by the @ prefix to their name, and they are usually located as standalone statements above the element they decorate, including a method payload or not.

We can define up to four different types of decorators, depending on what element each type is meant to decorate:

- Class decorators
- Property decorators
- Method decorators
- Parameter decorators

Let's take a look at each of them!

Class decorators

Class decorators allow us to augment a class or perform operations over any of its members, and the decorator statement is executed before the class gets instanced.

Creating a class decorator just requires defining a plain function, whose signature is a pointer to the constructor belonging to the class we want to decorate, typed as function (or any other type that inherits from the function). The formal declaration defines a `ClassDecorator`, as follows:

```
declare type ClassDecorator = <TFunction extends Function>(Target:
TFunction) => TFunction | void;
```

Yes, it is really difficult to grasp what this gibberish means, right? Let's put everything in context through a simple example, like this:

```
function Banana(target: Function): void {
  target.prototype.banana = function(): void {
    console.log('We have bananas!');
  }
}

@Banana
class FruitBasket {
  constructor() {
    // Implementation goes here...
  }
}
var basket = new FruitBasket();
basket.banana();  // console will output 'We have bananas!'
```

As we can see, we have gained a `banana()` method that was not originally defined in the `FruitBasket` class just by properly decorating it with the `Banana` decorator. It is worth mentioning though that this won't actually compile. The compiler will complain that `FruitBasket` does not have a `banana()` method, and rightfully so. TypeScript is typed. In ES5, we could do anything we wanted and any wrong doing would be discovered in runtime. So at this point, we need to tell the compiler that this is OK. So, how do we do that? One way is that when we create our basket instance, we give it the type any like so:

```
var basket: any = new FruitBasket();
basket.banana();
```

What we did here is actively give the variable basket the `any` type and thereby fight the TypeScript compilers urge to infer the type to be `FruitBasket`. By being of type any TypeScript has no idea of knowing whether what we have done to it is correct or not. Another way of essentially accomplishing the same effect is to type like this instead:

```
var basket = new FruitBasket();
(basket as any).banana();
```

Here, we are doing a conversion on the fly with the `as`-operator and thereby we tell the compiler that this is OK.

Extending the class decorator function signature

Sometimes, we might need to customize the way our decorator operates upon instancing it. No worries! We can design our decorators with custom signatures and then have them returning a function with the same signature we defined when designing class decorators with no parameters. As a rule of thumb, decorators taking parameters just require a function whose signature matches the parameters we want to configure. Such a function must return another function, whose signature matches that of the decorator we want to define.

The following piece of code illustrates the same functionality as the previous example, but it allows developers to customize the greeting message:

```
function Banana(message: string) {
  return function(target: Function) {
    target.prototype.banana = function(): void {
      console.log(message);
    }
  }
}

@Greeter('Bananas are yellow!')
class FruitBasket {
  constructor() {
    // Implementation goes here...
  }
}
var basket = new FruitBasket();
basket.banana();  // console will output 'Bananas are yellow'
```

Property decorators

Property decorators are meant to be applied on class fields and can be easily defined by creating a `PropertyDecorator` function, whose signature takes two parameters:

- **Target**: This is the prototype of class we want to decorate
- **Key**: This is the name of the property we want to decorate

Possible use cases for this specific type of decorator may encompass from logging the value assigned to class fields when instancing objects of such a class and even reacting to data changes on such fields. Let's see an actual example that encompasses both of these behaviors:

```
function Jedi(target: Object, key: string) {
  var propertyValue: string = this[key];
  if (delete this[key]) {
    Object.defineProperty(target, key, {
      get: function() {
        return propertyValue;
      },
      set: function(newValue){
        propertyValue = newValue;
        console.log(`${propertyValue} is a Jedi`);
      }
    });
  }
}

class Character {
  @Jedi
  name: string;
}

var character = new Character();
character.name = 'Luke';  // console outputs 'Luke is a Jedi'
character.name = 'Yoda';  // console outputs 'Yoda is a Jedi'
```

The same logic for parameterized class decorators applies here, although the signature of the returned function is slightly different in order to match that of the parameter-less decorator declaration we already saw.

The following example depicts how we can log changes on a given class property and trigger a custom function when this occurs:

```
function NameChanger(callbackObject: any): Function {
  return function(target: Object, key: string): void {
    var propertyValue: string = this[key];
    if (delete this[key]) {
      Object.defineProperty(target, key, {
        get: function() {
          return propertyValue;
        },
        set: function(newValue) {
          propertyValue = newValue;
          callbackObject.changeName.call(this, propertyValue);
```

```
        }
      });
    }
  }
}

class Fruit {
  @NameChanger ({
    changeName: function(string,newValue: string): void {
      console.log(`You are now known as ${newValue}`);
    }
  })
 name: string;
}

var character = new Character();
character.name 'Anakin';   // console: 'You are now known as Anakin'
character.name = 'Lord Vader';   //console: 'You are now known as Lord
Vader'
```

Method decorators

These special decorators can detect, log, and intervene in how methods are executed. To do so, we just need to define a `MethodDecorator` function whose payload takes the following parameters:

- **Target**: This is typed as an object and represents the method being decorated.
- **Key**: This is a string that gives the actual name of the method being decorated.
- **Value**: This is a property descriptor of the given method. In fact, it's a hash object containing, among other things, a property named value with a reference to the method itself.

Let's see how we can leverage the `MethodDecorator` function in an actual example. The syntax to this has changed in later TypeScript versions. The idea, however, is to intercept before and after the execution of the method. So, why would you want to do that? Well, there are a couple of interesting cases:

- You want to know more of how a method is called, what `args`, what were the results, and so on
- You want to know how long it took for a certain method to run

Let's create a decorator for each of these cases:

```
function Log(){
   return function(target, propertyKey: string,
                   descriptor: PropertyDescriptor) {
     var oldMethod = descriptor.value;
     descriptor.value = function newFunc( ...args:any[]){
       let result = oldMethod.apply(this, args);
       console.log(`${propertyKey} is called with ${args.join(',') and
                   result ${result}`);
       return result;
     }
   }
}

class Hero {
  @Log()
  attack(...args:[]) { return args.join(); }
}

var hero = new Hero();
hero.attack();
```

Here, we are talking to the `descriptor.value`, which contains our actual function and as you can see, we:

- Save a reference to the old method
- We redefine the method by replacing what `descriptor.value` points to
- Inside of our new function we execute the old method
- We log to the console what args was used and what the result became

So far, we have explained how to add logging information to a method, but there was another scenario we wanted to describe as well, namely measuring execution time. We can use a very similar approach to the previous one, but with some subtle differences:

```
function Timer(){
   return function(target, propertyKey: string, descriptor:
PropertyDescriptor) {
     var oldMethod = descriptor.value;
     descriptor.value = function() {
       var start = new Date();
       let result = oldMethod.apply(this, args);
       var stop = new Date();
       console.log(`Method took ${stop.getMilliseconds() -
                   start.getMilliseconds()}ms to run`);
       return result;
```

```
        }
    }
}
```

We still do much of the same, but let's summarize it in a few bullet points:

- Save a reference to the old method
- Redefine `descriptor.value`
- Start a timer before method execution
- Execute method
- Stop the timer after method execution

Remember that decorator functions are scoped within the class represented in the target parameter, so we can take advantage of that for augmenting the class with our own custom members. Be careful when doing this, since this might override the already existing members. For the sake of this example, we won't apply any due diligence over this, but handle this with care in your code in the future. Method decorators are quite a powerful thing, but do not use them all the time, but rather in cases like the previous where they shine.

Parameter decorator

Our last round of decorators will cover the `ParameterDecorator` function, which taps into parameters located in function signatures. This sort of decorator is not intended to alter the parameter information or the function behavior, but to look into the parameter value and then perform operations elsewhere, such as, for argument's sake, logging or replicating data. The `ParameterDecorator` function takes the following parameters:

- **Target**: This is the object prototype where the function, whose parameters are decorated, usually belongs to a class
- **Key**: This is the name of the function whose signature contains the decorated parameter
- **Parameter index**: This is the index in the parameters array where this decorator has been applied

The following example shows a working example of a parameter decorator:

```
function Log(target: Function, key: string, parameterIndex: number) {
  var functionLogged = key || target.prototype.constructor.name;
  console.log(`
    The parameter in position
    ${parameterIndex} at ${functionLogged} has been decorated`
  );
}

class Greeter {
  greeting: string;
  constructor (@Log phrase: string) {
    this.greeting = phrase;
  }
}
// The console will output right after the class above is defined:
// 'The parameter in position 0 at Greeter has been decorated'
```

You have probably noticed the weird assignation of the `functionLogged` variable. This is because the value of the target parameter will vary depending on the function whose parameters are being decorated. Therefore, it is different if we decorate a constructor parameter or a method parameter. The former will return a reference to the class prototype and the latter will just return the constructor function. The same applies for the key parameter, which will be undefined when decorating the constructor parameters.

As we mentioned in the beginning of this section, parameter decorators are not meant to modify the value of the parameters decorated or alter the behavior of the methods or constructors where these parameters live. Their purpose is usually to log or prepare the container object for implementing additional layers of abstraction or functionality through higher-level decorators, such as method or class decorators. Usual case scenarios for this encompass logging component behavior or managing dependency injection, as we will see in `Chapter 5`, *Enhancing Our Components with Pipes and Directives.*

Organizing our applications with modules

As our applications scale and grow in size, there will be a time when we will need to better organize our code to make it sustainable and more reusable. Modules are the response for this need, so let's take a look at how they work and how we can implement them in our application. Modules can be either internal or external. In this book, we will mostly focus on external modules, but it is a good idea to overview the two types now.

Internal modules

In a nutshell, internal modules are singleton wrappers containing a range of classes, functions, objects, or variables that are scoped internally, away from the global or outer scope. We can publicly expose the contents of a module by prefixing the keyword `export` to the element we want to be accessible from the outside, like this:

```
module Greetings {
  export class Greeting {
    constructor(public name: string) {
      console.log(`Hello ${name}`);
    }
  }

  export class XmasGreeting {
    constructor(public name: string){
      console.log(`Merry Xmas ${name}`);
    }
  }
}
```

Our `Greetings` module contains two classes that will be accessible from outside the module by importing the module and accessing the class we want to use by its name:

```
import XmasGreeting = Greeting.XmasGreeting;
var xmasGreeting = XmasGreeting('Joe');
// console outputs 'Merry Xmas Joe'
```

After looking at the preceding code, we can conclude that internal modules are a good way to group and encapsulate elements in a namespace context. We can even split our modules into several files, as long as the module declaration keeps the same name across these files. In order to do so, we will want to reference the different files where we have scattered objects belonging to this module with reference tags:

```
/// <reference path="greetings/XmasGreeting.ts" />
```

The major drawback of internal modules though is that in order to put them to work outside the domain of our IDE, we need to have all of them in the same file or application scope. We can include all the generated JavaScript files as script inserts in our web pages, leverage task runners such as Grunt or Gulp for that, or even use the `--outFile` flag in the TypeScript compiler to have all the `.ts` files found in your workspace compiled into a single bundle using a bootstrap file with reference tags to all the other modules as the starting point for our compilation:

```
tsc --outFile app.js module.ts
```

This will compile all the TypeScript files following the trail of dependent files referenced with reference tags. If we forget to reference any file this way, it will not be included in the final build file, so another option is to enlist all the files containing standalone modules in the compiling command or just add a `.txt` file containing a comprehensive list of the modules to bundle. Alternatively, we can just use external modules instead.

External modules

External modules are pretty much the solution we need when it comes to building applications designed to grow. Basically, each external module works at a file level, where each file is the module itself and the module name will match the filename without the .js extension. We do not use the module keyword anymore and each member marked with the export prefix will become part of the external module API. The internal module depicted in the previous example would turn into this once conveniently saved in the `Greetings.ts` file:

```
export class Greeting {
  constructor(public name: string) {
    console.log(`Hello ${name}`);
  }
}

export class XmasGreeting {
  constructor(public name: string) {
    console.log(`Merry Xmas ${name}`);
  }
}
```

Importing this module and using its exported classes would require the following code:

```
import greetings = require('Greetings');
var XmasGreetings = greeting.XmasGreetings();
var xmasGreetings = new XmasGreetings('Pete');
// console outputs 'Merry Xmas Pete'
```

Obviously, the require function is not supported by traditional JavaScript, so we need to instruct the compiler about how we want that functionality to be implemented in our target JavaScript files. Fortunately, the TypeScript compiler includes the `--module` parameter in its API, so we can configure the dependency loader of choice for our project: `commonjs` for node-style imports, `amd` for RequireJS-based imports, `umd` for a loader implementing the Universal Module Definition specification, or system for SystemJS-based imports. We will focus on the SystemJS module loader throughout this book:

```
tsc --outFile app.js --module commonjs
```

The resulting file will be properly shimmed, so modules can load dependencies across files using our module loader of choice.

ES6 like modules per TypeScript > 1.5

The way you will be using modules in your Angular projects is by using external modules with ES6 syntax, so let's go through the basics of what that means. As mentioned before in this section, there is one file per module and we can export it by using the export keyword. How you consume dependencies, however, differs syntactically; let's illustrate this by creating an ES6 module `service.ts` and another module `consumer.ts`, which is meant to consume the former:

```
//service.ts
export class Service {
  getData() {}
}
```

```
//consumer.ts
import {} from './service';
```

Two things to notice here is in the `consumer.ts` file:

- Importing with curly brackets {}
- Using the from keyword to find our file

The curly bracket {} gives us the opportunity to pick and choose what construct we actually want to import. Imagine if `service.ts` was more complicated like this:

```
//service-v2.ts
export class Service {
  getData(){}
}

export const PI = 3.14
```

As a consumer, we could now choose to import `Service` and/or `PI` like so:

```
//consumer-v2.ts
import { Service, PI } from './service-v2'
```

It is however possible to use an alternate syntax to export your constructs. So far, we have been typing `export` for each thing we wanted to export; we could type it like this instead in the third installment of our `service.ts` called `service-v3.ts`:

```
//service-v3.ts
class Service {}

const PI = 3.14;

export { Service, PI }
```

The third way of doing exports is default `export`. There is such a thing as a `default` keyword, which means we don't have to use the curly braces `{}` when importing it:

```
//service-v4.ts
export default function(a, b) {
 return a + b;
}

//consumer-v3.ts
import service from './service-v4';
```

Summary

This was definitely a long read, but this introduction to TypeScript was absolutely necessary in order to understand the logic behind many of the most brilliant parts of Angular. It gave us the chance to not only introduce the language syntax, but also explain the rationale behind its success as the syntax of choice for building the Angular framework. We reviewed its type architecture and how we can create advanced business logic designing functions with a wide range of alternatives for parameterized signatures, and we even discovered how to bypass issues related to scope by using the powerful new arrow functions. Probably the most relevant part of this chapter encompassed the overview of classes, methods, properties, and accessors and how we can handle inheritance and better application design through interfaces. Modules and decorators were some other major features explored in this chapter and, as we will see very soon, having a sound knowledge of these mechanisms is paramount to understand how dependency injection works in Angular.

With all this knowledge at our disposal, we can now resume our investigation of Angular and confront the relevant parts of component creation, such as style encapsulation, output formatting, and so on with confidence. Chapter 4, *Implementing Properties and Events in Our Components*, will expose us to advanced template creation techniques, data-binding techniques, directives, and pipes. All these features will allow us to put into practice all this newly gained knowledge of TypeScript.

4

Implementing Properties and Events in Our Components

So far, we have had the opportunity to take a bird's eye overview of what components are in the new Angular ecosystem, what their role is, how they behave, and what tools are required to start building our own components to represent widgets and pieces of functionality. In addition, TypeScript turns out to be the perfect companion for this endeavor, so we seem to have everything that we need to further explore the possibilities that Angular brings to the game with regards to creating interactive components that expose properties and emit events.

In this chapter, we will:

- Discover all the syntactic possibilities at our disposal to bind content in our templates
- Create public APIs for our components so that we can benefit from their properties and event handlers
- See how to implement data binding in Angular
- Reduce the complexity of CSS management with view encapsulation

A better template syntax

In Chapter 1, *Creating Our Very First Component in Angular*, we saw how to embed HTML templates in our components, but we didn't even scratch the surface of template development for Angular. As we will see later in this book, template implementation is tightly coupled with the principles of Shadow DOM design and it brings out a lot of syntactic sugar to ease the task of binding properties and events in our views in a declarative fashion.

In a nutshell, Angular components may expose a public API that allows them to communicate with other components or containers. This API may encompass input properties, which we use to feed the component with data. It also may expose output properties we can bind event listeners to, thereby getting prompt information about changes in the state of the component.

Let's take a look at the way Angular solves the problem of injecting data in and out of our components through quick and easy examples. Please focus on the philosophy behind these properties. We will have a chance to see them in action later.

Data bindings with input properties

Let's revisit the timer component functionality that we already saw in Chapter 1, *Creating Our Very First Component in Angular*, and let's imagine that we want our component to have a configurable attribute so that we can increase or decrease the countdown time:

```
<timer [seconds]="25"></timer>
```

Please note the attribute wrapped between brackets. This informs Angular that this is an input property. The class that models the timer component will contain a setter function for the seconds property, which will react to changes in that value by updating its own countdown duration. We can inject a data variable or an actual hardcoded value, in which case we will have to wrap it around single quotes within the double quotes should such a value be a text string.

Sometimes we will see this syntax while injecting data into our component's custom properties, while at other times we will use this very bracket syntax to make native HTML attributes reactive to component fields, like this:

```
<h1 [hidden]="hideMe">
    This text will not be visible if 'hideMe' is true
</h1>
```

Some extra syntactic sugar when binding expressions

The Angular team has made some shortcuts available for performing common transformations in our component directives and DOM elements, such as tweaking attributes and class names or applying styles. Here, we have some examples of great time-savers when declaratively defining bindings in our properties:

```
<div [attr.hidden]="isHidden">...</div>
<input [class.is-valid]="isValid">
<div [style.width.px]="myWidth"></div>
```

In the first case, div will enable the hidden attribute should the isHidden expression evaluate to true. Besides Boolean values, we can bind any other data type, such as a string value. In the second case, the is-valid class name will be injected in the class attribute if the isValid expression evaluates to true. In our third example, div will feature a style attribute that shows off a width property meant to be set with the value of the myWidth expressions in pixels. You can find more examples of this syntactic sugar in the Angular cheat sheet (https://angular.io/guide/cheatsheet) available at the official Angular site.

Event binding with output properties

Let's imagine we want our timer component to notify us when the countdown is finished so that we can perform other actions outside the realm of the component. We can achieve such functionality with an output property like this:

```
<timer (countdownComplete)="onCountdownCompleted()"></timer>
```

Note the attribute wrapped between braces. This informs Angular that such an attribute is, in fact, an output property that will trigger the event handler we bind to it. In this case, we will want to create an onCountownCompleted event handler on the container object that wraps this component.

By the way, the camel case is not a coincidence. It is a naming convention applied to all output and input property names in Angular.

We will find output properties mapped to interaction events that we already know, such as click, mouseover, mouseout, focus, and more:

```
<button (click)="doSomething()">click me</button>
```

Input and output properties in action

The best way to grasp the concepts detailed in the earlier sections is by practice. In the first chapter, we learned how to build an application from scratch by using either Webpack or Angular-CLI to set up the project. As Angular-CLI is considered the standard way of setting up the project, let's use just that and scaffold ourselves a new project by typing:

```
ng new InputOutputDemo
```

At this point, we have a fully working project that we can easily serve up by typing `ng serve`.

Let's quickly remind ourselves of the anatomy of an Angular project so we know what to do with all the new constructs we are about to create. The following files are of extra interest:

- `main.ts`: This file bootstraps our application.
- `app/app.module.ts`: This file declares our root module, any new constructs will have to be added to the declarations property of this module or you will need to add a dedicated module for those future constructs. It is generally recommended to have a dedicated module for new constructs we have.

In the previous bullet list, we mentioned the concept *root module*. We mentioned this concept to remind ourselves of Angular modules in general. An Angular module holds a bunch of constructs that belong together. You will recognize an Angular module by using the `@NgModule` decorator; the module itself is just a plain class. The `@NgModule` decorator takes an object literal as input and it is within this object literal that we register everything that belongs to the module.

As mentioned in the preceding bullet list, it is considered good practice to add a dedicated module for our new constructs, so let's do just that:

```
@NgModule({
  declarations: []
})
export class InputModule {}
```

At this point, we are leaving the `declarations` property array empty. Once we have declared our component, we will add it to that array.

This module doesn't belong to the application just yet, but it will need to be registered with the root module. Open up the `app.module.ts` file and add the newly created module to the `import` array, like so:

```
@NgModule({
    declarations: [AppComponent],
    imports: [
        BrowserModule,
        InputModule
    ],
    providers: [],
    bootstrap: [AppComponent]
})
export class AppModule { }
```

Let's strip down the timer example that we saw in Chapter 1, *Creating Our Very First Component in Angular*, and discuss a simpler example. Let's have a look at the `TimerComponent` file and replace its contents with the following component class:

```
import { Component } from '@angular/core';

@Component({
    selector : 'countdown-timer',
    template : '<h1>Time left: {{seconds}}</h1>'
})
export class CountdownTimerComponent {
    seconds: number = 25;
    intervalId: any;

    constructor() {
        this.intervalId = setInterval(() => this.tick(), 1000);
    }

    private tick(): void {
        if(--this.seconds < 1) {
            clearInterval(this.intervalId);
        }
    }
}
```

Great! We have just defined a simple but highly effective countdown timer component that will count down to 0 from 25 seconds (do you see the `seconds` field up there? TypeScript supports the initialisation of members upon declaring them). A simple `setInterval()` loop executes a custom private function named `tick()` that decreases the value of seconds until it reaches zero, in which case we just clear the interval.

However, now we just need to embed this component somewhere, so let's create another component with no functionality other than acting as an HTML wrapper host for the previous component. Create this new component right after the `CountdownTimerComponent` class in the same file:

```
@Component({
  selector: 'timer',
  template: '<countdown-timer></countdown-timer>'
})
export class TimerComponent {}
```

As promised earlier, we will also add our newly created components to the `declarations` array of the module it belongs to, like so:

```
@NgModule({
  declarations: [CountdownTimerComponent, TimerComponent]
})
export class InputModule {}
```

The reason for doing this in the first place is to ensure that these components are made available for one another, as is the case with `CountdownTimerComponent` being used inside the template of `TimerComponent`.

Components in Angular are basically directives with a view template. We can also find directives with no view, which basically add new functionalities to their host element, or they just act as custom elements without a UI that wraps other elements. Alternatively, they simply provide further functionalities to other components by means of their API.

We will explore directives in detail in the next chapter and also throughout the book. You must be wondering why we have created this host or parent `TimerComponent` component with no implementation. Soon, we will flesh it out with some more features, but for now let's use it as a proof of concept for how to initiate a component tree.

Setting up custom values declaratively

You will probably agree on the fact that having the functionality of setting up custom countdown timers would be nice, right? Input properties turn out to be an excellent way to achieve this. In order to leverage this functionality, we will have to tweak the `import` statement at the top of the file:

```
import { Component, Input } from '@angular/core';

@Component({
  selector: 'countdown-timer',
```

```
    template: '<h1>Time left: {{ seconds }}</h1>'
})
export class CountdownTimerComponent {
  @Input() seconds : number;
  intervalId;
  // rest of the implementation remains the same
}
```

You might have already noticed that we are no longer initializing the seconds field, and it is now decorated with a property decorator (as we saw in Chapter 3, *Introducing TypeScript*). We have just started to define the API of our component.

Property naming is case sensitive. The convention enforced by Angular is to apply camel case to component input and, as we will see shortly, output properties alike.

Next, we just need to add the desired property in our container component's template:

```
@Component({
  selector: 'timer',
  template: `
    <div class="container text-center">
      <countdown-timer [seconds]="25"></countdown-timer>
    </div>`
})
```

Please note that we have not updated the TimerComponent at all. We only updated its CountdownComponent child component. However, its brand new API becomes available to any component that eventually includes it in its own template as a child component, so we can set up its properties declaratively right from the template, or even bind a value imperatively from a property located in the TimerComponent controller class if we wish.

When flagging a class property with @Input(), we can configure the name we want this property to have upon instantiating the component in the HTML. To do so, we just need to introduce our name of choice in the decorator signature, like this: @Input('name_of_the_property'). In any event, this practice is discouraged since exposing property names in the component API distinct from the ones defined in its controller class can only lead to confusion.

Communicating between components through custom events

Now that our child component is being configured by its parent component, how can we achieve communication from the child to the parent? This is where custom events come to the rescue! In order to create proper event bindings, we just need to configure an output property in our component and attach an event handler function to it.

In order to trigger custom events, we will need to bring EventEmitter to the party, along with the @Output decorator, whose functionality is exactly the opposite to what we learned regarding the @Input decorator:

```
import { Component, Input, Output, EventEmitter } from '@angular/core';
```

EventEmitter is the built-in event bus of Angular. In a nutshell, the EventEmitter class provides support for emitting Observable data and subscribing Observer consumers to data changes. Its simple interface, which basically encompass two methods, emit() and subscribe(), can therefore be used to trigger custom events and listen to events as well, both synchronously and asynchronously. We will discuss Observables in more detail in Chapter 7, *Asynchronous Data Services with Angular*. For the time being, we can get away with the idea that we will be using the EventEmitter API to spawn events that listener methods in the components hosting our event-emitting component can observe and attach event handlers to. These events acquire visibility outside the scope of the component through any of its properties annotated with the @Input() decorator.

The following code shows an actual implementation that follows up from the previous example:

```
@Component({
  selector : 'countdown-timer',
  template : '<h1>Time left: {{ seconds }}</h1>'
})
export class CountdownTimerComponent {
  @Input() seconds : number;
  intervalId: any;
  @Output() complete: EventEmitter<any> = new EventEmitter();
  constructor() {
    this.intervalId = setInterval( () => this.tick(), 1000 );
  }
  private tick(): void {
    if(--this.seconds < 1) {
      clearTimeout(this.intervalId);
      // an event is emitted upon finishing the countdown
```

```
        this.complete.emit(null);
    }
  }
}
```

A new property named `complete` is conveniently annotated with the `EventEmitter` type and initialized on the spot. Later on, we will access its emit method to spawn a custom event as soon as the countdown ends. The `emit()` method needs one mandatory parameter of any type, so we can send a data value to the event subscribers (or null if not required).

Now, we just need to set up our host component so that it will listen to this complete event or output property and subscribe an event handler to it:

```
@Component({
  selector : 'timer',
  template :  `
    <div class="container text-center">
      <img src="assets/img/timer.png" />
      <countdown-timer [seconds]="25"
                (complete)="onCountdownCompleted()">
      </countdown-timer>`
})
export class TimerComponent {
  onCountdownCompleted(): void {
    alert('Time up !')
  }
}
```

Why `complete` and not `onComplete`? Angular provides support for an alternative syntax named canonical form for both input and output properties. In the case of input properties, a property represented as `[seconds]` could be represented as `bind-seconds`, without the need for brackets. With regards to output properties, these can be represented as `on-complete` instead of `(complete)`. That is why we never prefix output property names with an `on` prefix, since that would occur on output properties such as `on-complete` in case we eventually decide to favor the canonical syntax form in our projects.

We have learned to use input data with our component. The data would live in the container and the component would be rendered inside of the container template. This means the component could suddenly gain access to the container's data by us typing this:

```
<component [property]="propertyOnContainer">
```

And on the component side, the code looks as follows:

```
@Component({
  selector : 'component'
})
export class Component {
  @Input() property;
}
```

We've also learned about output, that is, how to communicate back from component to container. To make this happen, we added another property on the component like so:

```
<component (event)="methodOnContainer()" [property]="propertyOnContainer">
```

And on the component side, we would instead use a decorator called `Output`, like so:

```
@Component({
  selector : 'component'
})
export class Component {
  @Output() event = new EventEmitter<any>();
}
```

And to actively invoke that bonded method, we would type:

```
event.emit();
```

Then next thing coming up is to learn how to pass data from component to container.

Emitting data through custom events

Now that we know how to emit custom events from our component API, why don't we take a step further and send data signals beyond the scope of the component? We already discussed that the `emit()` event of the `EventEmitter<T>` class accepts in its signature any given data of the type represented by the `T` annotation. Let's extend our example to notify the progress of the countdown. Why would we ever want to do this? Basically, our component displays onscreen a visual countdown, but we might want to watch the countdown progress programmatically in order to take action once the countdown is finished or reaches a certain point.

Let's update our timer component with another output property that matches the original and emits a custom event on each iteration of the `seconds` property, as follows:

```
class CountdownTimerComponent {
```

```
@Input() seconds: number;
@Output() complete: EventEmitter<any> = new EventEmitter();
@Output() progress: EventEmitter<number> = new EventEmitter();
intervalId;

constructor() {
  this.intervalId = setInterval(() => this.tick(), 1000);
}

private tick(): void {
  if(--this.seconds < 1) {
    clearTimeout(this.intervalId);
    this.complete.emit(null);
  }
  this.progress.emit(this.seconds);
}
}
```

Now, let's rebuild our host component's template to reflect the actual progress of the countdown. We already do so by displaying the countdown, but that is a feature handled internally by the CountdownTimerComponent. Now, we will keep track of the countdown outside this component:

```
@Component({
  selector: 'timer',
  template: `
    <div class="container text-center">
      <countdown-timer [seconds]="25"
                   (progress)="timeout = $event"
                   (complete)="onCountdownCompleted()" >
      </countdown-timer>
      <p *ngIf="timeout < 10">
        Beware! Only
        <strong>{{ timeout }} seconds</strong>
      </p>
    </div>`
})
export class TimerComponent {
  timeout: number;
  onCountdownCompleted(): void {
    alert('Time up')
  }
}
```

We took advantage of this round of changes to formalize the timeout value as a property of the host component. This allows us to bind new values to that property in our custom event handlers, as we did in the preceding example. Rather than binding an event handler method to the (`progress`) handler, we refer to the `$event` reserved variable. It is a pointer to the payload of the `progress output` property that reflects the value we pass to the `emit()` function when executing `this.progress.emit(this.seconds)`. In short, `$event` is the value assumed by `this.seconds` inside `CountdownTimerComponent`. By assigning such a value to the `timeout` class property within the template, we are also updating the binding expressed in the paragraph we just inserted into the template. This paragraph will only become visible when `timeout` is lower than `10`:

```
<countdown-timer [seconds]="25"
          (progress)="timeout = $event"
          (complete)="onCountdownCompleted()">
</countdown-timer>
```

What we saw in this section was how we could send data from the component to the container. There are essentially two ways of doing that:

- Assign `$event` to the container property
- Invoke the container method with `$event` as the function parameter

The first version is what we demonstrated, that is:

```
<countdown [seconds]="25" (progress)="timeout = $event" >
</countdown>
```

With the component invoking it as follows:

```
progress.emit(data);
```

The second version is a small rewrite of the preceding example:

```
<countdown [seconds]="25" (progress)="onProgress($event)">
</countdown>
```

We would invoke it the same way in the component, but the difference would be that we need to declare a container method, `onProgress`, so the `timeout` property gets set that way instead:

```
onProgress(data) {
  this.timeout = data;
}
```

Local references in templates

We have previously seen how we can bind data to our templates using data interpolation with the double curly braces syntax. Besides this, we will quite often spot named identifiers prefixed by a hash symbol (#) in the elements belonging to our components or even regular HTML controls. These reference identifiers, namely local names, are used to refer to the components flagged with them in our template views and then access them programmatically. They can also be used by components to refer to other elements in the virtual DOM and access its properties.

In the previous section, we saw how we could subscribe to the countdown progress through the `progress` event. But what if we could inspect the component in depth, or at least its public properties and methods, and read the value that the `seconds` property takes on each tick interval without having to listen to the `progress` event? Well, setting a local reference on the component itself will open the door to its public façade.

Let's flag the instance of our `CountdownTimerComponent` in the `TimerComponent` template with a local reference named #counter. From that very moment, we will be able to directly access the component's public properties, such as `seconds`, and even bind it in other locations of the template. This way, we do not even need to rely on the `progress` event emitter or the `timeout` class field, and we can even manipulate the value of such properties. This is shown in the following code:

```
@Component({
  selector: 'timer',
  template: `
    <div class="container text-center">
      <countdown-timer [seconds]="25"
                  (complete)="onCountdownCompleted()"
                  #counter >
      </countdown-timer>
      <p>
        <button class="btn btn-default"
                (click)="counter.seconds = 25">
          reset
        </button>
      </p>
      <p *ngIf="counter.seconds < 10">
        Beware, only !
        <strong>{{ counter.seconds }} seconds</strong>
      </p>
    </div>`
})
export class TimerComponent {
  // timeout: any /* No longer required */
```

```
onCountdownCompleted(): void {
  alert('Time up');
}
}
```

Alternative syntax for input and output properties

Besides the @Input() and @Output() decorators, there is an alternative syntax where we can define input and output properties in our components by means of the @Component decorator. Its metadata implementation provides support for both features through the inputs and outputs property names, respectively.

The CountdownTimerComponent API could therefore be implemented like this:

```
@Component({
  selector : 'countdown-timer',
  template : '<h1>Time left: {{seconds}}</h1>',
  inputs : ['seconds'],
  outputs : ['complete','progress']
})
export class CountdownTimerComponent {
  seconds: number;
  intervalId;
  complete: EventEmitter<any> = new EventEmitter();
  progress: EventEmitter<any> = new EventEmitter();
  // And so on..
}
```

All in all, this syntax is discouraged and has been included here for reference purposes only. In the first place, we duplicate code by defining the names of our API endpoints in two places at the same time, increasing the risk of errors when refactoring code. It is also a common convention to keep the decorator implementations as lean as possible in order to improve readability.

 I strongly suggest that you stick to the @Input and @Output decorators.

Configuring our template from our component class

The component metadata also supports several settings that contribute to easy template management and configuration. On the other hand, Angular takes advantage of the CSS encapsulation functionalities of web components.

Internal and external templates

As our applications grow in size and complexity, chances are that our templates will grow as well, hosting other components and bigger chunks of HTML code. Embedding all this code in our component class definitions will become a cumbersome and unpleasant task and it will also be quite prone to errors. In order to prevent this from happening, we can leverage the `templateUrl` property, pointing to a standalone HTML file that contains our component HTML markup.

Back to our previous example, we can refactor the `@Component` decorator of our `TimerComponent` class to point to an external HTML file containing our template. Create a new file named `timer.component.html` in the workspace where our `timer.component.ts` file lives and populate it with the same HTML we configured in our `TimerComponent` class:

```
<div class="container text-center">
    <countdown [seconds]="25"
               (complete)="onCountdownCompleted()"
               #counter >
    </countdown>
    <p>
       <button class="btn btn-default"
               (click)="counter.seconds = 25">
         Reset countdown to 25 seconds
       </button>
    </p>
    <p *ngIf="counter.seconds < 10">
      Beware only !
      <strong>{{ seconds }} seconds</strong> left
    </p>
</div>
```

Now, we can polish our `@Component` decorator to point to that file instead of defining the HTML inside the decorator metadata:

```
@Component({
  selector: 'timer',
  templateUrl: './timer.component.html'
})
export class TimerComponent {
  // Class follows below
}
```

External templates follow a certain convention in Angular, enforced by the most popular Angular coding style guide out there, which is to share the same filename as the component they belong to, including any filename prefix or suffix we might append to the component filename. We will see this when exploring component naming conventions in Chapter 6, *Building an Application with Angular Components*. This way, it is easier to recognize, or even search with your IDE's search built-in fuzzy finder tool, which HTML file is in fact the template of a specific component.

What is the threshold for creating standalone templates rather than keeping the template markup inside the component? It depends on the complexity and size of the template. Common sense will be your best advisor in this case.

Encapsulating CSS styling

In order to better encapsulate our code and make it more reusable, we can define CSS styling within our components. These internal style sheets are a good way to make our components more shareable and maintainable. There are three different ways of defining CSS styling for our components.

The styles property

We can define `styles` for our HTML elements and class names through the `styles` property in the component decorator, like this:

```
@Component({
  selector : 'my-component',
  styles : [`
    p {
      text-align: center;
    }
    table {
      margin: auto;
```

```
      }
    `]
})
export class ExampleComponent {}
```

This property will take an array of strings, each containing CSS rules, and apply them to the template markup by embedding those rules at the head of the document as soon as we bootstrap our application. We can either inline the styling rules in a single line, or take advantage of ES2015 template strings to indent the code and make it more readable, as depicted in the preceding example.

The styleUrls property

Just like `styles`, `styleUrls` will accept an array of strings, although each one will represent a link to an external style sheet though. This property can be used alongside the `styles` property as well, defining different sets of rules where required:

```
@Component({
    selector: 'my-component',
    styleUrls: ['path/to/my-stylesheet.css'], // use this
    styles : [
        `
        p { text-align : center; }
        table { margin: auto; }
        `
    ]  // and this at the same time
})
export class MyComponent {}
```

Inline style sheets

We can also attach the styling rules to the template itself, no matter whether it's an inline template or a template served through the `templateUrl` parameter:

```
@Component({
    selector: 'app',
    template: `
        <style> p { color : red; } </style>
        <p>I am a red paragraph </p>
        `
})
export class AppComponent {}
```

Managing view encapsulation

All the preceding sections (`styles`, `styleUrls`, and inline style sheets) will be governed by the usual rules of CSS specificity (`https://developer.mozilla.org/en/docs/Web/CSS/Specificity`). CSS management and specificity becomes a breeze on browsers that support Shadow DOM, thanks to scoped styling. CSS styles apply to the elements contained in the component, but they do not spread beyond its boundaries.

On top of that, Angular will embed these style sheets at the head of the document, so they might affect other elements of our application. In order to prevent this from happening, we can set up different levels of view encapsulation.

In a nutshell, encapsulation is the way Angular needs to manage CSS scoping within the component for both shadow DOM-compliant browsers and those that do not support it. For all this, we leverage the `ViewEncapsulation enum`, which can take any of these values:

- **Emulated**: This is the default option, and it basically entails an emulation of native scoping in Shadow DOM, through sandboxing the CSS rules under a specific selector that points to our component. This option is preferred to ensure that our component styles will not be affected by other existing libraries on our site.
- **Native**: Use the native Shadow DOM encapsulation mechanism of the renderer, and it only works on browsers that support Shadow DOM.
- **None**: Template or style encapsulation is not provided. The styles will be injected as is into the document's header.

Let's check out an actual example. First, import the `ViewEncapsulation enum` into the script, and then create an encapsulation property with the emulated value. Then, let's create a style rule for our countdown text so any `<h1>` (!) tag is rendered in dark red:

```
import {
  Component,
  EventEmitter,
  Input,
  Output,
  ViewEncapsulation
} from '@angular/core';
@Component({
  selector: 'countdown-timer',
  template: '<h1>Time left: {{seconds}}</h1>',
  styles: ['h1 { color: #900}'],
  encapsulation: ViewEncapsulation.Emulated
})
```

```
export class CountdownTimerCoponent {
  // Etc
}
```

Now, click on the browser's dev tools inspector and check the generated HTML to discover how Angular injected the CSS inside the page `<head>` block. The just injected style sheet has been sandboxed to ensure that the global CSS rule we defined at the component setup in a very non-specific way for all `<h1>` elements only applies to matching elements scoped by the `CountdownTimerComponent` component exclusively.

We recommend that you try out different values and see how the CSS code is injected into the document. You will immediately notice the different grades of isolation that each variation provides.

Summary

This chapter guided us through the options available in Angular for creating powerful APIs for our components, so we can provide high levels of interoperability between components, configuring its properties by assigning either static values or managed bindings. We also saw how a component can act as a host component for another child component, instantiating the former's custom element in its own template, setting the ground up for larger component trees in our applications. Output parameters give the layer of interactivity we need by turning our components into event emitters so they can properly communicate in an agnostic fashion with any parent component that might eventually host them. Template references paved the way to create references in our custom elements that we can use as accessors to their properties and methods from within the template in a declarative fashion. We also discussed how we could isolate the component's HTML template in an external file in order to ease its future maintainability and how to do the same with any style sheet we wanted to bind to the component, in case we do not want to bundle the component styles inline. An overview of the built-in features for handling view encapsulation in Angular gave us some additional insights on how we can benefit from Shadow DOM's CSS scoping on a per-component basis and how we can polyfill it when not supported.

We still have much more to learn regarding template management in Angular, mostly with regards to the two concepts that you will use extensively along your journey with Angular. I am referring to Directives and Pipes, which we will cover extensively in `Chapter 5`, *Enhancing Our Components with Pipes and Directives*.

5
Enhancing Our Components with Pipes and Directives

In the previous chapters, we built several components that rendered data on screen with the help of input and output properties. We will leverage the knowledge in this chapter to take our components to the next level with the use of directives and pipes. In a nutshell, while pipes give us the opportunity to digest and transform the information we bind in our templates, directives allow us to conduct more ambitious functionalities where we can access the host element properties and also bind our very own custom event listeners and data bindings.

In this chapter, we will:

- Have a comprehensive overview of the built-in directives of Angular
- Discover how we can refine our data output with pipes
- See how we can design and build our own custom pipes and directives
- Leverage built-in objects for manipulating our templates
- Put all the preceding topics and many more into practice to build a fully interactive to-do items table

Directives in Angular

Angular defines directives as components without views. In fact, a component is a directive with an associated template view. This distinction is used because directives are a prominent part of the Angular core and each (plain directives and component directives) needs the other to exist. Directives can basically affect the way HTML elements or custom elements behave and display their content.

Core directives

Let's take a closer look at the framework's core directives, and then you will learn how to build your own directives later on in this chapter.

NgIf

As the official documentation states, the `ngIf` directive removes or recreates a portion of the DOM tree based on an expression. If the expression assigned to the `ngIf` directive evaluates to `false`, then the element is removed from the DOM. Otherwise, a clone of the element is reinserted into the DOM. We could enhance our countdown timer by leveraging this directive, like this:

```
<timer> [seconds]="timeout"></timer>
<p *ngIf="timeout === 0">Time up!</p>
```

When our timer reaches 0, the paragraph that displays the `Time up!` text will be rendered on the screen. You have probably noticed the asterisk that prepends the directive. This is because Angular embeds the HTML control marked with the `ngIf` directive (and all its HTML subtrees, if any) in a `<ng-template>` tag, which will be used later on to render the content on the screen. Covering how Angular treats templates is definitely out of the scope of this book, but let's just point out that this is syntactic sugar provided by Angular to act as a shortcut to other, more verbose syntax based on template tags.

Perhaps you are wondering what difference does it make to render some chunk of HTML on screen with `*ngIf="conditional"` rather than with `[hidden]="conditional"`. The former will clone and inject pieces of templated HTML snippets in the markup, removing it from the DOM when the condition evaluates to `false`, while the latter does not inject or remove any markup from the DOM. It simply sets the visibility of the already existing chunk of HTML annotated with that DOM attribute.

NgFor

The `ngFor` directive allows us to iterate through a collection (or any other iterable object) and bind each of its items to a template of our choice, where we can define convenient placeholders to interpolate the item data. Each instantiated template is scoped to the outer context, where the loop directive is placed, so we can access other bindings. Let's imagine we have a component named `Staff`: it features a field named employees, which represents an array of `Employee` objects. We can enlist those employees and job titles in this way:

```
<ul>
  <li *ngFor="let employee of employees">
    Employee {{ employee.name }}, {{ employee.position }}
  </li>
</ul>
```

As we can see in the example provided, we turn each item fetched from the iterable object on each loop into a local reference so that we can easily bind this item in our template. A thing to highlight is that the expression starts with the keyword `let`.

This directive observes changes in the underlying iterable object and will add, remove, or sort the rendered templates as items are added, removed, or reordered in the collection.

Advanced looping

Besides from just looping all the items in a list, it is possible to keep track of other usable properties as well. Every property can be used the same way by us adding another statement after the declaration of the items:

```
<div *ngFor="let items of items; let property = property">{{ item }}</div>
```

First/last, this is a Boolean that keeps track of whether we are on the first or last item in our loop, should we want to render that item differently. It can be accessed in the following way:

```
<div *ngFor="let item of items; let first = first">
  <span [ngClass]="{ 'first-css-class': first, 'item-css-class' : !first
}">
    {{ item }}
  </span>
</div>
```

Index, is a number to tell us what index we are on; it starts at 0.

Even/odd is a Boolean to indicate whether we are even on an even or odd index.

TrackBy, to explain what `trackBy` does, let's first talk about the problem it attempts to solve. The problem is that the data the `*ngFor` is pointing to may change, elements may be added or removed, and even the whole list may be replaced. The naive approach to the adding/removing of elements is to carry out create/remove on the DOM tree for all those elements. If same naive approach is used for displaying a new list instead of the old list we used to display this, it will be very expensive and slow. Angular deals with this by keeping DOM elements in memory because creation is costly. Internally, Angular uses something called object identity to keep track of every item in a list. `trackBy`, however, allows you to change from object identity to a specific property on your item. The default object identity is good in most cases, but if you start experiencing performance problems consider changing what property on your item `*ngFor` should look at like so:

```
@Component({
  template : `
  <*ngFor="let item of items; trackBy: trackFunction">{{ item }}</div>
  `
})
export class SomeComponent {
  trackFunction(index, item) {
    return item ? item.id : undefined;
  }
}
```

Else

Else is a new construct per Angular 4.0 and is a short hand you can use to help you with conditional statements. Imagine you have the following:

```
<div *ngIf="hero">
  {{ hero.name }}
</div>
<div *ngIf="!hero">
  No hero set
</div>
```

Our use case here is pretty clear; if we have a person set then display its name, otherwise show a default text. We can write this in another way using `else`:

```
<div *ngIf="person; else noperson">{{person.name}}</div>
<div #noperson>No person set</div>
```

What's happening here is how we define our conditional:

```
person; else noperson
```

We are saying if `person` is set then go ahead, if not display the template `noperson`. `noperson` can be applied to a normal HTML element as well as an `ng-template`.

Applying style

There are three ways to apply styling in your markup:

- Interpolation
- NgStyle
- NgClass

Interpolation

This version is about using the curly brackets and have them resolve what class/classes should be applied. You would write an expression that looks like this:

```
<div class="item {{ item.selected ? 'selected' : ''}}"
```

This reads as if your item has a selected property then apply the CSS class selected, or else apply empty string, which is no class. While this might be sufficient in a lot of cases, it has drawbacks especially if more than one style needs to be applied as there is more than one condition that needs checking.

 Interpolation expression is considered costly in terms of performance, and is normally discouraged.

NgStyle

As you probably have guessed already, this directive allows us to bind CSS styles by evaluating a custom object or expression. We can bind an object whose keys and values map CSS properties, or just define specific properties and bind data to them:

```
<p [ngStyle]="{ 'color': myColor, 'font-weight': myFontWeight }">
  I am red and bold
</p>
```

If our component defines the `myColor` and `myFontWeight` properties with the `red` and `bold` values, respectively, the color and weight of the text will change accordingly. The directive will always reflect the changes made within the component, and we can also pass an object instead of binding data on a per property basis:

```
<p [ngStyle]="myCssConfig">I am red and bold</p>
```

NgClass

Similar to `ngStyle`, `ngClass` allows us to define and toggle class names programmatically in a DOM element using a convenient declarative syntax. This syntax has its own intricacies, however. Let's see each one of the three case scenarios available for this example:

```
<p [ngClass]="{{myClassNames}}">Hello Angular!</p>
```

For instance, we can use a string type so that if `myClassNames` contains a string with one or several classes delimited by a space, all of them will be bound to the paragraph.

We can use an array as well so that each element will be added.

Last but not least, we can use an object in which each key corresponds to a CSS class name referred to by a Boolean value. Each key name marked as `true` will become an active class. Otherwise, it will be removed. This is usually the preferred way of handling class names.

There is an alternate syntax to `ngClass`, which is in the following format:

```
[ngClass]="{ 'class' : boolean-condition, 'class2' : boolean-condition-two }"
```

In short it is a comma separated version where it will apply a class when a condition is `true`. More than one class can be applied if more than one condition is `true`. It would look something like this if used in a more realistic scenario:

```
<span [ngClass] ="{
  'light' : jedi.side === 'Light',
  'dark' : jedi.side === 'Dark'
}">
{{ jedi.name }}
</span>
```

The resulting markup could be the following if `jedi.side` has the value `light` then add CSS class light to the span element:

```
<span class="light">Luke</span>
```

NgSwitch, ngSwitchCase, and ngSwitchDefault

The ngSwitch directive is used to switch templates within a specific set depending on the condition required for displaying each one. The implementation follows several steps; therefore, three different directives are explained in this section.

The ngSwitch will evaluate a given expression and then toggle and display those child elements marked with an ngSwitchCase attribute directive, whose value matches the value thrown by the expression defined in the parent ngSwitch element. A special mention is required about the children element marked with the ngSwitchDefault directive attribute. This attribute qualifies the template that will be displayed when no other value defined by its ngSwitchCase siblings matches the parent conditional expression.

We'll see all of this in an example:

```
<div [ngSwitch]="weatherForecaseDay">
  <ng-template ngSwitchCase="today">{{weatherToday}}</ng-template>
  <ng-template ngSwitchCase="tomorrow">{{weatherTomorrow}}</ng-template>
  <ng-template ngSwitchDefault>
  Pick a day to see the weather forecast
  <ng-template>
</div>
```

The parent [ngSwitch] parameter evaluates the weatherForecastDay context variable, and each nested ngSwitchCase directive will be tested against it. We can use expressions instead, but we want to wrap ngSwitchCase in brackets so that Angular can properly evaluate its content as context variables instead of taking it as a text string.

Coverage for the NgPlural and NgPluralCase sits outside of the scope of this book, but basically provide a convenient way to render or remove templates DOM blocks that match a switch expression, either strictly numeric or just a string, in a similar fashion to how the ngSwitch and ngSwitchWhen directives do.

Manipulating template bindings with pipes

So, we saw how we can use directives to render content depending on the data that our component classes manage, but there is another powerful feature that we will be using thoroughly in our daily practice with Angular. We are talking about pipes.

Pipes allow us to filter and funnel the outcome of our expressions on a view level to transform or just better display the data we are binding. Their syntax is pretty simple, basically consisting of the pipe name following the expression that we want to transform, separated by a pipe symbol (hence the name):

```
@Component({
  selector: 'greeting',
  template: 'Hello {{ name | uppercase }}'
})
export class GreetingComponent{ name: string; }
```

In the preceding example, we are displaying an uppercase greeting on the screen. Since we do not know whether the name will be in uppercase or not, we ensure a consistent output by transforming the value of the name whenever it is not an uppercase version at the view level. Pipes are chainable, and Angular has a wide range of pipe types already baked in. As we will see further in this chapter, we can also build our own pipes to fine-grain data output in cases where the built-in pipes are simply not enough.

The uppercase/lowercase pipe

The name uppercase/lowercase pipe says it all. As in the example provided previously, this pipe sets the string output in uppercase or lowercase. Insert the following code anywhere in your view and check out the output for yourself:

```
<p>{{ 'hello world' | uppercase}}</p>  // outputs HELLO WORLD
<p>{{ 'wEIrD hElLo' | lowercase}}</p>  // outputs weird hello
```

The decimal, percent, and currency pipes

Numeric data can come in a wide range of flavors, and this pipe is especially convenient when it comes to better formatting and localizing the output. These pipes use the Internationalization API, and therefore they are reliable in Chrome and Opera browsers only.

The decimal pipe

The decimal pipe will help us define the grouping and sizing of numbers using the active locale in our browser. Its format is as follows:

```
number_expression | number[:digitInfo[:locale]]
```

Here, `number_expression` is a number and `digitInfo` has the following format:

```
{minIntegerDigits}.{minFractionDigits}-{maxFractionDigits}
```

Each binding would correspond to the following:

- `minIntegerDigits`: The minimum number of integer digits to use. It defaults to 1.
- `minFractionDigits`: The minimum number of digits after the fraction. It defaults to 0.
- `maxFractionDigits`: The maximum number of digits after the fraction. It defaults to 3.

Keep in mind that the acceptable range for each of these numbers and other details will depend on your native internationalization implementation. Let's try to explain how this works by creating the following component:

```
import { Component, OnInit } from '@angular/core';

@Component({
  selector: 'pipe-demo',
  template: `
     <div>{{ no | number }}</div>    <!-- 3.141 -->
     <div>{{ no | number:'2.1-5' }}</div> <! -- 03.14114 -->
     <div>{{ no | number:'7.1-5' }}</div> <!-- 0,000,003.14114 -->
     <div>{{ no | number:'7.1-5':'sv' }}</div> <!-- 0 000 003,14114 -->
  `
})
export class PipeDemoComponent {
 no: number = 3.1411434344;

 constructor() { }
}
```

Here we have an example of four different expressions that showcases us manipulating the number, fractions as well as locale. In the first case, we don't give any instructions other than to use the number pipe. In the second example, we are are specifying the number of fractions as well as numbers to show, by typing number: '2.1-5'. This means we show the two number on the left side of the fraction marker and 5 on the right side. Because we only we have a 3 to the left we need to pad it with a zero. On the right side we just show 5 decimals. In the third example, we instruct it to show 7 numbers to the left and 5 to the right of the fraction marker. This means we need to pad the left side with 6 zeros. This also means that the thousand markers are being added. Our fourth example demonstrates the locale functionality. We see that the displayed result is space character for thousand separator and comma instead of point as fraction sign.

There is one thing to remember, though; for locale setting to work, we need to install the correct locale in our root module. The reason is that Angular only have en-US locale set up from the beginning. It is quite easy to add more locales though. We need to add the following code to app.module.ts:

```typescript
import { BrowserModule } from '@angular/platform-browser';
import { NgModule } from '@angular/core';
import { AppComponent } from './app.component';
import { PipeDemoComponent } from "./pipe.demo.component";

import { registerLocaleData } from '@angular/common';
import localeSV from '@angular/common/locales/sv';

registerLocaleData(localeSV);

@NgModule({
  declarations: [
    AppComponent, PipeDemoComponent
  ],
  imports: [
    BrowserModule
  ],
  providers: [],
  bootstrap: [AppComponent]
})
export class AppModule { }
```

The percent pipe

The percent pipe formats a number as local percent. Other than this, it inherits from the number pipe so that we can further format the output to provide a better integer and decimal sizing and grouping. Its syntax is as follows:

```
number_expression | percent[:digitInfo[:locale]]
```

The currency pipe

This pipe formats a number as a local currency, providing support for selecting the currency code such as USD for the US dollar or EUR for the euro and setting up how we want the currency info to be displayed. Its syntax is as follows:

```
number_expression | currency[:currencyCode[:display[:digitInfo[:locale]]]]
```

In the preceding statement, `currencyCode` is obviously the ISO 4217 currency code, while `display` is a string that

can either be `code`, assume the value `symbol` or `symbol-narrow`. The value `symbol-narrow` indicates whether to use the currency symbol (for example, $). The value `symbol` instructs to use the currency code (for example, USD) in the output. Similar to the decimal and percent pipes, we can format the output to provide a better integer and decimal sizing and grouping through the `digitInfo` value, we can also format based on locale.

In the following, example, we demonstrate all three forms:

```
import { Component, OnInit } from '@angular/core';

@Component({
  selector: 'currency-demo',
  template: `
  <p>{{ 11256.569 | currency:"SEK":'symbol-narrow':'4.1-2' }}</p> <!--
kr11,256.57 -->
  <p>{{ 11256.569 | currency:"SEK":'symbol':'4.1-3' }}</p> <!--
SEK11,256.569 -->
  <p>{{ 11256.569 | currency:"SEK":'code' }}</p> <!--SEK11,256.57 -->
  `
})
export class CurrencyDemoComponent {
  constructor() { }
}
```

The slice pipe

The purpose of this pipe is equivalent to the role played by `Array.prototype.slice()` and `String.prototype.slice()` when it comes to subtracting a subset (slice) of a collection list, array, or string, respectively. Its syntax is pretty straightforward and follows the same conventions as those of the aforementioned `slice()` methods:

```
expression | slice: start[:end]
```

Basically, we configure a starting index where we will begin slicing either the items array or the string on an optional end index, which will fall back to the last index on the input when omitted.

Both start and end arguments can take positive and negative values, as the JavaScript `slice()` methods do. Refer to the JavaScript API documentation for a full rundown on all of the available scenarios.

Last but not least, please note that when operating on a collection, the returned list is always a copy—even when all elements are being returned.

The date pipe

You must have already guessed that the date pipe formats a date value as a string based on the requested format. The time zone of the formatted output will be the local system time zone of the end user's machine. Its syntax is pretty simple:

```
date_expression | date[:format[:timezone[:locale]]]
```

The expression input must be a date object or a number (milliseconds since the UTC epoch). The format argument is highly customizable and accepts a wide range of variations based on date-time symbols. For our convenience, some aliases have been made available as shortcuts to the most common date formats:

- `'medium'`: This is equivalent to `'yMMMdjms'` (for example, Sep 3, 2010, 12:05:08 PM for en-US)
- `'short'`: This is equivalent to `'yMdjm'` (for example, 9/3/2010, 12:05 PM for en-US)
- `'fullDate'`: This is equivalent to `'yMMMMEEEEd'` (for example, Friday, September 3, 2010 for en-US)
- `'longDate'`: This is equivalent to `'yMMMMd'` (for example, September 3, 2010)

- `'mediumDate'`: This is equivalent to `'yMMMd'` (for example, Sep 3, 2010 for en-US)

- `'shortDate'`: This is equivalent to `'yMd'` (for example, 9/3/2010 for en-US)

- `'mediumTime'`: This is equivalent to `'jms'` (for example, 12:05:08 PM for en-US)

- `'shortTime'`: This is equivalent to `'jm'` (for example, 12:05 PM for en-US)

- The `json` pipe

The JSON pipe

JSON is probably the most straightforward pipe in its definition; it basically takes an object as an input and outputs it in JSON format:

```
import { Component } from '@angular/core';

@Component({
  selector: 'json-demo',
  template: `
    {{ person | json }}
    <!--{ "name": "chris", "age": 38, "address": { "street": "Oxford
Street", "city": "London" } } -->
  `
})
export class JsonDemoComponent {
  person = {
    name: 'chris',
    age: 38,
    address: {
      street: 'Oxford Street',
      city: 'London'
    }
  }

  constructor() { }
}
```

The output using the Json pipe is the following `{ "name": "chris", "age": 38, "address": { "street": "Oxford Street", "city": "London" } }`. This shows that the pipe has turned single quotes to double quotes and thereby produced valid JSON. So, why do we need this? One reason is debugging; it's a nice way to see what a complex object contains and have it nicely printed to the screen. As you can see from the preceding field `person`, it contains some simple properties but also the complex `address` property. The deeper the object is the nicer it is, to have the json pipe.

The i18n pipes

As part of Angular's strong commitment to providing a strong internationalization toolset, a reduced set of pipes targeting common i18n use cases have been made available. This book will only cover the two major ones, but it is quite likely that more pipes will be released in the future. Please refer to the official documentation for further information after finishing this chapter.

The i18nPlural pipe

The i18nPlural pipe has a simple usage, where we just evaluate a numeric value against an object mapping different string values to be returned depending on the result of the evaluation. This way, we can render different strings on our template depending if the numeric value is zero, one, two, more than *N*, and so on. The syntax is the following:

```
expression | i18nPlural:mapping[:locale]
```

Let's look at how this could look for a numeric field jedis on your component class:

```
<h1> {{ jedis | i18nPlural:jediWarningMapping }} </h1>
```

Then, we can have this mapping as a field of our component controller class:

```
export class i18DemoComponent {
  jedis: number = 11;
  jediWarningMapping: any = {
    '=0': 'No jedis',
    '=1' : 'One jedi present',
    'other' : '# jedis in sight'
  }
}
```

We even bind the numeric value evaluated in the expression by introducing the '#' placeholder in the string mappings. When no matching value is found, the pipe will fall back to the mapping set with the key 'other'.

The i18nSelect pipe

The `i18nSelect` pipe is similar to the `i18nPlural` pipe, but it evaluates a string value instead. This pipe is perfect for localizing text interpolations or providing distinct labels depending on state changes, for instance. For example, we could recap on our timer and serve the UI in different languages:

```
<button (click)="togglePause()">
  {{ languageCode | i18nSelect:localizedLabelsMap }}
</button>
```

In our controller class, we can populate `localizedLabelsMap`, as follows:

```
export class TimerComponent {
  languageCode: string ='fr';
  localizedLabelsMap: any = {
    'en' : 'Start timer',
    'es' : 'Comenzar temporizador',
    'fr' : 'Demarrer une sequence',
    'other' : 'Start timer'
  }
}
```

It is important to note that we can put this convenient pipe to use in use cases other than localizing components, but to provide string bindings depending on map keys and the like. Same as the `i18nPlural` pipe, when no matching value is found, the pipe will fall back to the mapping set with the `'other'` key.

The async pipe

Sometimes, we manage observable data or only data that is handled asynchronously by our component class, and we need to ensure that our views promptly reflect the changes in the information once the observable field changes or asynchronous loading has been accomplished after the view has been rendered. The async pipe subscribes to an observable or promise and returns the latest value it has emitted. When a new value is emitted, the async pipe marks the component to be checked for changes. We will return to this concept in `Chapter 7`, *Asynchronous Data Services with Angular*.

Putting it all together in a task list

Now that you have learned all the elements that allow you to build full-blown components, it's time to put all of this fresh knowledge into practice. In the next pages, we are going to build a simple task list manager. In it, we will see a tasks table containing the to-do items we need to build.

We will also queue up tasks straight from the backlog of tasks available. This will help showing the time required to accomplish all the queued tasks and see how many tasks are defined in our working agenda.

Setting up our main HTML container

Before building the actual component, we need to set up our work environment first and in order to do so, we will reuse the same HTML boilerplate file we used in the previous component. Please set aside the work you've done so far and keep the `package.json`, `tsconfig.json`, `typings.json`, and `index.html` files we used in previous examples. Feel free to reinstall the modules required in case you need to, and replace the contents of the body tag in our `index.html` template:

```html
<nav class="navbar navbar-default navbar-static-top">
  <div class="container">
    <div class="navbar-header">
      <strong class="navbar-brand">My Tasks</strong>
    </div>
  </div>
</nav>
<tasks></tasks>
```

In a nutshell, we have just updated the title of the header layout above our new `<tasks>` custom elements, which replaces the previous `<timer>`. You might want to update the `app.module.ts` file and make sure to point out tasks as a component that can be visible outside of our module by entering it in the `exports` key array:

```
@NgModule({
  declarations : [ TasksComponent ],
  imports : [ ],
  providers : [],
  exports : [ TasksComponent ]
})
export class TaskModule{}
```

Let's highlight here that the application has two modules so far: our root module called `AppModule` and our `TaskModule`. Our root module should import our `TaskModule` like so:

```
@NgModule({
  imports : [
    BrowserModule,
    TaskModule
  ]
})
export class AppModule {}
```

Building our task list table with Angular directives

Create an empty `tasks.ts` file. You might want to use this newly created file to build our new component from scratch and embed on it the definitions of all the accompanying pipes, directives, and components we will see later in this chapter.

Real-life projects are never implemented this way, since our code must conform to the "one class, one file" principle, taking advantage of ECMAScript modules for gluing things together. `Chapter 6`, *Building an Application with Angular Components*, will introduce you to a common set of good practices for building Angular applications, including strategies for organizing your directory tree and your different elements (components, directives, pipes, services, and so on) in a sustainable way. This chapter, on the contrary, will leverage `tasks.ts` to include all the code in a central location and then provide a bird's eye view of all the topics we will cover now without having to go switching across files. Bear in mind that this is in fact an anti-pattern, but for instructional purposes, we will take this approach in this chapter for the last time. The order in which elements are declared within the file is important. Refer to the code repository in GitHub if exceptions rise.

Before moving on with our component, we need to import the dependencies required, formalize the data model we will use to populate the table, and then scaffold some data that will be served by a convenient service class.

Let's begin by adding to our `tasks.ts` file the following code block, importing all the tokens we will require in this chapter. Pay special attention to the tokens we are importing from the Angular library. We have covered components and input already, but all the rest will be explained later in this chapter:

```
import {
  Component,
  Input,
```

```
  Pipe,
  PipeTransform,
  Directive,
  OnInit,
  HostListener
} from '@angular/core';
```

With the dependency tokens already imported, let's define the data model for our tasks, next to the block of imports:

```
/// Model interface
interface Task {
  name: string;
  deadline: Date;
  queued: boolean;
  hoursLeft: number;
}
```

The schema of a `Task` model interface is pretty self-explanatory. Each task has a name, a deadline, a field informing how many units need to be shipped, and a Boolean field named `queued` that defines if that task has been tagged to be done in our next session.

You might be surprised that we define a model entity with an interface rather than a class, but this is perfectly fine when the entity model does not feature any business logic requiring implementation of methods or data transformation in a constructor or setter/getter function. When the latter is not required, an interface just suffices since it provides the static typing we require in a simple and more lightweight fashion.

Now, we need some data and a service wrapper class to deliver such data in the form of a collection of `Task` objects. The `TaskService` class defined here will do the trick, so append it to your code right after the `Task` interface:

```
/// Local Data Service
class TaskService {
  public taskStore: Array<Task> = [];
  constructor() {
    const tasks = [
      {
        name : 'Code and HTML table',
        deadline : 'Jun 23 2015',
        hoursLeft : 1
      },
      {
        name : 'Sketch a wireframe for the new homepage',
        deadline : 'Jun 24 2016',
        hoursLeft : 2
      },
```

```
    {
      name : 'Style table with bootstrap styles',
      deadline : 'Jun 25 2016',
      hoursLeft : 1
    }
  ];

  this.taskStore = tasks.map( task => {
    return {
      name : task.name,
      deadline : new Date(task.deadline),
      queued : false,
      hoursLeft : task.hoursLeft
    };
  })
  }
}
```

This data store is pretty self-explanatory: it exposes a `taskStore` property returning an array of objects conforming to the `Task` interface (hence benefiting from static typing) with information about the name, deadline, and time estimate.

Now that we have a data store and a model class, we can begin building an Angular component that will consume this data source to render the tasks in our template view. Insert the following component implementation after the code you wrote before:

```
/// Component classes
// - Main Parent Component
@Component({
  selector : 'tasks',
  styleUrls : ['tasks.css'],
  templateUrl : 'tasks.html'
})
export class TaskComponent {
  today: Date;
  tasks: Task[];
  constructor() {
    const TasksService: TaskService = new TasksService();
    this.tasks = tasksService.taskStore;
    this.today = new Date();
  }
}
```

As you can see, we have defined and instantiated through the bootstrap function a new component named `TasksComponent` with the selector `<tasks>` (we already included it when we were populating the main `index.html` file, remember?). This class exposes two properties: today's date and a tasks collection that will be rendered in a table contained in the component's view, as we will see shortly. To do so, it instantiates in its constructor the data source that we created previously, mapping it to the array of models typed as `Task` objects represented by the tasks field. We also initialize the today property with an instance of the JavaScript built-in `Date` object, which contains the current date.

As you have seen, the component selector does not match its controller class naming. We will delve deeper into naming conventions at the end of this chapter, as a preparation for `Chapter 6`, *Building an Application with Angular Components*.

Let's create the stylesheet file now, whose implementation will be really simple and straightforward. Create a new file named `tasks.css` at the same location where our component file lives. You can then populate it with the following styles ruleset:

```css
h3, p {
  text-align : center;
}

table {
  margin: auto;
  max-width: 760px;
}
```

This newly created stylesheet is so simple that it might seem a bit too much to have it as a standalone file. However, this comes as a good opportunity to showcase in our example the functionalities of the `styleUrls` property of the component metadata.

Things are quite different in regards to our HTML template. This time we will not hardcode our HTML template in the component either, but we will point to an external HTML file to better manage our presentation code. Please create an HTML file and save it as `tasks.html` in the same location where our main component's controller class exists. Once it is created, fill it in with the following HTML snippet:

```html
<div class="container text-center">
  <img src="assets/img/task.png" alt="Task" />
  <div class="container">
    <h4>Tasks backlog</h4>
    <table class="table">
      <thead>
        <tr>
          <th> Task ID</th>
          <th>Task name</th>
```

```
            <th>Deliver by</th>
            <th></th>
            <th>Actions</th>
        </tr>
    </thead>
    <tbody>
        <tr *ngFor="let task of tasks; let i = index">
            <th scope="row">{{i}}</th>
            <td>{{ task.name | slice:0:35 }}</td>
                <span [hidden]="task.name.length < 35">...</span>
            </td>
            <td>
            {{ task.deadline | date:'fullDate' }}
                <span *ngIf="task.deadline < today"
                     class="label label-danger">
                  Due
                </span>
            </td>
            <td class="text-center">
                {{ task.hoursLeft }}
            </td>
            <td>[Future options...]</td>
    </tbody>
    </table>
</div>
```

We are basically creating a table that features a neat styling based on the Bootstrap framework. Then, we render all our tasks using the always convenient `ngFor` directive, extracting and displaying the index of each item in our collection as we explained while overviewing the `ngFor` directive earlier in this chapter.

Please look at how we formatted the output of our task's name and deadline interpolations by means of pipes, and how conveniently we display (or not) an ellipsis to indicate when the text exceeds the maximum number of characters we allocated for the name by turning the HTML hidden property into a property bound to an Angular expression. All this presentation logic is topped with a red label, indicating whether the given task is due whenever its end date is prior to this day.

You have probably noticed that those action buttons do not exist in our current implementation. We will fix this in the next section, playing around with state in our components. Back in Chapter 1, *Creating Our Very First Component in Angular,* we touched upon the click event handler for stopping and resuming the countdown, and then delved deeper into the subject in Chapter 4, *Implementing Properties and Events in Our Components,* where we covered output properties. Let's continue on our research and see how we can hook up DOM event handlers with our component's public methods, adding a rich layer of interactivity to our components.

Toggling tasks in our task list

Add the following method to your TasksComponent controller class. Its functionality is pretty basic; we just literally toggle the value of the queued property for a given Task object instance:

```
toggleTask(task: Task): void {
  task.queued = !task.queued;
}
```

Now, we just need to hook it up with our view buttons. Update our view to include a click attribute (wrapped in braces so that it acts as an output property) in the button created within the ngFor loop. Now that we will have different states in our Task objects, let's reflect this in the button labels by implementing an ngSwitch structure all together:

```
<table class="table">
  <thead>
    <tr>
      <th>Task ID</th>
      <th>Task name</th>
      <th>Deliver by</th>
      <th>Units to ship</th>
      <th>Actions</th>
    </tr>
  </thead>
  <tbody>
    <tr *ngFor="let task of tasks; let i = index">
      <th scope="row">{{i}}
        <span *ngIf="task.queued" class="label label-info">Queued</span>
      </th>
      <td>{{task.name | slice:0:35}}
        <span [hidden]="task.name.length < 35">...</span>
      </td>
      <td>{{ task.deadline | date:'fullDate'}}
        <span *ngIf="task.deadline < today" class="label label-
```

```
danger">Due</span>
    </td>
    <td class="text-center">{{task.hoursLeft}}</td>
    <td>
        <button type="button"
                class="btn btn-default btn-xs"
                (click)="toggleTask(task)"
                [ngSwitch]="task.queued">
          <ng-template ngSwitchCase="false">
            <i class="glyphicon glyphicon-plus-sign"></i>
            Add
          </ng-template>
          <ng-template ngSwitchCase="true">
            <i class="glyphicon glyphicon-minus-sign"></i>
            Remove
          <ng-template>
          <ng-template ngSwitchDefault>
            <i class="glyphicon glyphicon-plus-sign"></i>
            Add
          </ng-template>
        </button>
    </td>
  </tbody>
</table>
```

Our brand new button can execute the `toggleTask()` method in our component class, passing as an argument the `Task` object that corresponds to that iteration of `ngFor`. On the other hand, the preceding `ngSwitch` implementation allows us to display different button labels and icons depending on the state of the `Task` object at any given time.

We are decorating the newly created buttons with font icons fetched from the Glyphicons font family. The icons are part of the Bootstrap CSS bundle we installed previously and are in no means related to Angular. Feel free to skip its use or to replace it by another icon font family.

Execute the code as it is now and check out the results yourself. Neat, isn't it? But, maybe we can get more juice from Angular by adding more functionality to the task list.

Displaying state changes in our templates

Now that we can pick the tasks to be done from the table, it would be great to have some kind of visual hint of how many units we are meant to ship. The logic is as follows:

- The user reviews the tasks on the table and picks the ones to be done by clicking on each one

- Every time a row is clicked, the underlying `Task` object state changes and its Boolean queued property is toggled
- The state change is reflected immediately on the surface by displaying a `queued` label on the related task item
- The user gets prompt information of the amount of units they need to ship and a time estimation to deliver them all
- We see how a row of icons are displayed above the table, displaying the sum of all units from all the tasks set to be done

This functionality will have to react to the state changes of the set of `Task` objects we're dealing with. The good news is that thanks to Angular's very own change detection system, making components fully aware of state changes is extremely easy.

Thus, our very first task will be to tweak our `TasksComponent` class to include some way to compute and display how many tasks are queued up. We will use that information to render or not a block of markup in our component where we will inform how many tasks we have lined up and how much aggregated time it will take to accomplish them all.

The new `queuedTasks` field of our class will provide such information, and we will want to insert a new method named `updateQueuedTasks()` in our class that will update its numeric value upon instantiating the component or enqueueing tasks. On top of that, we will create a key/value mapping that we can use later on to render a more expressive title header depending on the amount of queued tasks thanks to the `I18nPlural` pipe:

```
class TasksComponent {
  today: Date;
  tasks: Task[];
  queuedTasks: number;
  queuedHeaderMapping: any = {
    '=0': 'No tasks',
    '=1': 'One task',
    'other' : '# tasks'
  };

  constructor() {
    const TasksService: TasksService = new TasksService();
    this.tasks = tasksService.tasksStore;
    this.today = new Date();
    this.updateQueuedTasks();
  }

  toggleTask(task: Task) {
    task.queued = !task.queued;
    this.updateQueuedTasks();
```

```
      }

      private updateQueuedTasks() {
        this.queuedTasks = this.tasks
          .filter( task:Task => task.queued )
          .reduce((hoursLeft: number, queuedTask: Task) => {
            return hoursLeft + queuedTask.hoursLeft;
          }, 0)
      }
    }
```

The `updateQueuedTasks()` method makes use of JavaScript's
native `Array.filter()` and `Array.reduce()` methods to build a list of queued tasks out
of the original task's collection property. The `reduce` method applied over the resulting
array gives us the total number of units to ship. With a stateful computation of the number
of queued units to ship now available, it's time to update our template accordingly. Go to
`tasks.html` and inject the following chunk of HTML right before the `<h4>Tasks
backlog</h4>` element. The code is as follows:

```
<div>
  <h3>
    {{queuedTasks | i18nPlural:queueHeaderMapping}}
    for today
    <span class="small" *ngIf="queuedTasks > 0">
      (Estimated time: {{ queuedTasks > 0 }})
    </span>
  </h3>
</div>
<h4>Tasks backlog</h4>
<!-- rest of the template remains the same -->
```

The preceding block renders an informative header title at all times, even when no tasks
have been queued up. We also bind that value in the template and use it to estimate
through an expression binding the amount of minutes required to go through each and
every session required.

We are hardcoding the duration of each task in the template. Ideally, such constant values
should be bound from an application variable or a centralized setting. Don't worry, we will
see how we can improve this implementation in the next chapters.

Save your changes and reload the page, and then try to toggle some task items on the table
to see how the information changes in real time. Exciting, isn't it?

Embedding child components

Now, let's start building a tiny icon component that will be nested inside the TasksComponent component. This new component will display a smaller version of our big icon, which we will use to display on the template the amount of tasks lined up to be done, as we described earlier in this chapter. Let's pave the way towards component trees, which we will analyze in detail in Chapter 6, *Building an Application with Angular Components*. For now, just include the following component class before the TasksComponent class you built earlier.

Our component will expose a public property named task in which we can inject a Task object. The component will use this Task object binding to replicate the image rendered in the template as many times as sessions are required by this task in its hoursLeft property, all this by means of an ngFor directive.

In our tasks.ts file, inject the following block of code before our TasksComponent:

```
@Component({
  selector : 'task-icons',
  template : `
    <img *ngFor="let icon of icons"
         src="/assets/img/task.png"
         width="50">`
})
export class TaskIconsComponent implements OnInit {
  @Input() task: Task;
  icons: Object[] = [];
  ngOnInit() {
    this.icons.length = this.task.hoursLeft;
    this.icons.fill({ name : this.task.name });
  }
}
```

Before we continue and iterate over our component, it is important to ensure we register our component with a module, so that other constructs may know its existence, so they can use said component in their template. We register it by adding it to the declarations property of its module object like so:

```
@NgModule({
  imports : [ /* add needed imports here */ ]
  declarations : [
   TasksComponent,
   TaskIconsComponent
   ]
})
export class TaskModule {}
```

Now that the `TaskModule` knows about our component, we can continue and improve it.

Our new `TaskIconsComponent` features a pretty simple implementation, with a very intuitive selector matching its camel-cased class name and a template where we duplicate the given `<img>` tag as many times as objects are populated in the icons array property of the controller class, which is populated with the native fill method of the `Array` object in the JavaScript API (the fill method fills all the elements of an array with a static value passed as an argument), within `ngOnInit()`. Wait, what is this? Shouldn't we implement the loop populating the icons array member in the constructor instead?

This method is one of the life cycle hooks that we will overview in the next chapter, and probably the most important one. The reason why we populate the icons array field here and not in the constructor method is because we need each and every data-bound property to be properly initialized before proceeding to run the for loop. Otherwise, it will be too soon to access the input value task since it will return an undefined value.

The `OnInit` interface demands an `ngOnInit()` method to be integrated in the controller class that implements such -interface, and it will be executed once all input properties with a binding defined have been checked. We will take a bird's eye overview of component lifecycle hooks in `Chapter 6`, *Building an Application with Angular Components*.

Still, our new component needs to find its way to its parent component. So, let's insert a reference to the component class in the directives property of the `TasksComponent` decorator settings:

```
@Component({
  selector : 'tasks',
  styleUrls : ['tasks.css'],
  templateUrl : 'tasks.html'
})
```

Our next step will be to inject the `<task-icons>` element in the `TasksComponent` template. Go back to `tasks.html` and update the code located inside the conditional block meant to be displayed when `hoursLeft` is greater than zero. The code is as follows:

```
<div>
  <h3>
    {{ hoursLeft | i18nPlural:queueHeaderMapping }}
    for today
    <span class="small" *ngIf="hoursLeft > 0">
    (Estimated time : {{ hoursLeft * 25 }})
    </span>
  </h3>
  <p>
    <span *ngFor="let queuedTask of tasks">
```

```
        <task-icons
        [task]="queuedTask"
        (mouseover)="tooltip.innerText = queuedTask.name"
        (mouseout)="tooltip.innerText = 'Mouseover for details'">
        </task-icons>
    </span>
    </p>
    <p #tooltip *ngIf="hoursLeft > 0">Mouseover for details</p>
</div>
<h4>Tasks backlog</h4>
<!-- rest of the template remains the same -->
```

There is still some room for improvement though. Unfortunately, the icon size is hardcoded in the `TaskIconsComponent` template and that makes it harder to reuse that component in other contexts where a different size might be required. Obviously, we could refactor the `TaskIconsComponent` class to expose a `size` input property and then bind the value received straight into the component template in order to resize the image accordingly:

```
@Component({
  selector : 'task-icon',
  template : `
    <img *ngfor="let icon of icons"
         src="/assets/img/task.png"
         width="{{size}}">`
})
export class TaskIconsComponent implements OnInit {
  @Input() task: Task;
  icons : Object[] = [];
  @Input() size: number;
  ngOnInit() {
    // initialise component here
  }
}
```

Then, we just need to update the implementation of `tasks.html` to declare the value we need for the size:

```
<span *ngFor="let queuedTask of tasks">
  <task-icons
    [task]="queuedTask"
    size="50"
    (mouseover)="tooltip.innerText = queuedTask.name">
  </task-icons>
</span>
```

Please note that the `size` attribute is not wrapped between brackets because we are binding a hardcoded value. If we wanted to bind a component variable, that attribute should be properly declared as `[size]="{{mySizeVariable}}"`.

We inserted a new DOM element that will show up only when we have hours left. We displayed an actual header telling us how many hours we have left, by binding the `hoursLeft` property in an H3 DOM element, plus a total estimation in minutes for accomplishing all of this contained in the `{{ hoursLeft * 25 }}` expression.

The `ngFor` directive allows us to iterate through the tasks array. In each iteration, we render a new `<task-icons>` element.

We bound the `Task` model object of each iteration, represented by the `queuedTask` reference, in the task input property of the `<task-icons>` in the loop template.

We took advantage of the `<task-icons>` element to include additional mouse event handlers that point to the following paragraph, which has been flagged with the `#tooltip` local reference. So, every time the user hovers the mouse over the task icon, the text beneath the icons row will display the respective task name.

We ran the extra mile, turning the size of the icon rendered by `<task-icons>` into a configurable property as part of the component API. We now have icons that get updated in real time as we toggle the information on the table. New problems have arisen, however. Firstly, we are displaying icon components matching the hours left of each task, without filtering out those that are not queued. On the other hand, the overall estimation of time required to achieve all our tasks displays the gross number of minutes, and this information will make no sense as we add more tasks to the working plan.

Perhaps, it's time to amend this. It's a good thing that custom pipes have come to the rescue!

Building our own custom pipes

We have already seen what pipes are and what their purpose is in the overall Angular ecosystem, but now we are going to dive deeper into how we can build our own set of pipes to provide custom transformations to data bindings.

Anatomy of a custom pipe

Pipes are very easy to define. We essentially need to do the following:

- Import `Pipe` and `PipeTransform`
- Implement the `PipeTransform` interface
- Add the `Pipe` component to modules

The full code for implementing the `Pipe` would look something like this:

```
import { Pipe, PipeTransform, Component } from '@angular/core';

@Pipe({
  name : 'myPipeName'
})
export class MyPipe implements PipeTransform {
  transform( value: any, ...args: any[]): any {
    // We apply transformations to the input value here
    return something;
  }
}
@Component({
  selector : 'my-selector',
  template : '<p>{{ myVariable | myPipeName: "bar"}}</p>'
})
export class MyComponent {
  myVariable: string = 'Foo';
}
```

Let's break down the code in the upcoming subsections.

Imports

We import the following constructs:

```
import { Pipe, PipeTransform, Component }
```

Defining our pipe

The `Pipe` is a decorator that takes an object literal; we need to at least give it a name property:

```
@Pipe({ name : 'myPipeName' })
```

This means that once used, we will refer to its name property like so:

```
{{ value | myPipeName }}
```

The `PipeTransform` is an interface that we need to implement. We can easily do so by adding it to our class like so:

```
@Pipe({ name : 'myPipeName' })
export class MyPipeClass {
  transform( value: any, args: any[]) {
    // apply transformation here
    return 'add banana ' + value;
  }
}
```

Here, we can see that we have a transform method, but also the first argument being the value itself and the rest is `args`, an array with any number of arguments you provide it. We've already shown how to use this `Pipe`, but if supplying arguments, it looks a little bit different, like so:

```
{{ value | myPipeName:arg1:arg2 }}
```

It is worth noting that for every argument we supply, it ends up in the `args` array and we separate it with a colon.

Registering it

To make a construct usable, in this case a pipe, you need to tell the module it exists. Just like with components, we need to add to the declarations property like so:

```
@NgModule({
  declarations : [ MyPipe ]
})
export ModuleClass {}
```

The pure property

We can add a property to our `@Pipe` decorator, `pure`, like so:

```
@Pipe({ name : 'myPipe', pure : false })
export class MyPipe implements PipeTransform {
  transform(value: any, ...args: any[]) {}
}
```

"Why would we do that in the first place?" you ask. Well, there are situations where this might be necessary. If you have a pipe that works on primitives like so:

```
{{ "decorate me" |  myPipe }}
```

We don't have an issue. However, if it looks like this:

```
{{ object | myPipe }}
```

We might have a problem. Consider the following code in a component:

```
export class Component {
  object = { name : 'chris', age : 37 }

  constructor() {
    setTimeout(() => this.object.age = 38 , 3000)
  }
}
```

Imagine that we have the following `Pipe` implementation to go with it:

```
@Pipe({ name : 'pipe' })
export class MyPipe implements PipeTransform {
  transform(value:any, ...args: any[]) {
    return `Person: ${value.name} ${value.age}`
  }
}
```

This would at first be the output:

Chris 37

However, you expect the output to change to `Chris 38` after 3 seconds, but it doesn't. The pipe only looks at whether the reference have changed or not. In this case, it hasn't because the object is still the same, but a property on the object has changed. A way to tell it to react to changes is to specify the `pure` property, like we did in the beginning. So, we update our `Pipe` implementation to look like this:

```
@Pipe({ name : 'pipe', pure: false })
export class MyPipe implements PipeTransform {
  transform(value: any, ...args:any[]) {
    return `Person: ${value.name} ${value.age}`
  }
}
```

Now, we suddenly see the change happen. A word of caution though. This actually means the `transform` method is called every time the change detection cycle is being triggered. So, this might actually be damaging for performance. You could try and cache the value if setting the `pure` property, but you could also try to work with reducers and immutable data to solve this in a better way:

```
// instead of altering the data like so
this.jedi.side = 'Dark'

// instead do
this.jedi = Object.assign({}, this.jedi, { side : 'Dark' });
```

The preceding code would change the reference and our Pipe wouldn't kill performance. All in all, it's good to know what the pure property does, but be careful.

A custom pipe to better format time output

Watching the gross number of minutes summed up when lining up tasks to be done is not very intuitive, so we need a way to deconstruct this value into hours and minutes. Our pipe will have the name `formattedTime` and will be implemented by the `formattedTimePipe` class, whose unique transform method receives a number representing a total number of minutes and returns a string (proving that pipes do not need to return the same type as they receive in the payload) in a readable time format:

```
@Pipe({
  name : 'formattedTime'
})
export class FormattedTimePipe implements PipeTransform {
  transform(totalMinutes : number) {
    let minutes : number = totalMinutes % 60;
    let hours : numbers = Math.floor(totalMinutes / 60);
    return `${hours}h:{minutes}m`;
  }
}
```

We should not skip the opportunity to highlight that the naming convention for pipes is, the same as we saw with components, the name of the pipe class with the `Pipe` suffix plus a selector matching that name without the suffix. Why this mismatch between the pipe controller's class name and the selector? It is common practice to prefix the selector strings of our custom pipes and directives with a custom prefix in order to prevent collisions with other selectors defined by third party pipes and directives:

```
@Component({
  selector : 'tasks',
  styleUrls : [ 'tasks.css' ],
  templateUrl : 'tasks.html'
})
export class TasksComponent {}
```

Finally, we just need to tweak the HTML in the `tasks.html` template file to ensure that our EDT expression is properly formatted:

```
<span class="small">
  (Estimated time: {{ queued * 25 | formattedTime }})
</span>
```

Now, reload the page and toggle some tasks. The estimated time will be properly rendered in hours and minutes.

Lastly, we must not forget to add our `Pipe` construct to its module `tasks.module.ts`:

```
@NgModule({
  declarations: [TasksComponent, FormattedTimePipe]
})
export class TasksModule {}
```

Filtering out data with custom filters

As we noticed already, we are displaying at this moment an icon component for each and every task in the collection served from the tasks service, without filtering out what tasks are marked as queued and which aren't. Pipes provide a convenient way to map, transform, and digest data bindings, so we can leverage its functionalities for filtering out the tasks binding in our `ngFor` loop to return only those tasks that are marked as queued.

The logic will be pretty simple: since the tasks binding is an array of `Task` objects, we just need to make use of the `Array.filter()` method to fetch only those `Task` objects whose queued property is set to `true`. We might run the extra mile and configure our pipe to take one Boolean argument, indicating whether we want to filter out queued or unqueued tasks. The implementation of these requirements is as follows, where you can see again the conventions in place for the selector and class names:

```
@Pipe({
  name : 'queuedOnly'
})
export class QueuedOnlyPipe implements PipeTransform {
  transform(tasks: Task[]), ...args:any[]): Task[] {
    return tasks.filter( task:Task => task.queued === args[0])
  }
}
```

The implementation is pretty straightforward, so we will not get into detail about it here. However, there is something that is worth highlighting at this stage: this is an impure pipe. Bear in mind that the tasks binding is a collection of stateful objects that will change in length and content as the user toggles tasks on the table. For that reason, we need to instruct the pipe to take advantage of Angular's change detection system so its output is checked by the latter on every cycle regardless of whether its input has changed or not. Configuring the pure property of the pipe decorator as `false` will do the trick then.

Now, we just need to update the pipes property of the component using this pipe:

```
@Component({
  selector : 'tasks',
  styleUrls : ['tasks.css'],
  templateUrl : 'tasks.html'
})
export class TasksComponent {
  // Class implementation remains the same
}
```

Then, update the `ngFor` block in `tasks.html` to properly filter out the unqueued tasks:

```
<span *ngFor="queuedTask of tasks | queuedOnly:true">
  <task-icons
    [task]="queuedTask"
    (mouseover)="tooltip.innerText = queuedTask.name"
    (mouseout)="tooltip.innerText = 'Mouseover for details'">
  </task-icons>
</span>
```

Please check how we configured the pipe as `queuedOnly: true`. Replacing the Boolean parameter value by `false` will give us the chance to enlist the tasks pertaining to the queues we have not picked.

Save all your work and reload the page, toggling some tasks then. You will see how our overall UI reacts to the latest changes accordingly, and we only enlist the icons pertaining to the amount of hours left of queued tasks only.

Building our own custom directives

Custom directives encompass a vast world of possibilities and use cases, and we would need an entire book for showcasing all the intricacies and possibilities they offer.

In a nutshell, directives allow you to attach advanced behaviors to elements in the DOM. If a directive has a template attached, then it becomes a component. In other words, components are Angular directives with a view, but we can build directives with no attached views that will be applied to already existing DOM elements, making its HTML contents and standard behavior immediately accessible to the directive. This applies to Angular components as well, where the directive will just access its template and custom attributes and events when necessary.

Anatomy of a custom directive

Declaring and implementing a custom directive is pretty easy. We just need to import the `Directive` class to provide decorator functionalities to its accompanying controller class:

```
import { Directive } from '@angular/core';
```

Then, we define a controller class annotated by the `@Directive` decorator, where we will define the directive selector, input and output properties (if required), optional events applied to the host element, and injectable provider tokens, should our directive's constructor require specific types to be instantiated by the Angular injector when instancing itself (we will cover this in detail in Chapter 6, *Building an Application with Angular Components*):

Let's warm up by creating a very simple directive:

```
import { Directive, ElementRef } from '@angular/core';

@Directive({
  selector : '[highlight]'
})
export class HighLightDirective {
  constructor( private elementRef: ElementRef, private renderer : Renderer2
) {
    var nativeElement = elementRef.nativeElement;
    this.renderer.setProperty( nativeElement,'backgroundColor', 'yellow');
  }
}
```

And to use it is as simple as typing:

```
<h1 highlight></h1>
```

We use two actors here, `ElementRef` and `Renderer2`, to manipulate the underlying element. We could use `elementRef.nativeElement` directly, but this is discouraged as this might break server side rendering or when interacting with service workers. Instead, we do all manipulations using an instance of `Renderer2`.

Notice how we don't type the square bracket, but only the selector name.

A quick recap of what we did here was to inject the `ElementRef` and access the `nativeElement` property, which is the actual element. We also put a `@Directive` decorator on a class just like we do with components and pipes. The main mindset to have when creating directives is to think reusable functionality that not necessarily relates to a certain feature. The topic chosen previously was highlighting, but we could build other functionalities such as tooltip and collapsible or infinite scrolling features with relative ease.

Properties and decorators' such as selector, `@Input()`, or `@Output()` (same with inputs and outputs) will probably resonate to you from the time when we overviewed the component decorator spec. Although we haven't mentioned all the possibilities in detail yet, the selector may be declared as one of the following:

- `element-name`: Select by element name
- `.class`: Select by class name
- `[attribute]`: Select by attribute name
- `[attribute=value]`: Select by attribute name and value

- `not(sub_selector)`: Select only if the element does not match the `sub_selector`
- `selector1, selector2`: Select if either `selector1` or `selector2` matches

In addition to this, we will find the host parameter, which specifies the events, actions, properties, and attributes pertaining to the host element (that is, the element where our directive takes action) that we want to access from within the directive. We can therefore take advantage of this parameter to bind interaction handlers against the container component or any other target element of our choice, such as window, document, or body. In this way, we can refer to two very convenient local variables when writing a directive event binding:

- `$event`: This is the current event object that triggered the event.
- `$target`: This is the source of the event. This will be either a DOM element or an Angular directive.

Besides events, we can update specific DOM properties that belong to the host component. We just need to link any specific property wrapped in braces with an expression handled by the directive as a key-value pair in our directive's host definition.

The optional host parameter can also specify static attributes that should be propagated to a host element, if not present already. This is a convenient way of injecting HTML properties with computed values.

The Angular team has also made available a couple of convenient decorators so that we can more expressively declare our host bindings and listeners straight on the code, like this:

```
@HostBinding('[class.valid]')
isValid: boolean; // The host element will feature class="valid"
// is the value of 'isValid' is true.
@HostListener('click', ['$event'])
onClick(e) {
  // This function will be executed when the host
  // component triggers a 'click' event.
}
```

In the next chapters, we will cover the configuration interface of directives and components in more detail, paying special attention to its life cycle management and how we can easily inject dependencies into our directives. For now, let's just build a simple, yet powerful, directive that will make a huge difference to how our UI is displayed and maintained.

Listening to events

So far, we were able to create our first directive, but it wasn't very interesting. Adding the ability to listen to events, however, would make it more interesting, so let's do that. We will need to use a helper called `HostListener` to listen to events, so we start by importing that:

```
import { HostListener } from '@angular/core';
```

The next thing we need to do is to use it as a decorator and decorate a method; yes, a method, not a class. That would look like the following:

```
@Directive({
  selector : '[highlight]'
})
export class HighlightDirective {
  @HostListener('click')
  clicked() {
    alert('clicked')
  }
}
```

Clicking on an element using this directive will lead to an alert window showing up. It was quite painless to add events, so let's try to add the events `mouseover` and `mouseleave`:

```
@Directive({
  selector : '[highlight]'
})
export class HighlightDirective {
  private nativeElement;

  constructor(elementRef: ElementRef, renderer: Renderer2) {
    this.nativeElement = elementRef.nativeElement;
  }

  @HostListener('mousenter')
  onMouseEnter() {
    this.background('red');
  }

  onMouseLeave('mouseleave') {
    this.background('yellow');
  }

  private background(bg:string) {
    this.renderer.setAttribute(nativeElement,'backgroundColor', bg);
  }
}
```

This gives us a directive that makes the background red on mouseover and reverts back to yellow when the mouse cursor leaves the component.

Adding input data

Our directive is quite static on what colors are being used for what, so let's ensure that they can be set from the outside. To add the first input, we need to use our old friend the @Input decorator, but instead of giving it no parameters as input as we are used to, we need to supply the name of the directive itself like so:

```
<div highlight="orange"></div>

@Directive({ selector : '[highlight]' })
export class HighlightDirective
  private nativeElement;

  constructor(elementRef: ElementRef, renderer: Renderer2) {
    this.nativeElement = elementRef.nativeElement;
  }

  @Input('highlight') color:string;

  @HostListener('mousenter')
  onMouseEnter(){
    this.background(this.color);
  }

  onMouseLeave() {
    this.background('yellow');
  }

  private background(bg: string) {
    this.renderer( nativeElement, 'background', bg );
  }
}
```

At this point, we have taken care of the first input; we did that with the following:

```
@Input('highlight') color: string;
```

But, how do we add more inputs to our directive? We'll cover that in the next subsection.

Adding more than one input property

So you want to add another input, that is relatively easy as well. We just add a property to our HTML element like so:

```
<div [highlight]="orange" defaultColor="yellow">
```

And in the code we type:

```
@Directive({})
export class HighlightDirective {
  @Input() defaultColor
  constructor() {
    this.background(this.defaultColor);
  }
  // the rest omitted for brevity
}
```

We notice, however, that we have no color until we do our first `mousenter` + `mouseleave` and the reason for that is that the constructor runs before our `defaultColor` property has been set. To fix that, we need to set up the input a bit differently. We need to use a property instead like so:

```
private defaultColor: string;

@Input()
set defaultColor(value) {
  this.defaultColor = value;
  this.background(value);
}

get defaultColor(){ return this.defaultColor; }
```

To recap this section on using input, it is clear that we can use the `@Input` decorator for both one as well as several inputs. The first input, however, should refer to the selector name of the directive and the second is the name of the attribute you give it.

A second example – error validation

Let's take this new found knowledge on directives and build a directive that indicates that a field is erroneous. We take erroneous to mean we color elements and display an error text:

```
import { Directive, ElementRef, Input } from '@angular/core';
@Directive({
  selector: '[error]'
})
```

```
export class ErrorDirective {
  error:boolean;
  private nativeElement;
  @Input errorText: string;
  @Input()
  set error(value: string) {
    let val = value === 'true' ? true : false;
    if(val){ this.setError(); }
    else { this.reset(); }
  }

  constructor(
    private elementRef: ElementRef,
    private renderer: Renderer2
  ) {
    this.nativeElement = elementRef.nativeElement;
  }

  private reset() {
    this.renderer.setProperty(nativeElement, 'innerHTML', '');
    this.renderer.setProperty(nativeElement, 'background', '')
  }

  private setError(){
    this.renderer.setProperty(nativeElement, 'innerHTML', this.errorText);
    this.renderer.setProperty(nativeElement, 'background', 'red');
  }
}
```

And to use it we just type:

```
<div error="{{hasError}}" errorText="display this error">
```

Building a task tooltip custom directive

So far, we have built a highlight directive as well as an error displaying directive. We've learned how to deal with events as well as multiple inputs.

A short word on tooltip. A tooltip appears when we hover over an element. What you normally do to achieve that is to set the title property on the element like so:

```
<div title="a tooltip"></div>
```

There are several approaches to build tooltips generally over such a component. One way is to bind to the `title` property like so:

```
<task-icons [title]="task.name"></task-icons>
```

However, if you have more logic in mind it might not be so nice to add all that in the markup, so at this point, we can create a directive to hide away the tooltip bit like so:

```
@Directive({ selector : '[task]' })
export class TooltipDirective {
  private nativeElement;
  @Input() task:Task;
  @Input() defaultTooltip: string;
  constructor(private elementRef: ElementRef, private renderer : Renderer2)
{
    this.nativeElement = elementRef.nativeElement;
  }

  @HostListener('mouseover')
  onMouseOver() {
    let tooltip = this.task ? this.task.name : this.defaultTooltip;
    this.renderer.setProperty( this.nativeElement, 'title', tooltip );
  }
}
```

And using it would be:

```
<div [task]="task">
```

However, there is another approach we can take to this. What if we wanted to alter the `innerText` of another element while hovering over an element? That's quite easy to do, we just need to feed our directive the other element and update its `innerText` property like so:

```
<div [task]="task" [elem]="otherElement" defaultTooltip="default text" >
<div #otherElement>
```

This of course means we need to update our directive a little bit to this:

```
@Directive({ selector : '[task]' })
export class TooltipDirective {
  private nativeElement;
  @Input() task:Task;
  @Input() defaultTooltip: string;
  constructor(private elementRef: ElementRef, private renderer : Renderer2)
{
    this.nativeElement = elementRef.nativeElement;
  }
```

```
@HostListener('mouseover')
onMouseOver() {
  let tooltip = this.task ? this.task.name : this.defaultTooltip;
  this.renderer.setProperty( this.nativeElement, 'innerText', tooltip );
}
}
```

A word about naming conventions for custom directives and pipes

Talking about reusability, the common convention is to prepend a custom prefix to the selector. This prevents conflicts with other selectors defined by other libraries that we might be using in our project. The same applies to pipes as well, as we highlighted already when introducing our very first custom pipe.

Ultimately, it is up to you and the name convention you embrace, but it is generally a good idea to establish a naming convention that prevents this from happening. A custom prefix is definitely the easier way.

Summary

Now that we have reached this point, it is fair to say that you know almost everything it takes to build Angular components, which are indeed the wheels and the engine of all Angular 2 applications. In the forthcoming chapters, we will see how we can design our application architecture better, and therefore manage dependency injection throughout our components tree, consume data services, leverage the new Angular router to show and hide components when required, and manage user input and authentication.

Nevertheless, this chapter is the backbone of Angular development, and we hope that you enjoyed it as much as we did when writing about template syntax, component APIs based on properties and events, view encapsulation, pipes, and directives. Now, get ready to assume new challenges—we are about to move from learning how to write components to discovering how we can use them to build bigger applications, while enforcing good practices and rational architectures. We will see all this in the next chapter.

6
Building an Application with Angular Components

We have reached a point in our journey where we can successfully develop more complex applications by nesting components within other components, in a sort of component tree. However, bundling all our component logic in a unique file is definitely not the way to go. Our application might become unmaintainable very soon and, as we will see later in the chapter, we would be missing the advantages that Angular's dependency management mechanism can bring to the game.

In this chapter, we will see how to build application architectures based on trees of components, and how the new Angular dependency injection mechanism will help us to declare and consume our dependencies across the application with minimum effort and optimal results.

In this chapter, we will cover these topics:

- Best practices for directory structures and naming conventions
- Different approaches to dependency injection
- Injecting dependencies into our custom types
- Overriding global dependencies throughout the component tree
- Interacting with the host component
- Overviewing the directive lifecycle
- Overviewing the component lifecycle

Introducing the component tree

Modern web applications based on web component architectures often conform to a sort of tree hierarchy, wherein the top main component (usually dropped somewhere in the main HTML index file) acts as a global placeholder where child components turn into hosts for other nested child components, and so on and so forth.

There are obvious advantages to this approach. On one hand, reusability does not get compromised and we can reuse components throughout the component tree with little effort. Secondly, the resulting granularity reduces the burden required for envisioning, designing, and maintaining bigger applications. We can simply focus on a single piece of UI and then wrap its functionality around new layers of abstraction until we wrap up a full-blown application from the ground up.

Alternatively, we can approach our web application the other way around, and start from a more generic functionality just to end up breaking down the app into smaller pieces of UI and functionality, which become our web components. The latter has become the most common approach when building component-based architectures. We will stick to it for the rest of the book, undertaking architectures as the one depicted here:

```
Application bootstrap
Root module
  Root component that is Application component
  Component A
  Component B
  Component B-I
  Component B-II
  Component C
  Component D
Feature module
  Component E
  Component F
Common module
  Component G
  Component H
```

For the sake of clarity, this chapter will just borrow the code we wrote in the previous chapters, and we will deconstruct it into a component hierarchy. We will also allocate some room in the resulting application for all the supporting classes and models required to give shape to our Pomodoro tool. This will turn into a perfect opportunity to learn the intricacies of the dependency injection machinery baked into Angular, as we will see later in this chapter.

Common conventions for scalable applications

In all fairness, we have already tackled a good number of the common concerns that modern web developers confront when building applications, small and large alike, nowadays. Therefore, it makes sense to define an architecture that will separate the aforementioned concerns into separate domain folders, catering to media assets and shared code units.

Angular's approach to separating the code and assets into logical units is by organizing them into different folders, but also by introducing the concept of an Angular module. It is in these modules that the constructs are registered. By introducing modules, a lot of the noise have disappeared from our components and our components are free to use the other constructs of the same module and, in some cases, constructs from other modules, given that their containing module is imported first.

It's worth emphasizing that when we are talking about Angular modules, we mean the `@NgModule` decorator and when we otherwise talk about modules, we mean the ES2015 construct.

Sometimes, two contexts may require sharing the same entities, and that is fine (as long as it does not become a common thing in our project, which would denote a serious design issue). Also worth emphasizing is that we use the word *context* to describe a logical boundary of constructs. A context is best kept within an Angular module. So, every time the word *context* is used, think that it will in code translate to an Angular module.

The following example, applied to our previous work on Pomodoro components, depicts this scheme, essentially making out our entire application of contexts and different constructs:

- Task context:
    - Task module
    - Task model
    - Tasks service
    - Task table component
    - Task pomodoros component
    - Task tooltip directive

- Timer context:
  - Timer module
  - Timer feature
  - Timer component
- Admin context:
  - Admin module
  - Authentication service
  - Login component
  - Editor component
- Shared context:
  - Shared module
  - Components shared across features
  - Pipes shared across features
  - Directives shared across features
  - Global models and services
  - Shared media assets

As we can see, the first step is to define the different features our application needs, keeping in mind that each one should make sense on its own in isolation from the others. Once we define the set of features required, we will create a module for each one. Each module will then be filled with the components, directives, pipes, models, and services that shape the feature it represents. Always remember the principles of encapsulation and reusability when defining your features set.

Initially, when starting your project, you should name your constructs after what they are, so say we have the `Admin` context, it should look something like this:

```
//admin/

admin.module.ts
authentication.service.ts
login.component.ts
editor.component.ts
```

With a quick glance, you should be able to see what the construct contains, so use a naming standard that looks like this:

```
<name>.<type>.ts // example login.service.ts
```

This is not the only way to do it, of course. There is another perfectly acceptable way of doing it, namely to create subdirectories for each type, so your preceding `admin` directory could look like this instead:

```
//admin/

admin.module.ts
services/
  authentication.service.ts
components/
  login.component.ts
  login.component.html
  editor.component.ts
  create-user.component.ts
pipes/
  user.pipe.ts
```

It is worth noting that you should keep the type in the filename for clarity in debugging. Otherwise, when looking for a specific file to set a breakpoint in your browser, let's say the login service, it might be quite confusing if you start typing `login.ts` and you are presented with:

- `components/login.ts`
- `services/login.ts`
- `pipes/login.ts`

There is an official style guide in place for how you should organize your code and how to name your constructs. There are definitely benefits to following a guide; it's easy for newcomers, the code looks more consistent, and so on. You can read more here; `https://angular.io/guide/styleguide`. Remember that whether you choose to follow this style guide in its entirety or not, consistency is key as it will make it easier to maintain the code.

File and ES6 module naming conventions

Each one of our feature folders will host a wide range of files, so we need a consistent naming convention to prevent filename collisions while we ensure that the different code units are easy to locate.

The following list summarizes the current conventions enforced by the community:

- Each file should contain a single code unit. Simply put, each component, directive, service, pipe, and so on should live in its own file. This way, we contribute to a better organization of code.
- Files and directories are named in lower-kebab-case.
- Files representing components, directives, pipes, and services should append a type suffix to their name: `video-player.ts` will become `video-player.component.ts`.
- Any component's external HTML template or CSS style sheet filename will match the component filename, including the suffix. Our `video-player.component.ts` might be accompanied by `video-player.component.css` and `video-player.component.html`.
- Directive selectors and pipe names are camelCased, while component selectors are lower-kebab-cased. Plus, it is strongly advised to add a custom prefix of our choice to prevent name collisions with other component libraries. For example, following up our video player component, it may be represented as `<vp-video-player>`, where `vp-` (which stands for video-player) is our custom prefix.
- Modules are named by following the rule of taking a PascalCased self-descriptive name, plus the type it represents. For example, if we see a module named `VideoPlayerComponent`, we can easily tell it is a component. The custom prefix in use for selectors (`vp-`, in our example) should not be part of the module name.
- Models and interfaces require special attention, though. Depending on your application architecture, model types will feature more or less relevance. Architectures such as MVC, MVVM, Flux, or Redux tackle models from different standpoints and grades of importance. Ultimately, it will be up to you and your architectural design pattern of choice to approach models and their naming convention in one way or another. This book will not be opinionated in that sense, although we do enforce interface models in our example application and will create modules for them.
- Each component and shared context of business logic in our application is intended to integrate with the other pieces of the puzzle in a simple and straightforward way. Clients of each subdomain are not concerned about the internal structure of the subdomain itself. If our timer feature, for example, evolves to the point of having two dozen components and directives that need to be reorganized into different folder levels, external consumers of its functionalities should remain unaffected.

From facades/barrels to NgModule

There comes a need to group your constructs into logical groups as your application grows. As the application grows, you also realize that not all constructs should be able to talk to each other, so you also need to think about restricting this. Before @NgModule was added to the framework, the natural course of action was to think of facade modules, which essentially meant that we created a specific file with the sole purpose of deciding what would get exported to the outside world. This could look like the following:

```
import TaskComponent from './task.component';
import TaskDetailsComponent from './task-details.component';
// and so on
export {
  TaskComponent,
  TaskDetailsComponent,
  // other constructs to expose
}
```

Everything else not explicitly exported would be considered as private or internal to the feature. Using one of the exported constructs would be as easy as typing:

```
import { TaskComponent } from './task.component.ts';
// do something with the component above
```

This was a valid way of dealing with grouping as well as restricting access. We keep these two features in mind as we delve deeper into @NgModule in the next subsection.

Using NgModule

With the arrival of @NgModule, we suddenly had a more logical way of grouping our constructs and also a natural way of deciding what got to be exported or not. The following piece of code corresponds to the preceding facade code, but it uses @NgModule instead:

```
import { NgModule } from '@angular/core';
import { TaskDetailComponent } from './task.detail.component';
import { TaskDetailsComponent } from './task.details.component';
import { TaskComponent } from './task.component';

@NgModule({
  declarations: [TaskComponent, TaskDetailsComponent],
  exports: [TaskComponent, TaskDetailComponent]
})
export class TaskModule { }
```

This would create the same effect and the construct is called a feature module. The `exports` keyword is what says what is publicly accessible or not. Getting access to what is publicly exposed looks a bit different though. Instead of typing:

```
import { TaskDetailComponent } from 'app/tasks/tasks';
```

We would need to import our feature module into our root module. This means our root module would look like the following:

```
import { TaskModule } from './task.module';

@NgModule({
  imports: [ TasksModule ]
  // the rest is omitted for brevity
})
```

This would now give us access to the exported components in the template markup. So in your upcoming app building, think about what belongs in a root module, what is part of a feature, and what is more common and used everywhere in the app. This is how you need to break apart your app, first in modules and then in proper constructs like components, directives, pipes, and so on.

How dependency injection works in Angular

As our applications grow and evolves, each one of our code entities will internally require instances of other objects, which are better known as dependencies in the world of software engineering. The action of passing such dependencies to the dependent client is known as injection, and it also entails the participation of another code entity, named the injector. The injector will take responsibility for instantiating and bootstrapping the required dependencies so they are ready for use from the very moment they are successfully injected in the client. This is very important since the client knows nothing about how to instantiate its own dependencies and is only aware of the interface they implement in order to use them.

Angular features a top-notch dependency injection mechanism to ease the task of exposing required dependencies to any entity that might exist in an Angular application, regardless of whether it is a component, a directive, a pipe, or any other custom service or provider object. In fact, as we will see later in this chapter, any entity can take advantage of dependency injection (usually referred to as DI) in an Angular application. Before delving deeper into the subject, let's look at the problem that Angular's DI is trying to address.

Let's figure out if we have a music player component that relies on a `playlist` object to broadcast music to its users:

```
import { Component } from '@angular/core';
import { Playlist } from './playlist.model';

@Component({
  selector: 'music-player',
  templateUrl: './music-player.component.html'
})
export class MusicPlayerComponent {
  playlist: Playlist;
  constructor() {
    this.playlist = new Playlist();
  }}
}
```

The `Playlist` type could be a generic class that returns in its API a random list of songs or whatever. That is not relevant now, since the only thing that matters is that our `MusicPlayerComponent` entity does need it to deliver its functionality. Unfortunately, the previous implementation means that both types are tightly coupled, since the component instantiates the playlist within its own constructor. This prevents us from altering, overriding, or mocking up in a neat way the `Playlist` class if required. It also entails that a new `Playlist` object is created every time we instantiate a `MusicPlayerComponent`. This might be not desired in certain scenarios, especially if we expect a singleton to be used across the application and thus keep track of the playlist's state.

Dependency injection systems try to solve these issues by proposing several patterns, and the constructor injection pattern is the one enforced by Angular. The previous piece of code could be rethought like this:

```
import { Component } from '@angular/core';
import { Playlist } from './playlist.model';

@Component({
  selector: 'music-player',
  templateUrl: './music-player.component.html'
})
export class MusicPlayerComponent {
  constructor(private playlist: Playlist) {}
}
```

Now, the `Playlist` is instantiated outside our component. On the other hand, the `MusicPlayerComponent` expects such an object to be already available before the component is instantiated so it can be injected through its constructor. This approach gives us the opportunity to override it or mock it up if we wish.

Basically, this is how dependency injection, and more specifically the constructor injection pattern, works. However, what has this got to do with Angular? Does Angular's dependency injection machinery work by instantiating types by hand and injecting them through the constructor? Obviously not, mostly because we do not instantiate components by hand either (except when writing unit tests). Angular features its own dependency injection framework, which can be used as a standalone framework by other applications, by the way.

The framework offers an actual injector that can introspect the tokens used to annotate the parameters in the constructor and return a singleton instance of the type represented by each dependency, so we can use it straight away in the implementation of our class, as in the previous example. The injector ignores how to create an instance of each dependency, so it relies on the list of providers registered upon bootstrapping the application. Each one of those providers actually provides mappings over the types marked as application dependencies. Whenever an entity (let's say a component, a directive, or a service) defines a token in its constructor, the injector searches for a type matching that token in the pool of registered providers for that component. If no match is found, it will then delegate the search on the parent component's provider, and will keep conducting the provider's lookup upwards until a provider resolves with a matching type or the top component is reached. Should the provider lookup finish with no match, Angular will throw an exception.

The latter is not exactly true, since we can mark dependencies in the constructor with the `@Optional` parameter decorator, in which case Angular will not throw any exception and the dependency parameter will be injected as null if no provider is found.

Whenever a provider resolves with a type matching that token, it will return such type as a singleton, which will be therefore injected by the injector as a dependency. In fairness, the provider is not just a collection of key/value pairs coupling tokens with previously registered types, but a factory that instantiates these types and also instantiates each dependency's very own dependencies as well, in a sort of recursive dependency instantiation.

So, instead of instantiating the `Playlist` object manually, we could do this:

```
import { Component } from '@angular/core';
import { Playlist } from './playlist';

@Component({
```

```
    selector: 'music-player',
    templateUrl: './music-player.component.html',
    providers: [Playlist]
})
export class MusicPlayerComponent {
    constructor(private playlist: Playlist) {}
}
```

The `providers` property of the `@Component` decorator is the place where we can register dependencies on a component level. From that moment onwards, these types will be immediately available for injection at the constructor of that component and, as we will see next, at its own child components as well.

A note on providers

Before `@NgModule` was introduced, Angular applications and especially components were thought to be responsible for what they needed. Therefore, it was commonplace for a component to ask for what dependencies it needed in order to be instantiated correctly. In the example of the previous section, the `MusicPlayerComponent` asks for a `Playlist` dependency. While this is still technically possible to do, we should use our new `@NgModule` concept and provide constructs on a module level instead. This means that the previously mentioned example would instead register its dependencies in a module, like so:

```
@NgModule({
    declarations: [MusicComponent, MusicPlayerComponent],
    providers: [Playlist, SomeOtherService]
})
```

Here, we can see that `Playlist` and `SomeOtherService` would be available for injection, for all constructs declared in the declarations property. As you can see, the responsibility of where to provide a service has shifted somewhat. As mentioned before, this does not mean we can't provide constructs on a per component level, there exist use cases where this makes sense. We want to stress however that the normal case is to place your services or other constructs, which need injecting, in the `providers` property of the module rather than the component.

Injecting dependencies across the component tree

We have seen that the provider lookup is performed upwards until a match is found. A more visual example might help, so let's figure out that we have a music app component that hosts in its directives property (and hence its template) a music library component with a collection of all our downloaded tunes that also hosts, in its own directives property and template, a music player component so we can playback any of the tunes in our library:

```
MusicAppComponent
  MusicLibraryComponent
    MusicPlayerComponent
```

Our music player component requires an instance of the `Playlist` object we mentioned before, so we declare it as a constructor parameter, conveniently annotated with the `Playlist` token:

```
MusicAppComponent
  MusicLibraryComponent
    MusicPlayerComponent(playlist: Playlist)
```

When the `MusicPlayerComponent` entity is instantiated, the Angular DI mechanism will go through the parameters in the component constructor with special attention to their type annotations. Then, it will check if that type has been registered in the component's provider property of the component decorator configuration. The code is as follows:

```
@Component({
  selector: 'music-player',
  providers: [Playlist]
})
export class MusicPlayerComponent {
  constructor(private playlist: Playlist) {}
}
```

But, what if we want to reuse the `Playlist` type in other components throughout the same component tree? Maybe the `Playlist` type contains functionalities in its API that are required by different components at once across the application. Do we have to declare the token in the provider's property for each one? Fortunately not, since Angular anticipates that necessity and brings transversal dependency injection through the component tree.

In the previous section, we mentioned that components conduct a provider lookup upwards. This is because each component has its own built-in injector, which is specific to it. Nevertheless, that injector is in reality a child instance of the parent's component injector (and so on and so forth), so it is fair to say that an Angular application has not a single injector, but many instances of the same injector, so to say.

We need to extend the injection of the `Playlist` object to other components in the component tree in a quick and reusable fashion. Knowing beforehand that components perform a provider lookup starting from itself and then passing up the request to its parent component's injectors, we can then address the issue by registering the provider in the parent component, or even the top parent component, so the dependency will be available for injection for each and every child component found underneath it. In this sense, we could register the `Playlist` object straight at `MusicAppComponent`, regardless to whether it might not need it for its own implementation:

```
@Component({
  selector: 'music-app',
  providers: [Playlist],
  template: '<music-library></music-library>'
})
export class MusicAppComponent {}
```

The immediate child component might not require the dependency for its own implementation either. Since it has been already registered in its parent `MusicAppComponent` component, there is no need to register it there again:

```
@Component({
  selector: 'music-library',
  template: '<music-player></music-player>'
})
export class MusicLibraryComponent {}
```

We finally reach our music player component, but now it no longer features the `Playlist` type as a registered token in its `providers` property. In fact, our component does not feature a providers property at all. It no longer requires this, since the type has been already registered somewhere above the component's hierarchy, being immediately available for all child components, no matter where they are:

```
@Component({
  selector: 'music-player'
})
export class MusicPlayerComponent {
  constructor(private playlist: playlist) {}
}
```

Now, we see how dependencies are injected down the component hierarchy and how the provider lookup is performed by components just by checking their own registered providers and bubbling up the request upwards in the component tree. However, what if we want to constrain such injection or lookup actions?

Restricting dependency injection down the component tree

In our previous example, we saw how the music app component registered the Playlist token in its providers collection, making it immediately available for all child components. Sometimes, we might need to constrain the injection of dependencies to reach only those directives (and components) that are immediately next to a specific component in the hierarchy. We can do that by registering the type token in the `viewProviders` property of the component decorator, instead of using the providers property we've seen already. In our previous example, we can restrain the downwards injection of `Playlist` one level only:

```
@Component({
  selector: 'music-app',
  viewProviders : [Playlist],
  template: '<music-library></music-library>'
})
export class MusicAppComponent {}
```

We are informing Angular that the `Playlist` provider should only be accessible by the injectors of the directives and components located in the `MusicAppComponent` view, but not for the children of such components. The use of this technique is exclusive of components, since only they feature views.

Restricting provider lookup

Just like we can restrict dependency injection, we can constrain dependency lookup to the immediate upper level only. To do so, we just need to apply the `@Host()` decorator to those dependency parameters whose provider lookup we want to restrict:

```
import {Component, Host} from '@angular/core';

@Component {
  selector: 'music-player'
}
export class MusicPlayerComponent {
  constructor(@Host() playlist:Playlist) {}
}
```

According to the preceding example, the `MusicPlayerComponent` injector will look up a `Playlist` type at its parent component's providers collection (`MusicLibraryComponent`, in our example) and will stop there, throwing an exception because `Playlist` has not been returned by the parent's injector (unless we also decorate it with the `@Optional()` parameter decorator).

To clarify this functionality, let's do another example:

```
@Component({
  selector: 'granddad',
  template: 'granddad <father>'
  providers: [Service]
})
export class GranddadComponent {
  constructor(srv:Service){}
}

@Component({
  selector: 'father',
  template: 'father <child>'
})
export class FatherComponent {
  constructor(srv:Service) {} // this is fine, as GranddadComponent
provides Service
}
```

```
@Component({
  selector: 'child',
  template: 'child'
})
export class ChildComponent {
  constructor(@Host() srv:Service) {} // will cause an error
}
```

In this case, we would get an error as the Child component only looks one level up, to try and find the service. As it is two levels up, it does not find it.

Overriding providers in the injector hierarchy

We've seen so far how Angular's DI framework uses the dependency token to introspect the type required and return it right from any of the provider sets available along the component hierarchy. However, we might need to override the class instance corresponding to that token in certain cases where a more specialized type is required to do the job. Angular provides special tools to override the providers or even implement factories that will return a class instance for a given token, not necessarily matching the original type.

We will not cover all the use cases in detail here, but let's look at a simple example. In our example, we assumed that the Playlist object was meant to be available across the component tree for use in different entities of the application. What if our MusicAppComponent directive hosts another component whose child directives require a more specialized version of the Playlist object? Let's rethink our example:

```
MusicAppComponent
  MusicChartsComponent
    MusicPlayerComponent
  MusicLibraryComponent
    MusicPlayerComponent
```

This is a bit of a contrived example, but it will definitely help us to understand the point of overriding dependencies. The `Playlist` instance object is available right from the top component downwards. The `MusicChartsComponent` directive is a specialized component that caters only for music featured in the top seller's charts and hence its player must playback big hits only, regardless of the fact it uses the same component as `MusicLibraryComponent`. We need to ensure that each player component gets the proper playlist object, and this can be done at the `MusicChartsComponent` level by overriding the object instance corresponding to the `Playlist` token. The following example depicts this scenario, leveraging the use of the `provide` function:

```
import { Component } from '@angular/core';
import { Playlist } from './playlist';

import { TopHitsPlaylist } from './top-hits/playlist';

@Component({
  selector: 'music-charts',
  template: '<music-player></music-player>',
  providers: [{ provide : Playlist, useClass : TopHitsPlaylist }]
})
export class MusicChartsComponent {}
```

The `provide` keyword creates a provider mapped to the token specified in the first argument (`Playlist`, in this example) and the property `useClass` essentially overwrites the playlist with `TopHitsPlaylist` from this component and downstream.

We could refactor the block of code to use `viewProviders` instead, so we ensure that (if required) the child entities still receive an instance of `Playlist` instead of `TopHitsPlaylist`. Alternatively, we can go the extra mile and use a factory to return the specific object instance we need, depending on other requirements. The following example will return a different object instance for the `Playlist` token, depending on the evaluation of a Boolean condition variable:

```
function playlistFactory() {
  if(condition) {
    return new Playlist();
  }
  else {
    return new TopHitsPlaylist();
  }
}

@Component({
  selector: 'music-charts',
  template: '<music-player></music-player>',
```

```
    providers: [{ provide : Playlist, useFactory : playlistFactory }]
})
export class MusicChartsComponent {}
```

So, you can see how powerful this is. We could, for example, make sure that our data service suddenly would be replaced by a mock data service when testing. The point is it is really easy to tell the DI mechanism to change its behavior based on a condition.

Extending injector support to custom entities

Directives and components require dependencies to be introspected, resolved, and injected. Other entities such as service classes often require such functionality too. In our example, our `Playlist` class might rely on a dependency on a HTTP client to communicate with a third party to fetch the songs. The action of injecting such dependency should be as easy as declaring the annotated dependencies in the class constructor and have an injector ready to fetch the object instance by inspecting the class provider or any other provider available somewhere.

It is only when we think hard about the latter that we realize there is a gap in this idea: custom classes and services do not belong to the component tree. Hence, they do not benefit from anything such as a built-in injector or a parent injector. We cannot even declare a providers property, since we do not decorate these types of class with a `@Component` or `@Directive` decorator. Let's take a look at an example:

```
class Playlist {
  songs: Song[];
  constructor(songsService: SongsService) {
    this.songs = songsService.fetch();
  }
}
```

We might try this in the hope of having Angular's DI mechanism introspecting the `songsService` parameter of the `Playlist` class constructor when instantiating this class in order to inject it into `MusicPlayerComponent`. Unfortunately, the only thing we will eventually get is an exception like this:

It cannot resolve all parameters for Playlist (?). Make sure they all have valid type or annotations.

This is kind of misleading, since all constructor parameters in `Playlist` have been properly annotated, right? As we said before, the Angular DI machinery resolves dependencies by introspecting the types of the constructor parameters. To do so, it needs some metadata to be created beforehand. Each and every Angular entity class decorated with a decorator features this metadata as a by-product of the way TypeScript compiles the decorator configuration details. However, dependencies that also require other dependencies have no decorator whatsoever and no metadata is then created for them. This can be easily fixed thanks to the `@Injectable()` decorator, which will give visibility to these service classes for the DI mechanism:

```
import { Injectable } from '@angular/core';

@Injectable()
class Playlist {
  songs: string[];

  constructor(private songsService: SongsService) {
    this.songs = this.songsService.fetch();
  }
}
```

You will get used to introducing that decorator in your service classes, since they will quite often rely on other dependencies not related to the component tree in order to deliver the functionality.

It is actually a good practice to decorate all your service classes with the `@Injectable()` decorator, irrespective of whether its constructor functions have dependencies or not. This way, we prevent errors and exceptions because of skipping this requirement once the service class grows, and it requires more dependencies in the future.

Initializing applications with bootstrapModule()

As we have seen in this chapter, the dependency lookup bubbles up until the first component at the top. This is not exactly true, since there is an additional step that the DI mechanism will check on: the `bootstrapModule()` function.

As far as we know, we use the `bootstrapModule()` function to kickstart our application by declaring in its first argument the root module, that in turn points out the root component, that initiates the application's component tree.

A typical bootstrap will look like the following in the file `main.ts`:

```
import { enableProdMode } from '@angular/core';
import { platformBrowserDynamic } from '@angular/platform-browser-dynamic';
import { AppModule } from './app/app.module';
import { environment } from './environments/environment';

if (environment.production) {
  enableProdMode();
}

platformBrowserDynamic().bootstrapModule(AppModule);
```

The takeaway from the preceding code is that Angular has changed how it bootstraps things. With the addition of `@NgModule`, we now bootstrap a root module rather than a root component. However, the root module still needs to point to an entry point where the application starts. Let's have a look at the root module to see how this is done:

```
import { NgModule } from '@angular/core';
import { AppComponent } from './app.component';

@NgModule({
  bootstrap: [AppComponent]
  // the rest omitted for brevity
})
```

Note the existence of the `bootstrap` key, how we point out the root component `AppComponent`. Also, note how the `bootstrap` property is an array. This means we can have multiple root components. Each one of these root components will feature its own set of injectors and service singletons, with no relationship whatsoever among them. Next up, let's talk about the different modes we can alter in-between.

Switching between development and production modes

Angular applications are bootstrapped and initialized by default in development mode. In the development mode, the Angular runtime will throw warning messages and assertions to the browser console. While this is quite useful for debugging our application, we do not want those messages to be displayed when the application is in production. The good news is that the development mode can be disabled in favor of the more silent production mode. This action is usually performed before bootstrapping our application:

```
import { environment } from './environments/environment';
// other imports omitted for brevity
if(environment.production) {
  enableProdMode();
```

```
  }

  //bootstrap
  platformBrowserDynamic().bootstrapModule(AppModule);
```

What we can see here is that the call to `enableProdMode()` is what enables production mode.

Different modes in Angular CLI

It is worth noting that it's a good idea to keep different environment configurations in different files, as follows:

```
  import { environment } from './environments/environment';
```

The environments directory consists of two different files:

- `environment.ts`
- `environment.prod.ts`

With the first file looking like this:

```
  export const environment = {
    production: false
  }
```

And the second looking like this:

```
  export const environment = {
    production: true
  }
```

Depending on how we call the `ng build` command, one of the two files will be used:

```
  ng build --env=prod // uses environment.prod.ts
  ng build // by default uses environment.ts
```

To find out which files map to which environment, you should have a look at the `angular-cli.json` file:

```
  // config omitted for brevity
  "environments" : {
    "dev": "environments/environment.ts",
    "prod": "environments/environment.prod.ts"
  }
```

Introducing the app directory structure

In the previous chapters and sections in this chapter, we have seen different approaches and good practices for laying out Angular applications. These guidelines encompassed from naming conventions to pointers about how to organize files and folders. From this point onwards, we are going to put all this knowledge to practice by refactoring all the different interfaces, components, directives, pipes, and services in an actual Angular architecture, conforming to the most commonly agreed community conventions.

By the end of this chapter, we will have a final application layout that wraps everything we have seen so far in the following site architecture:

```
app/
 assets/ // global CSS or image files are stored here
 core/
  (application wide services end up here)
  core.module.ts
 shared/
   shared.module.ts // Angular module for shared context
 timer/
 ( timer-related components and directives )
   timer.module.ts // Angular module for timer context
 tasks/
 ( task-related components and directive )
   task.module.ts // Angular module for task context
 app
   app.component.ts
   app.module.ts // Angular module for app context
main.ts // here we bootstrap the application
index.html
package.json
tsconfig.json
typings.json
```

It is easy to understand the whole rationale of the project. Now, we will put together an application that features two main contexts: a timer feature and tasks listing feature. Each feature can encompass a different range of components, pipes, directives, or services. The inner implementation of each feature is opaque to the other features or contexts. Each feature context exposes an Angular module that exports the pieces of functionality (that is, the component, one or many) that each context delivers to the upper-level context or application. All the other pieces of functionality (inner directives and components) are concealed from the rest of the application.

It is fair to say that it is difficult to draw a line in the sand differentiating what belongs to a specific context or another. Sometimes, we build pieces of functionality, such as certain directives or pipes, which can be reused throughout the application. So, locking them down to a specific context does not make much sense. For those cases, we do have the shared context, where we store any code unit that is meant to be reusable at an application level, apart from media files such as style sheets or bitmap images that are component-agnostic.

The main `app.component.ts` file contains and exports the application root component, which declares and registers in its own injector the dependencies required by its child components. As you know already, all Angular applications must have at least one root module and one root component, initialized by the `bootstrapModule()` function. This operation is actually performed in the `main.ts` file, which is fired by the `index.html` file.

Defining a component or a group of related components within a context like this improves reusability and encapsulation. The only component that is tightly coupled with the application is the top root component, whose functionality is usually pretty limited and entails basically rendering the other child components in its template view or acting as a router component, as we will see in further chapters.

The last bit of the puzzle is the JSON files that contain the TypeScript compiler, typings, and `npm` configuration. Since versioning on the Angular framework keeps evolving, we will not look at the actual content of these files here. You are supposed to know their purpose, but some specifics such as the peer dependency versions change quite often, so you'd better refer to the book's GitHub repository for the latest up-to-date version of each one. The `package.json` file requires a special mention though. There are a few common industry conventions and popular seed projects, like the one provided by the Angular official site itself. We have provided several `npm` commands to ease the overall installation process and the development endeavor.

Refactoring our application the Angular way

In this section, we will split the code we created in earlier chapters into code units, following the single responsibility principle. So, do not expect many changes in the code, apart from allocating each module in its own dedicated file. This is why we will focus more on how to split things rather than explaining each module, whose purpose you should know already. In any event, we will take a minute to discuss changes if required.

Let's begin by creating in your work folder the same directory structure we saw in the previous section. We will populate each folder with files on the go.

The shared context or store it all in a common module

The shared context is where we store any construct whose functionality is meant to be used by not one, but many contexts at once, as it is agnostic to those contexts as well. A good example is the Pomodoro bitmap we've been using to decorate our components, which should be stored in the `app/shared/assets/img` path (please do save it there, by the way).

Another good example is the interfaces that model data, mostly when their schema can be reused across a different context of functionality. For instance, when we defined the `QueuedOnlyPipe` in Chapter 4, *Implementing Properties and Events in Our Components*, we actioned only over the queued property of items in the recordset. We can then seriously consider implementing a Queued interface that we can use later on to provide type-checking for modules that feature that property. This will make our pipes more reusable and model-agnostic. The code is as follows:

```
//app/shared/queueable.model.ts

export interface Queueable {
  queued: boolean;
}
```

Pay attention to this workflow: first, we define the module corresponding to this code unit, and then we export it, flagging it as default so we can import it by name from elsewhere. Interfaces need to be exported this way, but for the rest of the book we will usually declare the module and export it in the same statement.

With this interface in place, we can now safely refactor the `QueuedOnlyPipe` to make it fully agnostic from the `Task` interface so that it is fully reusable in any context where a recordset, featuring items implementing the `Queueable` interface, needs to be filtered, regardless of what they represent. The code is as follows:

```
// app/shared/queued.only.pipe.ts
import { Pipe, PipeTransform } from '@angular/core';
import { Queueable } from '../interfaces/queuable';

@Pipe({ name : 'queuedOnly' })
export class QueuedOnlyPipe implements PipeTransform {
  transform(queueableItems: Queueable[], ...args) :Queueable[] {
    return queuableItems.filter(
      queueableItem:Queueable => queueableItem.queued === args[0]
    )
  }
```

```
}
```

As you can see, each code unit contains a single module. This code unit conforms to the naming conventions set for Angular filenames, clearly stating the module name in camel case, plus the type suffix (.pipe, in this case). The implementation does not change either, apart from the fact that we have annotated all queue-able items with the Queuable type, instead of the Task annotation we had earlier. Now, our pipe can be reused wherever a model implementing the Queueable interface is present.

However, there is something that should draw your attention: we're not importing the Queuable interface from its source location, but from a file named shared.ts located in the upper level. This is the facade file for the shared context, and we will expose all public shared modules from that file, not only to the clients consuming the shared context modules, but to those inside the shared context as well. There is a case for this: if any module within the shared context changes its location, we need to update the facade so that any other element referring to that module within the same context remains unaffected since it consumes it through the facade. This is actually a good moment to start introducing our shared module that before @NgModule would have been a facade file:

```
//app/shared/shared.module.ts

import { QueuedOnlyPipe } from './pipes/queued-only.pipe';

@NgModule({
  declarations: [QueuedOnlyPipe],
  exports: [QueuedOnlyPipe]
})
export class SharedModule {}
```

The main difference from a facade file is that we can add all sorts of business logic to our SharedModule by adding methods and injecting services and so on to SharedModule.

This far we have only exposed pipes, directives, and components through the exports property of our SharedModule, but what about other things such as classes and interfaces? Well, we can require them directly when we need them, like so:

```
import { Queueable } from '../shared/queueable';

export class ProductionService {
  queueable: Queueable;
}
```

Now that we have a working `Queueable` interface and a `SharedModule`, we can create the other interface we will require throughout the book, corresponding to the `Task` entity, along with the other pipe we required:

```
//app/task/task.model.ts

import { Queueable } from './queueable';

export interface Task extends Queueable {
  name: string;
  deadline: Date;
  pomodorosRequired: number;
}
```

We implement an interface onto another interface in TypeScript by using extends (instead of implements). Now, for the `FormattedTimePipe`:

```
//app/shared/formatted.time.pipe.ts

import { Pipe, PipeTransform } from '@angular/core';

@Pipe({ name : 'formattedTime' })
export class FormattedTimePipe {
  transform(totalMinutes: number) {
    let minutes: number = totalMinutes % 60;
    let hours: number = Math.floor( totalMinutes / 60 );
    return `${hours}h:${minutes}m`;
  }
}
```

Finally, we need to update our `SharedModule` to contain this `Pipe` as well:

```
//app/shared/shared.module.ts

import { QueuedOnlyPipe } from './pipes/queued-only.pipe';
import { FormattedTimePipe } from './pipes/formatted-time.pipe';

@NgModule({
 declarations: [QueuedOnlyPipe, FormattedTimePipe],
 exports: [QueuedOnlyPipe, FormattedTimePipe]
})
export class SharedModule {}
```

To sum up what we did here, we created two interfaces, Task and Queueable. We also created two pipes, QueuedOnlyPipe and FormattedTimePipe. We added the latter to the declarations keyword for our @NgModule, and as for the interfaces, we will pull them into the application as we need them, using the import keyword. There is no need to expose them through a facade file anymore.

Services in the shared context

Let's talk about what the impact of having services in a shared context and what the addition of @NgModule has brought to the table. There are two types of services we need to care about:

- A transient service; this service creates a new copy of itself and may or may not contain an inner state; for each copy created it has its own state
- A singleton, there can only be one of this service and if it has a state, we need to ensure that there is only a copy of this service in our entire application

Using dependency injection in Angular, placing services in the providers of the modules will ensure they end up on on the root injector and thereby there will be only one copy of them created if we have this situation:

```
// app/task/task.module.ts

@NgModule({
  declarations: [TaskComponent],
  providers: [TaskService]
})
export class TaskModule {}
```

Earlier, we had a declaration of a TaskModule in which we provided the TaskService. Let's look at defining another module:

```
@NgModule({
  declarations: [ProductsComponent]
  providers: [ProductsService]
})
export class ProductsModule {}
```

Providing we import both of these modules in the root module, like so:

```
//app/app.module.ts

@NgModule({
   imports: [TaskModule, ProductsModule]
})
export class AppModule {}
```

We have now created a situation where `ProductsService` and `TaskService` can be injected in the constructor of `ProductsComponent` or `TaskComponent`, thanks to `ProductsModule` and `TaskModule` both being imported into the `AppModule`. So far, we don't have an issue. However, were we to start using lazy loading, we have an issue on our hands. In lazy loading, the user navigates to a certain route and our module, together with its constructs, which are loaded into the bundle. If the lazy loaded module, or one of its constructs, actually injects, let's say `ProductsService`, it would not be the same `ProductsService` instance that `TaskModule` or `ProductsModule` is using and this might become a problem, especially if the state is shared. The way to solve this is to create a core module, a module that is imported by the `AppModule`; this would ensure that services is never subjected to the risk of being instantiated again, by mistake. So, if `ProductsService` is used in more than one module, especially in a lazy loaded module, it is advisable to move it to a core module. So essentially, we go from doing this:

```
@NgModule({
   providers: [ProductsService],
})
export class ProductsModule {}
```

To moving our `ProductService` to a core module:

```
@NgModule({
   providers: [ProductsService]
})
export class CoreModule {}
```

And of course, we need to add the newly created `CoreModule` to our root module, like so:

```
@NgModule({
   providers: [],
   imports: [CoreModule, ProductsModule, TasksModule]
})
export class AppModule {}
```

One can argue that if our application is small enough, creating a core module early on might be seen as somewhat of an overkill. An argument against that is that the Angular framework has a mobile first approach and that you as a developer should lazy load most of your modules, unless there is a good reason not to. This means that when you deal with services which might be shared, you should move them to a core module.

We built a data service in the previous chapter to serve a tasks dataset to populate our data table with. As we will see later in this book, the data service will be consumed by other contexts of the application. So, we will allocate it in the shared context, exposing it through our shared module:

```typescript
//app/task/task.service.ts

import { Injectable } from '@angular/core';
import { Task } from '../interfaces/task';

@Injectable()
export class TaskService {
  taskStore: Task[] = [];
  constructor() {
    const tasks = [
      {
        name : 'task 1',
        deadline : 'Jun 20 2017 ',
        pomodorosRequired : 2
      },
      {
        name : 'task 2',
        deadline : 'Jun 22 2017',
        pomodorosRequired : 3
      }
    ];
    this.taskStore = tasks.map( task => {
      return {
        name : task.name,
        deadline : new Date(task.deadline),
        queued : false,
        pomodorosRequired : task.pomodorosRequired
      }
    });
  }
}
```

Please pay attention to how we imported the `Injectable()` decorator and implemented it on our service. It does not require any dependency in its constructor, so other modules depending on this service will not have any issues anyway when declaring it in its constructors. The reason is simple: it is actually a good practice to apply the `@Injectable()` decorator in our services by default to ensure they keep being injected seamlessly as long as they begin depending on other providers, just in case we forget to decorate them.

Configuring application settings from a central service

In the previous chapters, we hardcoded a lot of stuff in our components: labels, durations, plural mappings, and so on. Sometimes, our contexts are meant to have a high level of specificity and it's fine to have that information there. At other times, we might require more flexibility and a more convenient way to update these settings application-wide.

For this example, we will make all the `118n` pipes mappings and settings available from a central service located in the shared context and exposed, as usual, from the `shared.ts` facade.

The following code describes a `SettingsService` that will hold all the configuration for the application:

```
// app/core/settings.service.ts
import { Injectable } from '@angular/core';

@Injectable()
export class SettingsService {
  timerMinutes: number;
  labelsMap: any;
  pluralsMap: any;

  contructor() {
    this.timerMinutes = 25;
    this.labelsMap = {
      timer : {
        start : 'Start Timer',
        pause : 'Pause Timer',
        resume : 'Resume Countdown',
        other : 'Unknown'
      }
    };

    this.pluralsMap = {
      tasks : {
```

```
              '=0' : 'No pomodoros',
              '=1' : 'One pomodoro',
              'other' : '# pomodoros'
            }
          }
        }
      }
```

Please note how we expose context-agnostic mapping properties, which are actually namespaced, to better group the different mappings by context.

It would be perfectly fine to split this service into two specific services, one per context, and locate them inside their respective context folders, at least with regard to the 118n mappings. Keep in mind that data such as the time duration will be used across different contexts, though, as we will see later in this chapter.

Putting it all together in our shared module

With all the latest changes, our `shared.module.ts` should look like this:

```
// app/shared/shared.module.ts

import { NgModule } from '@angular/core';
import { FormattedTimePipe } from './pipes/formatted-time-pipe';
import { QueuedOnlyPipe } from './pipes/queued-only-pipe';

import { SettingsService } from './services/settings.service';
import { TaskService } from './services/task.service';

@NgModule({
  declarations: [FormattedTimePipe, QueuedOnlyPipe],
  providers: [SettingsService, TaskService],
  exports: [FormattedTimePipe, QueuedOnlyPipe]
})
export class SharedModule {}
```

Our `SharedModule` exposes `FormattedTimePipe` and `QueuedOnlyPipe` from before, but there are some new additions; namely, we added things to the `provider` keyword. We added our services, `SettingsService` and `TaskService`.

Now, an interesting thing happens when this module is consumed by another module; so, let's take a look at such a scenario in the following code:

```
// app/app.module.ts

import { NgModule } from '@angular/core';
import { SharedModule } from './shared/shared.module';

@NgModule({
  imports: [SharedModule]
  // the rest is omitted for brevity
})
export class AppModule {}
```

The effect of importing another module is partly known from before. We know that everything included in the `export` keyword from `SharedModule` is now readily available in the `AppModule`, but there is more. Anything mentioned in the `provider` keyword of `SharedModule` is ready to be injected. So, let's say we have the following `app.component.ts` file:

```
// app/app.component.ts

import { AppComponent } from './app.component';

@Component({
  selector: 'app',
  template: 'app'
})
export class AppComponent {
  constructor(
    private settingsService:SettingsService,
    private taskService: TaskService
  ) {}
}
```

As you can see, we can now freely inject services from other modules as long as they are:

- Mentioned in the `providers` keyword for their module
- The module they reside in gets imported by another module

To sum up, so far, we have learned how to add components as well as services to a shared module and we have also learned that we need to register components in declarations and `export` keywords, and for services, we need to place them in the `provider` keyword. Lastly, we need to `import` the module they reside in and all your shared constructs are ready for use in your application.

Creating our components

With our shared context sorted out, the time has come to cater to our other two contexts: timer and tasks. Their names are self-descriptive enough of the scope of their functionalities. Each context folder will allocate the component, HTML view template, CSS, and directive files required to deliver their functionality, plus a facade file that exports the public components of this feature.

Introduction to life cycle hooks

Life cycle hooks are your ability to spy on stages in the life cycle of a directive or component. The hooks themselves are completely optional to use, but might be of valuable help if you understand how to use them. Some hooks are considered best practice to use, while other hooks help with debugging and understanding what happens in your app. A hook comes with an interface that defines a method you need to implement. The Angular framework makes sure the hook is called, provided you have added the interface to the component or directive and fulfilled the contract by implementing the methods the interface specifies. As we are just starting to learn how to build your app, it might not make sense to use certain hooks yet. So, we will have a reason to return to this topic in later chapters.

The hooks you can use are as follows:

- `OnInit`
- `OnDestroy`
- `OnChanges`
- `DoCheck`
- `AfterContentInit`
- `AfterContentChecked`
- `AfterViewInit`
- `AfterViewChecked`

In this section, we will cover the top three ones in this chapter as the rest are touching on more complex topics. We will revisit the remaining five hooks in later chapters in the book.

OnInit - the beginning of it all

Using this hook is as easy as adding the `OnInit` interface and implementing the `ngOnInit()` method:

```
export class ExampleComponent implements OnInit {
  ngOnInit() {}
}
```

Let's talk about why this hook exists though. Constructors should be relatively empty and devoid of logic other than setting initial variables. There should be no surprises when constructing an object because sometimes you construct an object meant for business use and sometimes it is created in unit testing scenarios.

The following is an example of suitable things to carry out in the constructor of the class. Here, we are showing assignment of the class's member variables:

```
export class Component {
  field: string;
  constructor(field: string) {
    this.field = field;
  }
}
```

The following example shows what NOT to do. In the code, we are subscribing to an Observable in the constructor. This can be acceptable in some scenarios, but it is usually a better idea to place this kind of code inside an `ngOnInit()` method:

```
export class Component {
  data:Entity;
  constructor(private http:Http) {
    this.http.get('url')
    .map(mapEntity)
    .subscribe( x => this.data = x);
  }
}
```

It's better to set up subscription, as shown previously with the `ngOnInit()` method provided by the `OnInit` interface.

This is, of course, a recommendation and not a law. If you are not using this hook, then obviously you need to use the constructor or similar to perform the preceding HTTP call. Other than just saying that the constructor should be empty for aesthetic reasons and when dealing with testing, there is another aspect, namely that of binding of input values. An input variable won't be set immediately, so relying on the input value to be there when in the constructor will lead to a runtime error. Let's illustrate the mentioned scenario:

```
@Component({
  selector: 'father',
  template: '<child [prop]='title'></child>'
})
export class FatherComponent {
  title: string = 'value';
}

@Component({
  selector: 'child',
  template: 'child'
})
export class ExampleComponent implements OnInit {
  @Input prop;

  constructor(private http:Http) {
    // prop NOT set, accessing it might lead to an error
    console.log('prop constructor',prop)
  }

  ngOnInit() {
    console.log('prop on init', prop) // prop is set and is safe to use
  }
}
```

At this stage, you can make sure that all bindings have been properly set and you can safely use the value of prop. If you are familiar with jQuery, then ngOnInit acts much like a $(document).ready() like construct, the bottom line is that the ceremony that happens when a component is being set up has happened at this point.

OnDestroy - called when a component is removed from a DOM tree

The typical use case for this is to do some custom clean up when the component is about to leave the DOM tree. It consists of the interface OnDestroy and the ngOnDestroy() method.

To demonstrate its use, let's look at the following code snippet where we implement the `OnDestroy` interface:

```
@Component({
  selector: 'todos',
  template: `
    <div *ngFor="let todo of todos">
      <todo [item]="todo" (remove)="remove($event)">
    </div>
  `
})
export class TodosComponent {
  todos;

  constructor() {
    this.todos = [{
      id : 1,
      name : 'clean'
    }, {
      id : 2,
      name : 'code'
    }]
  }

  remove(todo) {
    this.todos = this.todos.filter( t => t.id !== todo.id );
  }
}

@Component({
  selector: 'todo',
  template: `
    <div *ngIf="item">{{item.name}} <button
(click)="remove.emit(item)">Remove</button></div>
  `
})
export class TodoComponent implements OnDestroy {
  @Output() remove = new EventEmitter<any>();
  @Input() item;
  ngOnDestroy() { console.log('todo item removed from DOM'); }
}
```

Our preceding snippet tries to highlight when an instance of `TodoComponent` gets removed from the DOM tree. The `TodosComponent` renders a list of `TodoComponents` and when the `remove()` method is invoked, the targeted `TodoComponent` is removed, thereby triggering the `ngOnDestroy()` method on the `TodoComponent`.

OK, great, so we have a way to capture that exact moment in time when our component is being disposed... so what?

This is where we do a clean up of resources; by clean up, we mean:

- Timeout, interval should be unsubscribed to here
- Observable streams should be unsubscribed to
- Other clean up

Essentially, anything that causes a footprint should be cleaned up here.

OnChanges - a change has occurred

This hook is used in the following way:

```
export class ExampleComponent implements OnChanges {
  ngOnChanges(changes: SimpleChanges) { }
}
```

Note how our method takes an input parameter `changes`. This is an object with all properties that changed as keys on the `changes` object. Each key points to an object with the previous value and the current value, like so:

```
{
  'prop' : { currentValue : 11, previousValue : 10 }
  // below is the remaining changed properties
}
```

The preceding code assumes we have a class with a `prop` field, like so:

```
export class ExampleComponent {
  prop: string;
}
```

So, what causes things to change? Well, it's a change in the binding, that is, we have the `@Input` property set up, like so:

```
export class TodoComponent implements OnChanges {
  @Input() item;
  ngOnChanges(changes: SimpleChanges) {
    for (let change in changes) {
      console.log(`
        '${change}' changed from
        '${changes[change].previousValue}' to
        '${changes[change].currentValue}'
      `)
```

```
        )
      }
    }
  }
```

A little heads up worth noting here is that what we are tracking are reference changes, not property changes on an object. If, for example, we have the following code:

```
<todo [item]="todoItem">
```

And the name property on the `todoItem` changed so that `todoItem.name` is `code` instead of `coding`, this would not lead to a change being reported. However, if the whole item is replaced, as in the following code:

```
this.todoItem = { ...this.todoItem, { name : 'coding' });
```

Then this would lead to a change event being emitted as the `todoItem` now points to a completely new reference. I hope this clears it up a bit.

The timer feature

Our first feature is the one belonging to the timer functionality, which happens to be the simpler one as well. It comprises of a unique component with the countdown timer we built in the previous chapters:

```
import { Component } from '@angular/core';
import { SettingsService } from "../core/settings.service";

@Component({
  selector: 'timer-widget',
  template: `
  <div class="text-center">
    <h1> {{ minutes }}:{{ seconds | number }}</h1>
    <p>
      <button (click)="togglePause()" class="btn btn-danger">
      {{ buttonLabelKey | i18nSelect: buttonLabelsMap }}
      </button>
    </p>
  </div>
  `
})
export class TimerWidgetComponent {
  minutes: number;
  seconds: number;
  isPaused: boolean;
  buttonLabelKey: string;
```

```
  buttonLabelsMap: any;

  constructor(private settingsService: SettingsService) {
    this.buttonLabelsMap = this.settingsService.labelsMap.timer;
  }

  ngOnInit() {
    this.reset();
    setInterval(() => this.tick(), 1000);
  }

  reset() {
    this.isPaused = true;
    this.minutes = this.settingsService.timerMinutes - 1;
    this.seconds = 59;
    this.buttonLabelKey = 'start';
  }

  private tick(): void {
    if (!this.isPaused) {
      this.buttonLabelKey = 'pause';
      if (--this.seconds < 0) {
        this.seconds = 59;
        if (--this.minutes < 0) {
          this.reset();
        }
      }
    }
  }

  togglePause(): void {
    this.isPaused = !this.isPaused;
    if (this.minutes < this.settingsService.timerMinutes ||
      this.seconds < 59
    ) {
      this.buttonLabelKey = this.isPaused ? 'resume' : 'pause';
    }
  }
}
```

As you can see, the implementation is pretty much the same to what we saw already back in Chapter 1, *Creating Our Very First Component in Angular,* with the exception of initializing the component at the init lifecycle stage through the OnInit interface hook. We leverage the l18nSelect pipe to better handle the different labels required for each state of the timer, consuming the label information from the SettingsService, which is injected in the constructor. Later on in this chapter, we will see where to register that provider. The duration in minutes is also consumed from the service, once the latter is bound to a class field.

The component is exported publicly through the TimerModule file timer.module.ts by us adding it to the declarations keyword as well as the exported keyword, the latter to enable outside access:

```
import { NgModule } from '@angular/core';

@NgModule({
  // tell other constructs in this module about it
  declarations: [TimerWidgetComponent],
  // usable outside of this module
  exports: [TimerWidgetComponent]
})
export class TimerModule() {}
```

And we also need to remember to import our newly created module to the root module in app.module.ts:

```
import { NgModule } from '@angular/core';
import { TimerModule } from './timer/timer.module';

@NgModule({
  imports: [TimerModule]
  // the rest is omitted for brevity
})
```

At this point, we have created a nice structure before we create more constructs for the timer feature.

The tasks feature

The tasks feature encompasses some more logic since it entails two components and a directive. Let's begin by creating the core unit required by `TaskTooltipDirective`:

```
import { Task } from './task.model';
import { Input, Directive, HostListener } from '@angular/core';

@Directive({
  selector: '[task]'
})
export class TaskTooltipDirective {
  private defaultTooltipText: string;
  @Input() task: Task;
  @Input() taskTooltip: any;

  @HostListener('mouseover')
  onMouseOver() {
    if (!this.defaultTooltipText && this.taskTooltip) {
      this.defaultTooltipText = this.taskTooltip.innerText;
    }
    this.taskTooltip.innerText = this.defaultTooltipText;
  }
}
```

The directive keeps all the original functionality in place and just imports the Angular core types and task-typing it requires. Let's look at the `TaskIconsComponent` now:

```
import { Component, Input, OnInit } from '@angular/core';
import { Task } from './task.model';

@Component({
  selector: 'task-icons',
  template: `
  <img *ngFor="let icon of icons"
       src="/app/shared/assets/img/pomodoro.png"
       width="{{size}}">`
})
export class TaskIconsComponent implements OnInit {
  @Input() task: Task;
  @Input() size: number;
  icons: Object[] = [];
  ngOnInit() {
    this.icons.length = this.task.noRequired;
    this.icons.fill({ name : this.task.name });
  }
}
```

So far so good. Now, let's jump to `TasksComponent`. This will consist of:

- The component file `tasks.component.ts`, where the logic is described in TypeScript
- The CSS file `tasks.component.css`, where the styles are defined
- The template file `tasks.component.html`, where the markup is defined

Starting with the CSS file, it will look like this:

```
// app/task/tasks.component.css

h3, p {
  text-align: center;
}

.table {
  margin: auto;
  max-width: 860px;
}
```

Continuing on with the HTML markup:

```
// app/task/tasks.component.html

<div class="container text-center">
  <h3>
  One point = 25 min, {{ queued | i18nPlural: queueHeaderMapping }}
  for today
  <span class="small" *ngIf="queued > 0">
  (Estimated time : {{ queued * timerMinutes | formattedTime }})
  </span>
  </h3>
  <p>
    <span *ngFor="let queuedTask of tasks | queuedOnly: true">
      <task-icons
        [task]="queuedTask"
        [taskTooltip]="tooltip"
        size="50">
      </task-icons>
    </span>
  </p>
  <p #tooltip [hidden]="queued === 0">
  Mouseover for details
  </p>
  <h4>Tasks backlog</h4>
  <table class="table">
    <thead>
```

```
      <tr>
        <th>Task ID</th>
        <th>Task name</th>
        <th>Deliver by</th>
        <th>Points required</th>
        <th>Actions</th>
      </tr>
  </thead>
  <tbody>
    <tr *ngFor="let task of tasks; let i = index">
      <th scope="row">{{ (i+1) }}
        <span *ngIf="task.queued" class="label label-info">
        Queued</span>
      </th>
      <td>{{ task.name | slice:0:35 }}
        <span [hidden]="task.name.length < 35">...</span>
      </td>
      <td>{{ task.deadline | date: 'fullDate' }}
        <span *ngIf="task.deadline < today" class="label label-danger">
        Due</span>
      </td>
      <td class="text-center">{{ task.noRequired }}</td>
      <td>
        <button
          type="button"
          class="btn btn-default btn-xs"
          [ngSwitch]="task.queued"
          (click)="toggleTask(task)">
          <ng-template [ngSwitchCase]="false">
            <i class="glyphicon glyphicon-plus-sign"></i>
            Add
          </ng-template>
          <ng-template [ngSwitchCase]="true">
            <i class="glyphicon glyphicon-minus-sign"></i>
            Remove
          </ng-template>
          <ng-template ngSwitchDefault>
            <i class="glyphicon glyphicon-plus-sign"></i>
            Add
          </ng-template>
        </button>
      </td>
    </tr>
  </tbody>
</table>
</div>
```

Please take a moment to check out the naming convention applied to the external component files, whose filename matches the component's own to identify which file belongs to what in flat structures inside a context folder. Also, please note how we removed the main bitmap from the template and replaced the hardcoded time durations with a variable named `timerMinutes` in the binding expression that computes the time estimation to accomplish all queued tasks. We will see how that variable is populated in the following component class:

```
// app/task/tasks.component.ts

import { Component, OnInit } from '@angular/core';
import { TaskService } from './task.service';
import { Task } from "./task.model";
import { SettingsService } from "../core/settings.service";

@Component({
  selector: 'tasks',
  styleUrls: ['tasks.component.css'],
  templateUrl: 'tasks.component.html'
})
export class TasksComponent implements OnInit {
  today: Date;
  tasks: Task[];
  queued: number;
  queueHeaderMapping: any;
  timerMinutes: number;
  constructor(
    private taskService: TaskService,
    private settingsService: SettingsService) {
    this.tasks = this.taskService.taskStore;
    this.today = new Date();
    this.queueHeaderMapping = this.settingsService.pluralsMap.tasks;
    this.timerMinutes = this.settingsService.timerMinutes;
  }

  ngOnInit(): void {
      this.updateQueued();
    }

  toggleTask(task: Task): void {
    task.queued = !task.queued;
    this.updateQueued();
  }

  private updateQueued(): void {
    this.queued = this.tasks
    .filter((Task: Task) => Task.queued)
```

```
      .reduce((no: number, queuedTask: Task) => {
        return no + queuedTask.noRequired;
      }, 0);
  }
}
```

Several aspects of the `TasksComponent` implementation are worth highlighting. Firstly, we can inject the `TaskService` and `SettingsService` in the component, leveraging Angular's DI system. The dependencies are injected with accessors right from the constructor, becoming private class members on the spot. The tasks dataset and the time duration are then populated from the bound services.

Let's now add all these constructs to the `TaskModule`, that is, the file `task.module.ts` and export everything that is either a directive or a component. It is worth noting, however, that we do this because we think all these constructs may need to be referred to somewhere else in the app. I urge you to strongly consider what to put in the `exports` keyword and what not to put there. Your default stance should be to put as little as possible for exporting:

```
import { NgModule } from '@angular/core';
@NgModule({
  declarations: [TasksComponent, TaskIconsComponent,
TasksTooltipDirective],
  exports: [TasksComponent],
  providers: [TaskService]
  // the rest omitted for brevity
})
```

We have now added the constructs to the `declarations` keyword so that the module is aware of them and also the `exports` keyword so that other modules importing our `TaskModule` are able to use them. The next task is to set up our `AppComponent`, or root component, as it is also known as.

Defining the top root component

With all our feature contexts ready, the time has come to define the top root component, which will kickstart the whole application as a cluster of components laid out in a tree hierarchy. The root component usually has a minimum implementation. The main child components will eventually evolve into branches of child components.

The following is an example of the template of the root component. This is the main visual component that your app is going to live in. Here, it makes sense to define application headers, menus, or viewports for routing:

```
//app/app.component.ts

import { Component } from '@angular/core';

@Component({
  selector: 'app',
  template: `
  <nav class="navbar navbar-default navbar-static-top">
    <div class="container">
      <div class="navbar-header">
        <strong class="navbar-brand">My App</strong>
      </div>
    </div>
  </nav>
  <tasks></tasks>
  `
})
export class AppComponent {}
```

It has been mentioned before, but it is worth repeating. Any constructs that we use in the `app.component.ts` file that do not belong to the `AppModule` need to be imported. Technically, it is the module these constructs belong to that is being imported. You also need to ensure that the constructs are properly exposed by being mentioned in said modules `exports` keyword. With the preceding root component, we can see that we use two different components in the template for `app.component.ts`, the `<timer-widget>` and `<pomodoro-tasks>`. These belong to different modules with the first component belonging to the `TimerModule` and the second belonging to the `TaskModule`. This means that the `AppModule` needs to import both of these modules for the preceding to compile. The `app.module.ts` should, therefore, look like this:

```
import { NgModule } from '@angular/core';
import { TimerModule } from './timer/timer.module';
import { TasksModule } from './tasks/tasks.module';

@NgModule({
  imports: [ TimerModule, TasksModule ]
  // omitted for brevity
})
export class AppModule {}
```

Summary

This chapter has definitely set the foundation for all the great applications that you will be building on top of Angular from now on. The Angular dependency management implementation is in fact one of the gems of this framework and a time saver. Application architectures based on component trees are not rocket science anymore, and we have followed this pattern to some extent while building web software in other frameworks such as AngularJS and React.

This chapter concludes our trip through the core of Angular and its application architecture, setting up the standards that we will follow from now on while building applications on top of this new and exciting framework.

In the following chapters, we will focus on very specific tools and modules that we can use to solve everyday problems when crafting our web projects. We will see how to develop better HTTP networking clients with Angular.

Asynchronous Data Services with Angular

7

Connecting to data services and APIs and handling asynchronous information is a common task in our everyday lives as developers. In this sense, Angular provides an unparalleled tool set to help its enthusiastic developers when it comes to consuming, digesting, and transforming all kinds of data fetched from data services.

There are so many possibilities that it would require an entire book to describe all that you can do to connect to APIs or to consume information from the filesystem asynchronously through HTTP. In this book, we will only scratch the surface, but the insights covered in this chapter about the HTTP API and its companion classes and tools will give you all that you need to connect your applications to HTTP services in no time, leaving all that you can do with them up to your creativity.

In this chapter, we will:

- Look at the different strategies for handling asynchronous data
- Introduce Observables and Observers
- Discuss functional reactive programming and RxJS
- Review the HTTP class and its API and learn some nice service patterns
- Learn about Firebase and how to connect it to your Angular app
- See all of the preceding points in action through actual code examples

Strategies for handling asynchronous information

Consuming information from an API is a common operation in our daily practice. We consume information over HTTP all the time—when authenticating users by sending out credentials to an authentication service, or when fetching the latest tweets in our favorite Twitter widget. Modern mobile devices have introduced an unparalleled way of consuming remote services by deferring requests and response consumption until mobile connectivity is available. Responsivity and availability have become a big deal. Although modern internet connections are ultra-fast, there is always a response time involved when serving such information that forces us to put in place mechanisms to handle states in our applications in a transparent way for the end user.

This is not specific to scenarios where we need to consume information from an external resource.

Asynchronous response - from callbacks to promises

Sometimes, we might need to build functionalities that depend on time as a parameter of something, and we need to introduce code patterns that handle this deferred change in the application state.

For all these scenarios, we have always used code patterns, such as the callback pattern, where the function that triggers the asynchronous action expects another function in its signature, which will emit a sort of notification as soon as the asynchronous operation is completed, as follows:

```
function notifyCompletion() {
  console.log('Our asynchronous operation has been completed');
}

function asynchronousOperation(callback) {
  setTimeout(() => {
    callback();
  }, 5000);
}

asynchronousOperation(notifyCompletion);
```

The problem with this pattern is that code can become quite confusing and cumbersome as the application grows and more and more nested callbacks are introduced. In order to avoid this scenario, `Promises` introduced a new way of envisioning asynchronous data management by conforming to a neater and more solid interface, in which different asynchronous operations can be chained at the same level and even be split and returned from other functions. The following code introduces how to construct a `Promise`:

```
function getData() {
  return new Promise((resolve, reject) => {
    setTimeout(() => {
      resolve(42);
    }, 3000);
  })
}

getData().then((data) => console.log('Data',data)) // 42
```

The preceding code example is perhaps a bit more verbose, but it definitely produces a more expressive and elegant interface for our function. As for chaining data, we need to understand what problem we are solving. We are solving something called callback hell, looking like this:

```
getData(function(data){
  getMoreData(data, function(moreData){
    getEvenMoreData(moreData, function(evenMoreData) {
      // done here
    });
  });
});
```

As can be seen in the preceding code, we have a situation where we are dependent on the previous async call and the data it brings back before we are able to do the next async call. This leads to us having to execute a method inside of a callback inside of a callback, and so on and so forth. You get the idea—the code quickly ends up looking horrible, also known as *callback hell*. Continuing with the subject of chaining async calls, chaining is the answer to *callback hell* and `Promises` allows us to chain them, like so:

```
getData()
  .then(getMoreData)
  .then(getEvenMoreData);

function getData() {
  return new Promise(resolve) => resolve('data');
}

function getMoreData(data) {
```

```
    return new Promise((resolve, reject) => resolve('more data'));
  }

  function getEvenMoreData(data) {
    return new Promise((resolve, reject) => resolve('even more data'));
  }
```

The chaining of the `.then()` method calls in the preceding code shows how we can clearly line up one async call after another, and that the previous async call has input its result in the upcoming `async` method.

So, `Promises` take over the coding arena by storm and no developer out there seems to question the great value they bring to the game. So, why do we need another paradigm? Well, because sometimes we might need to produce a response output that follows a more complex digest process as it is being returned, or even cancel the whole process. This cannot be done with `Promises`, because they are triggered as soon as they're being instantiated. In other words, `Promises` are not lazy. On the other hand, the possibility of tearing down an asynchronous operation after it has been fired but not completed yet can become quite handy in certain scenarios. `Promises` only allow us to resolve or reject an asynchronous operation, but sometimes we might want to abort everything before getting to that point. On top of that, `Promises` behave as one-time operations. Once they are resolved, we cannot expect to receive any further information or state change notification unless we run everything again from scratch. Moreover, we sometimes need a more proactive implementation of async data handling. This is where Observables come into the game. To summarize the limitations of promises:

- They cannot be cancelled
- They are immediately executed
- They are one-time operations only; there is no easy way to retry them
- They respond with only one value

Observables in a nutshell

An Observable is basically an async event emitter that informs another element, called the Observer, that the state has changed. In order to do so, the Observable implements all of the machinery that it needs to produce and emit such async events, and it can be fired and canceled at any time regardless of whether it has emitted the expected data events already or not.

This pattern allows concurrent operations and more advanced logic since the Observers that subscribe to the Observable async events will react to reflect the state change of the Observable they subscribe to.

These subscribers, which are the Observers we mentioned earlier, will keep listening to whatever happens in the Observable until the Observable is disposed, if that happens eventually. In the meantime, information will be updated throughout the application with no intention whatsoever of triggering routines.

We can probably see all this with more transparency in an actual example. Let's refactor the example we covered when assessing promise-based async operations and replace the `setTimeout` command with `setInterval`:

```
function notifyCompletion() {
  console.log('Our asynchronous operation has been completed');
}

function asynchronousOperation() {
  let promise = new Promise((resolve, reject) => {
    setInterval(resolve, 2000);
  });

  return promise;
}

asynchronousOperation().then(notifyCompletion);
```

Copy and paste the preceding snippet in your browser's console window and see what happens. The text `Our asynchronous operation has been completed` will show up at the dev tools' console only once after 2 seconds and will never be rendered again. The promise resolved itself and the entire async event was terminated at that very moment.

Now, point your browser to an online JavaScript code playground such as JSBIN (`https://jsbin.com/`), and create a new code snippet enabling just the JavaScript and the Console tabs. Then, make sure you add the RxJS library from the **Add library** option dropdown (we will need this library to create Observables, but don't panic; we will cover this later in this chapter) and insert the following code snippet:

```
let observable$ = Rx.Observable.create(observer => {
  setInterval(() => {
    observer.next('My async operation');
  }, 2000);
});

observable$.subscribe(response => console.log(response));
```

Run it and expect a message to appear on the right pane. 2 seconds later, we will see the same message showing up, and then again and again. In this simple example, we created an `observable` and then subscribed to its changes, throwing to the console whatever it emitted (a simple message, in this example) as a sort of push notification.

The Observable returns a stream of events and our subscribers receive prompt notification of those streamed events, so they can act accordingly. This is what the magic of Observables relies on—Observables do not perform an async operation and die (although we can configure them to do so), but start a stream of continuous events we can subscribe our subscribers to.

If we comment out the last line, nothing will happen. The console pane will remain silent and all the magic will begin only when we subscribe our source object.

That's not all, however. This stream can be the subject of many operations before they hit the Observers subscribed to them. Just as we can grab a collection object, such as an array, and apply functional methods over it such as `map()` or `filter()` in order to transform and play around with the array items, we can do the same with the stream of events that are emitted by our Observables. This is what is known as reactive functional programming, and Angular makes the most of this paradigm to handle asynchronous information.

Reactive functional programming in Angular

The Observable pattern stands at the core of what we know as reactive functional programming. Basically, the most basic implementation of a reactive functional script encompasses several concepts that we need to become familiar with:

- An Observable
- An Observer
- A timeline
- A stream of events featuring the same behavior as an object's collection
- A set of composable operators, also known as Reactive Extensions

Sounds daunting? It's not. Believe us when we tell you that all of the code you have gone through so far is much more complex than this. The big challenge here is to change your mindset and learn to think in a reactive fashion, and that is the main goal of this section.

To put it simply, we can just say that reactive programming entails applying asynchronous subscriptions and transformations to Observable streams of events. We can imagine your poker face right now, so let's put together a more descriptive example.

Think about an interaction device such as a keyboard. A keyboard has keys that the user presses. Each one of those key strokes triggers a key press event. That key press event features a wide range of metadata, including—but not limited to—the numeric code of the specific key the user pressed at a given moment. As the user continues hitting keys, more **keyUp** events are triggered and piped through an imaginary timeline. The timeline of keyUp events should look like the following diagram:

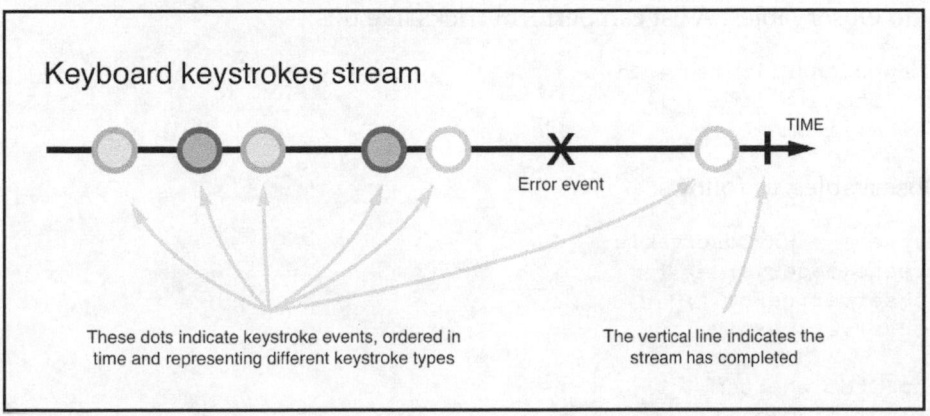

What you can see from the preceding timeline of keyUps is that it is a continuous stream of data where the keyUp event can happen at any time; after all, the user decides when to press those keys. Remember the Observable code we wrote, containing the `setTimeout`? That code was able to tell a concept Observer that every time 2 seconds passed, another value should be emitted. What's the difference between that code and our keyUps? Nothing. Well, we know how often a timer interval is triggered, and with keyUps, we don't really know because it is not in our hands. But that is really the only difference, which means keyUps can be thought of as an Observable as well:

```
let key = document.getElementId('.search');
/*
we assume there exist a button in the DOM like this
<input class="search" placeholder="searchfor"></input>
*/

let stream = Rx.Observable.fromEvent(key, 'keyUp');
stream.subscribe((data) => console.log('key up happened', data))
```

So, what I am really telling you is that timeout as well as keyUps can be thought as one and the same concept, the Observable. That makes it easier to understand all things async. There is, however, another observation we need to make, namely that whatever async concept occurs, it occurs in a list-like way.

Even though the time might differ, it's still a series of events, like a list. A list usually has a bunch of methods on it to project, filter, or in other ways manipulate its element, and guess what, so do Observables. A list can perform tricks like this:

```
let mappedAndFiltered = list
  .map(item => item + 1)
  .filter(item > 2);
```

So can Observables, as follows:

```
let stream = Rx.Observable
  .create(observer => {
    observer.next(1);
    observer.next(2);
  })
  .map(item => item + 1)
  .filter(item > 2);
```

The difference is just in the naming at this point. For a list, `.map()` and `.filter()` are called methods. For an Observable, the same methods are called Reactive Extensions or operators. Imagine at this point that `keyUps` and timeouts can be described as Observables and that we have operators to manipulate data. Now, take the bigger leap of realizing that anything async, even HTTP calls, can be thought of as Observables. This means that we can suddenly mix and match anything async. This enables something called **rich composition**. Whatever the async concept is, it and its data can be thought of as a stream, and you are a wizard that can bend it to your will. Feel empowered—you can now turn your application into a reactive architecture.

The RxJS library

As mentioned previously, Angular comes with a peer dependency on RxJS, the JavaScript flavor of the ReactiveX library that allows us to create Observables and Observable sequences out of a large variety of scenarios, such as:

- Interaction events
- Promises
- Callback functions
- Events

In this sense, reactive programming does not aim to replace asynchronous patterns such as promises or callbacks. All the way around, it can leverage them as well to create Observable sequences.

RxJS comes with built-in support for a wide range of composable operators to transform, filter, and combine the resulting event streams. Its API provides convenient methods to subscribe Observers to these streams so that our scripts and components can respond accordingly to state changes or interaction input. While its API is so massive that covering it in detail is out of the scope of this book, we will highlight some bits of its most basic implementation in order for you to better understand how HTTP connections are handled by Angular.

Before jumping into the HTTP API provided by Angular, let's create a simple example of an Observable event stream that we can transform with Reactive Extensions and subscribe observers to. To do so, let's use the scenario described in the previous section.

We envisioned how a user interacting with our application through the keyboard can't turn it into a timeline of keystrokes and, therefore, an event stream. Go back to JSBIN, delete the contents of the JavaScript pane, and then write down the following snippet:

```
let keyboardStream$ = Rx.Observable
  .fromEvent(document, 'keyup')
  .map(x => x.which);
```

The preceding code is pretty self-descriptive. We leverage the `Rx.Observable` class and its `fromEvent` method to create an event emitter that streams the `keyup` events that take place in the scope of the document object. Each of the event objects emitted is a complex object. So, we simplify the streamed objects by mapping the event stream onto a new stream that contains only the key codes pertaining to each keystroke. The map method is a Reactive Extension that features the same behavior as the JavaScript map functional method. This is why we usually refer to this code style as reactive functional programming.

All right, so now we have an event stream of numeric keystrokes, but we are only interested in observing those events that inform us of hits on the cursor keys. We can build a new stream out of an existing stream by applying more Reactive Extensions. So, let's do it with `keyboardStream` by filtering such a stream and returning only those events that are related to cursor keys. We will also map those events to their text correspondence for the sake of clarity. Append the following chunk of code, following the previous snippet:

```
let cursorMovesStream$ = keyboardStream
  .filter(x => {
    return x > 36 && x < 41;
  })
  .map(x => {
    let direction;
    switch(x) {
      case 37:
        direction = 'left';
        break;
      case 38:
        direction = 'up';
        break;
      case 39:
        direction = 'right';
        break;
      default:
        direction = 'down';
    }
    return direction;
  });
```

We could have done all of this in a single action by chaining the filter and map methods to the `keyboardStream` Observable and then subscribing to its output, but it's generally a good idea to separate concerns. By shaping our code in this way, we have a generic keyboard events stream that we can reuse later on for something completely different. So, our application can scale up while keeping the code footprint to a minimum.

Now that we have mentioned subscribers, let's subscribe to our cursor moves stream and print the `move` commands to the console. We type the following statement at the end of our script, then clear the console pane, and click on the **Output** tab so that we can have surface to input code in so we can try different code statements out:

```
cursorMovesStream$.subscribe(e => console.log(e));
```

Click anywhere on the **Output** pane to put the focus on it and start typing random keyboard keys and cursor keys.

You are probably wondering how we can apply this pattern to an asynchronous scenario such as consuming information from an HTTP service. Basically, you have so far become used to submitting async requests to AJAX services and then delegating the response handling a callback function or just piping it through a promise. Now, we will handle the call by returning an Observable. This Observable will emit the server response as an event in the context of a stream, which will be funneled through the Reactive Extensions to better digest the response.

Introducing the HTTP API

Now, before we dive into describing what the Angular framework has given us in terms of `HttpClient` service implementation, let's talk about how we can wrap an `XmlHttpRequest` into an Observable. To do that, we first need to realize that there is a contract that we need to fulfill to consider it a successful wrapping. The contract is made up of the following:

- Emit any arrived data using `observer.next(data)`
- When we don't expect any more data we should call `observer.complete()`
- Emit any errors using `observer.error(error)`

That's it; its pretty simple really. Let's see what a `XmlHttpRequest` call looks like:

```
const request = new XMLHttpRequest();

request.onreadystatechange = () => {
  if(this.readyState === 4 and this.state === 200) {
    // request.responseText
  } else {
  // error occurred here
  }
}

request.open("GET", url);
request.send();
```

Ok, so we have a typical callback pattern where the `onreadystatechange` property points to a method that is being invoked once the data arrives. That's all we need to know to wrap the following code, so let's do that:

```
let stream$ = Rx.Observable.create(observer => {
  let request = new XMLHttpRequest();
  request.onreadystatechange = () => {
    if(this.readyState === 4 && this.state === 200) {
      observer.next( request.responseText )
      observer.complete();
    } else {
      observer.error( request.responseText )
    }
  }
})
```

That's it, the wrapping is complete; you have now built your own HTTP service. Of course, this isn't much, there are a lot of cases we are not handling, POST, PUT, DELETE, caching, and so on. It was, however, important for you to realize all the heavy lifting the HTTP service in Angular was doing for you. Another important lesson here was how easy it is to take any kind of async API and turn that into an Observable that fits in nicely with the rest of our async concepts. So, let's continue with Angular's implementation of a HTTP service. We will use the `HttpClient` service from this point.

The `HttpClient` class provides a powerful API that abstracts all the operations required to handle asynchronous connections through a variety of HTTP methods, handling the responses in an easy and comfortable way. Its implementation was considered with a lot of care to ensure that programmers feel at ease while developing solutions that take advantage of this class to connect to an API or a data resource.

In a nutshell, instances of the `HttpClient` class (which has been implemented as an `Injectable` resource and can therefore be used in our class constructors just by injecting it as a dependency provider) expose a connection method named `request()` to perform any type of HTTP connection. The Angular team has created some syntax shortcuts for the most common request operations, such as GET, POST, PUT, and every existing HTTP verb. So, creating an async HTTP request is as easy as this:

```
let request = new HttpRequest('GET', 'jedis.json');
let myRequestStream:Observable<any> = http.request(request);
```

Also, all of this can be simplified into a single line of code:

```
let myRequestStream: Observable<any> = http.get('jedis.json');
```

As we can see, the `HttpClient` class connection methods operate by returning an Observable stream. This allows us to subscribe Observers to the stream, which will process the information accordingly once it is returned, as many times as required:

```
let myRequestStream = http
  .get<Jedi[]>('jedis.json')
  .subscribe(data => console.log(data));
```

In the preceding example, we give the `get()` method a templated type that does the type conversion for us. Let's highlight this bit more:

```
.get<Jedi[]>('jedis.json')
```

This very fact saves us from having to deal with a response object directly and performing a map operation to turn our JSON into a list of Jedi objects. All we have to remember is the URL to our resource and specify a type and what you subscribe to is instantly usable for the subscribe of our service.

By doing this, we can respawn the HTTP request as many times as we need, and the rest of our machinery will react accordingly. We can even merge the event stream represented by the HTTP call with other related calls, and compose more complex Observable streams and data threads. The possibilities are endless.

Working with headers

We mentioned the `HttpRequest` classes while introducing the `HttpClient` class. On a regular basis, you will not need to make use of low-level classes, mostly because of the shortcut methods provided by the `HttpClient` class abstract and the need to declare the HTTP verb in use (GET, POST, and so on) and the URL you want to consume. With that being said, you will sometimes want to introduce special HTTP headers in your requests or append query string parameters automatically to each request, for argument's sake. That is why these classes can become quite handy in certain scenarios. Think of a use case where you want to add an authentication token to each request in order to prevent unauthorized users from reading data from one of your API endpoints.

In the following example, we read an authentication token and append it as a header to our request to a data service. Contrary to our example, we will inject the `options` hash object straight into the `HttpRequest` constructor, skipping the step of creating an object instance. Angular provides a wrapper class for defining custom headers as well, and we will take advantage of it in this scenario. Let's suppose we do have an API that expects all requests to include a custom header named `Authorization`, attaching the `authToken` that is received when logging into the system, which is then persisted in the browser's local storage layer, for instance:

```
const authToken = window.localStorage.getItem('auth_token');

let headers = new HttpHeaders();
headers.append('Authorization', `Token ${authToken}`);
let request = new HttpRequest('products.json', { headers: headers });

let authRequest = http.request(request);
```

Again, we would like to note that apart from this scenario, you will seldom need to create custom request configurations, unless you want to delegate the creation of request configurations in a factory class or method and reuse the same `Http` wrapper all the time. Angular gives you all the flexibility to go as far as you wish when abstracting your applications.

Handling errors when performing HTTP requests

Handling errors raised in our requests by inspecting the information returned in the `Response` object is actually quite simple. We just need to inspect the value of its `Boolean` property, which will return `false` if the HTTP status of the response falls somewhere outside of the 2xx range, clearly indicating that our request could not be accomplished successfully. We can double-check that by inspecting the `status` property to understand the error code or the `type` property, which can assume the following values: `basic`, `cors`, `default`, `error`, or `opaque`. Inspecting the response headers and the `statusText` property of the `HttpResponse` object will provide insightful information about the origin of the error.

All in all, we are not meant to inspect those properties on every response message we get. Angular provides an Observable operator to catch errors, injecting in its signature the `HttpResponse` object we require, to inspect the previous properties:

```
http.get('/api/bio')
.subscribe(bio => this.bio = bio)
.catch(error: Response => Observable.of(error));
```

Worth noting is that we capture our error by using the `catch()` operator and return a new operator by calling `Observable.of(error)` and letting our error serve as input for the new Observable we create. This is a week for us to not crash the stream, but let it live on. Of course, in a more real scenario, we would probably not just create a new Observable, but maybe log the error and return something completely different potentially or add some retry logic. The point is that with the `catch()` operator, we have a way of capturing the error; how you handle it depends on your scenario.

In a normal scenario, you would want to inspect more data than the error properties, aside from logging that information in a more solid exception tracking system.

Injecting the HttpClient service

The `HttpClient` service can be injected into our own components and custom classes by leveraging Angular's unique dependency injection system. So, if we ever need to implement HTTP calls, we need to import the `HttpClientModule` and import the `HttpClient` service:

```
// app/biography/biography.module.ts
import { HttpClientModule } from '@angular/common/http';

@NgModule({
  imports: [ HttpClientModule ]
})
export class BiographyModule {}

// app/biography/biography.component.ts

import { Component } from '@angular/core';
import { HttpClient } from '@angular/http';

@Component({
  selector: 'bio',
  template: '<div>{{bio}}</div>'
})
export class BiographyComponent {
```

```
  bio: string;

  constructor(private http: HttpClient) {
    const options = {};
    this.http.get('/api/bio', { ...options, responseType: 'text' })
    .catch(err => Observable.of(err))
    .subscribe(x => this.bio= bio)
  }
}
```

In the code provided, we just follow up with the `bio` example that we pointed out in the previous section. Note how we are importing the `HttpClient` type and injecting it as a dependency in the `Biography` constructor.

Usually, we need to perform multiple HTTP calls in different parts of our application, so it's usually recommended to create a `DataService` and a `DataModule` that wraps the `HttpClientModule` and the `HttpClient` service.

The following is an example of creating such a `DataService`:

```
import {Http} from '@angular/http';
import {Injectable} from '@angular/core';

@Injectable()
export class DataService {
  constructor(private http:HttpClient) {}

  get(url, options?) {}
  post(url, payload, options?) {}
  put(url, payload, options?) {}
  delete(url) {}
}
```

The corresponding `DataModule` would look like the following:

```
import {DataService} from './data.service';
import {HttpModule} from '@angular/http';

@NgModule({
  imports: [HttpClientModule],
  providers: [DataService]
})
```

If you want to add your own caching or authorization logic for calling the backend, this is the place to do it. Another way is to use `HttpInterceptors`, an example of using `HttpInterceptors` will be provided in an upcoming section in this chapter.

Of course, any module that wanted to use this `DataModule` would need to import it, like so:

```
@NgModule({
  imports: [DataModule],
  declarations: [FeatureComponent]
})
export class FeatureModule {}
```

And any construct in our `FeatureModule` can now inject the `DataService`, like so:

```
import { Component } from '@angular/core';

@Component({})
export class FeatureComponent {
  constructor(private service: DataService) { }
}
```

A real case study – serving Observable data through HTTP

In the previous chapter, we refactored our entire app into models, services, pipes, directives, and component files. One of those services was the `TaskService` class, which is the bread and butter of our app since it delivers the data that we need to build our task list and other related components.

In our example, the `TaskService` class was contained within the information we wanted to deliver. In a real-world scenario, you need to fetch that information from a server API or backend service. Let's update our example to emulate this scenario. First, we will remove the task information from the `TaskService` class and wrap it into an actual JSON file. Let's create a new JSON file inside the shared folder and populate it with the task information that we had hardcoded in the original `TaskService.ts` file, now in JSON format, though:

```
[{
  "name": "Code an HTML Table",
  "deadline": "Jun 23 2015",
  "pomodorosRequired": 1

}, {
  "name": "Sketch a wireframe for the new homepage",
  "deadline": "Jun 24 2016",
  "pomodorosRequired": 2

}, {
```

```
  "name": "Style table with Bootstrap styles",
  "deadline": "Jun 25 2016",
  "pomodorosRequired": 1

}, {
  "name": "Reinforce SEO with custom sitemap.xml",
  "deadline": "Jun 26 2016",
  "pomodorosRequired": 3
}]
```

With the data properly wrapped in its own file, we can consume it as if it were an actual backend service from our `TaskService` client class. However, we will need to conduct relevant changes in our main.ts file for that. The reason is that despite installing the RxJS bundle when installing all the Angular peer dependencies, the reactive functional operators, such as `map()`, do not become available straight away. We could import all of them at once by inserting the following line of code in some step at the beginning of our application initialisation flow, such as the bootstrapping stage in `main.ts`:

```
import 'rxjs/Rx';
```

However, that would import all the reactive functional operators, which will not be used at all and will consume an unnecessarily huge amount of bandwidth and resources. Instead, the convention is to import only what is needed, so append the following import line at the top of the `main.ts` file:

```
import 'rxjs/add/operator/map';
import { bootstrap } from '@angular/platform-browser-dynamic';
import AppModule from './app.module';

bootstrapModule(AppModule);
```

When a reactive operator is imported this way, it gets automatically added to the Observable prototype, being then available for use throughout the entire application. It should be said that the concept of lettable operators was just introduced per RxJS 5.5. At the time of this book's writing we are just in the shift of patching the Operator prototype, as described above and moving into the lettable operator space. For the interested reader, please have a look at this article that describes in detail what this will mean for your code. The changes are not that big, but there is still change: https://blog.angularindepth.com/ rxjs-understanding-lettable-operators-fe74dda186d3

Leveraging HTTP – refactoring our TaskService to use HTTP service

With all the dependencies properly in place, the time has come to refactor our `TaskService.ts` file. Open the service file and let's update the import statements block:

```
import { Injectable } from '@angular/core';
import { HttpClient } from '@angular/common/http';
import { Observable } from 'rxjs/Observable';

import { Task } from './task.model';
```

First, we import in the `HttpClient` and `Response` symbols so that we can annotate our objects later on. The Observable symbol is imported from the RxJS library so that we can properly annotate the return types of our async HTTP requests. We also import `Task` as a model (it is an interface) from the file `task.model.ts`, as follows:

```
export interface Task {
  name: string;
  deadline: string;
  pomodorosRequired: number;
  queued: boolean;
}
```

We will refactor this service using two steps:

1. Rewrite the service to use the HTTP service.
2. Implement a store/feed pattern and give the service a state.

Using the Angular HTTP service

Now, we will replace the existing implementation using static data inside of the service to one using the HTTP service. To do this, we call the `http.get()` method on the HTTP service to fetch data, but we also need to use the map operator to get a result we can display outwards:

```
import { HttpClient } from '@angular/common/http';
import { Task } from './task.model';

export default class TaskService {
  constructor(private http:HttpClient) {}
```

```
getTasks(): Observable<Task[]> {
    return this.http.get<Task[]>(`tasks.json`)
}
}
```

To use the previously defined service, we just need to tell the module about it. We do so by adding it to the `providers` keyword:

```
// app/tasks/task.module.ts

@NgModule({
    imports: [ /* add dependant modules here */ ],
    declarations: [ ./* add components and directives here */ ]
    providers: [TaskService],
})
export class TaskModule {}
```

Thereafter, we need to inject the `TaskService` in a consumer component and display it in a suitable way:

```
// app/tasks/task.component.ts

@Component({
    template: `
    <div *ngFor="let task of tasks">
    {{ task.name }}
    </div>
    `
})
export class TasksComponent {
    tasks:Task[];
    constructor(private taskService:TaskService){
        this.taskService.getTasks().subscribe( tasks => this.tasks = tasks)
    }
}
```

A stateful TaskService for most scenarios

So far, we have covered how to inject an HTTP service into a service constructor and have been able to subscribe to such a service from a component. In some cases, a component might want to deal with the data directly and not with Observables. In fact, most of our cases are like that. So, we don't have to use Observables much; HTTP services are utilizing Observables, right? We are talking about the component layer. Currently, we have this happening inside of our component:

```
// app/tasks/task.service.ts

@Component({
  template: `
  <div *ngFor="let task of tasks$ | async">
    {{ task.name }}
  </div>
  `
})
export class TaskListComponent {
  tasks$:Observable<Task[]>;

  constructor(private taskService: TaskService ) {}

  ngOnInit() {
    this.tasks$ = this.taskService.getTasks();
  }
}
```

Here, we see that we assign `taskService.getTasks()` to a stream called `tasks$`. What is the `$` at the end of the `tasks$` variable? This is a naming convention that we use for streams; let's try to follow that for any future streams/Observable fields that we declare. We use the words Observable and stream interchangeably, as they come to mean the same thing in the context of Angular. We also let the `| async` async pipe handle it with `*ngFor` and display our tasks.

We can do this in an even simpler way, like so:

```
// app/tasks/tas.alt.component.ts

@Component({
  template: `
    <div *ngFor="let task of tasks">
      {{ task.name }}
    </div>
  `
})
```

```
export class TaskComponent {
  constructor(private taskService: TaskService ) {}
  get tasks() {
    return this.taskService.tasks;
  }
}
```

So, the following changes took place:

- `ngOnInit()` and the assigning to the `tasks$` stream was removed
- The async pipe was removed
- We replaced the `tasks$` stream with a `tasks` array

How can this still work? The answer lies in how we define our service. Our service needs to expose an array of items and we need to ensure the array is changed when we get some data back from HTTP, or when we receive data from elsewhere, such as from a web socket or a product like Firebase.

We just mentioned two interesting methods, sockets and Firebase. Let's explain what those are and how they relate to our service. A web socket is a technique that establishes a two-way communication, a so-called *full duplex connection*, with the help of the TCP protocol. So, why is it interesting to mention it in the context of HTTP? Most of the time, you have simple scenarios where you fetch data over HTTP, and you can leverage Angular's HTTP service. Sometimes, the data might come from a full duplex connection in addition to it coming from HTTP.

What about Firebase? Firebase is a product by Google that allows us to create a database in the cloud. As can be expected, we can perform CRUD operations on the database, but the strength lies in the fact that we can set up subscriptions to it and thereby listen to changes when they occur. This means we can easily create collaboration apps, where a number of clients are operating on the same data source. This is a very interesting topic. This means you can quickly supply your Angular app with a backend, so for that reason, it deserves its own chapter. It also happens to be the next chapter of this book.

Back to the point we were trying to make. On paper, it sounds like the addition of sockets or Firebase would complicate our service a whole lot. In practice, they don't. The only thing you need to keep in mind is that when such data arrives, it needs to be added to our `tasks` array. We make the assumption here that it is interesting to deal with tasks from a HTTP service as well as from full duplex connections like Firebase or web sockets.

Let's have a look at what it would look like to involve an HTTP service and sockets in our code. You can easily leverage sockets by using a library that wraps its API.

WebSockets are supported natively by most browsers, but it is considered experimental still. With that said, it still makes sense to rely on a library that helps us work with sockets, but it's worth keeping track of when WebSockets are becoming less experimental as we would no longer consider using a library. For the interested reader, please check the official documentation at `https://developer.mozilla.org/en-US/docs/Web/API/WebSockets_API`

One such library is the `socket.io` library; it can be installed in the following way:

```
npm install socket.io
```

To start using this in Angular, you need to:

1. Import the `socket.io-client`.
2. Establish a connection by calling `io(url)`; this will return a socket that you can add subscriptions to.
3. Wait for incoming events that will contain a payload that we want to display in our app.
4. Generate events and send the possible payload when you want to talk to a backend

The following code will only show you how to do these steps. There is more to socket implementation, though, such as creating a backend. To see what a full example with Angular and `socket.io` looks like, the interested reader is encouraged to have a look at the following article by Torgeir Helgwold:

`http://www.syntaxsuccess.com/viewarticle/socket.io-with-rxjs-in-angular-2.0`

This isn't really an HTTP topic, which is why we settle for only showing the points of interest in the code, which is where we would receive the data and add it to our tasks array. We also highlight the setting up and tearing down of the socket. Highlighting is done in bold, as follows:

```
import * as io from 'socket.io-client';

export class TaskService {
  subscription;
  tasks:Task[] = [];
  constructor(private http:HttpClient) {
    this.fetchData();

    this.socket = io(this.url);  // establishing a socket connection
```

```
    this.socket.on('task', (data) => {
      // receive data from socket based on the 'task' event happening
      this.tasks = [ ..this.tasks, data ];
    });
  }

  private fetchData() {
    this.subscription =
    this.http.get<Task[]>('/tasks')
      .subscribe( data => this.tasks = data );
  }

  // call this from the component when component is being destroyed
  destroy() {
    this.socket.removeAllListeners('task');   // clean up the socket
                                               connection
  }
}
```

This is a very simple example that works well for showing data in a template, as well updating the template when the `tasks` array changes. As you can see, if we involve a `socket`, it won't matter; our template will still be updated.

This way of doing it also comprises another scenario—how do two sibling components or more communicate? The answer is quite simple: they use the `TaskService`. If you want the other components template to be updated, then simply change the contents of the tasks array and it will be reflected in the UI. The code for this follows:

```
@Component({
  template: `
    <div *ngFor="let task of tasks">
      {{ task.name }}
    </div>
    <input [(ngModel)]="newTask" />
    <button (click)="addTask()" ></button>
  `
})
export class FirstSiblingComponent {
  newTask: string;

  constructor(private service: TaskService) {}

  get tasks() {
    return this.taskService.tasks;
  }

  addTask() {
```

```
      this.service.addTask({ name : this.newTask });
      this.newTask = '';
    }
  }
```

This means that we also need to add a addTask() method to our service, like so:

```
import * as io from 'socket.io-client';

export class TaskService {
  subscription;
  tasks: Task[] = [];
  constructor(private http:Http) {
    this.fetchData();

    this.socket = io(this.url);  // establishing a socket connection

    this.socket.on('task', (data) => {
      // receive data from socket based on the 'task' event happening
      this.tasks = [ ..this.tasks, data ];
    });
  }

  addTask(task: Task) {
    this.tasks = [ ...this.tasks, task];
  }

  private fetchData() {
    this.subscription =
    this.http.get('/tasks')
      .subscribe(data => this.tasks = data);
  }

  // call this from the component when component is being destroyed
  destroy() {
    this.socket.removeAllListeners('task');  // clean up the socket
                                                connection
  }
}
```

The other component would look pretty much identical in terms of the parts that relate to setting up the `taskService`, exposing a `tasks` property and manipulating the `tasks` list. Regardless of which one of the components takes the initiative to change the task list through user interaction, the other component would be notified. I want to highlight what makes this general approach work, though. For this approach to work, you need to expose the tasks array through a getter in the component, like so:

```
get tasks() {
  return this.taskService.tasks;
}
```

Otherwise, the changes to it won't be picked up.

There is one drawback, though. What if we wanted to know exactly when an item was added and, say, display some CSS based on that? In that case, you have two options:

- Set up the socket connection in the component and listen for the data changes there.
- Use a behavior subject inside of the task service instead of a task array. Any changes from HTTP or socket will write to the subject through `subject.next()`. If you do this, then you can simply subscribe to the subject when a change happens.

The last alternative is a bit complicated to explain in a few words, so the whole next section is dedicated to explaining how you can use a `BehaviourSubject` over an array.

Further improvements – turning TaskService into a stateful, more robust service

RxJS and Observables didn't arrive just to be a one-to-one match to Promises. RxJS and reactive programming arrived to promote a different kind of architecture, as well. From such an architecture emerged a store pattern suitable for services. The store pattern is about ensuring our service is stateful and can deal with data coming from more places than HTTP. The potential places where data can arrive from could be, for example:

- HTTP
- localStorage
- Sockets
- Firebase

Handling service calls when network connection intermittently goes offline

First of all, you owe it to the application users to ensure that your application still works if the network connection goes down, at least when it comes to reading data. For that situation, it would be nice if we could answer with `localStorage` if the HTTP response fails to deliver. This, however, means we need logic in our service that works in the following way:

```
if(networkIsDown) {
  /* respond with localStorage instead */
} else {
  /* respond with network call */
}
```

Let's take our service and modify it slightly to account for being offline:

```
export class TaskService {
  getTasks() {
    this.http
      .get<Task[]>('/data/tasks.json')
      .do( data => {
        localStorage.setItem('tasks', JSON.stringify(data))
      })
      .catch(err) => {
        return this.fetchLocalStorage();
      })
  }

  private fetchLocalStorage(){
    let tasks = localStorage.getItem('tasks');
    const tasks = localStorage.getItem('tasks') || [];
    return Observable.of(tasks);
  }
}
```

As you can see, we do two things:

- We add the `.do()` operator to carry out a side effect; in this case, we write the response to `localStorage`
- We add the `catch()` operator and respond with a new Observable that contains previously stored data or an empty array

There is nothing wrong with solving it this way, and in a lot of cases, it might even be good enough. What happens when data arrives from many different directions, though, as suggested earlier? If that is the case, then we must have the ability to push data into the stream. Normally, it's only Observers that can push data with `observer.next()`.

There is another construct, though, the `Subject`. The `Subject` has a dual nature. It has the ability to both push data to the stream and it can also be subscribed to. Let's rewrite our service to account for the external arrival of data and then add `Sock.io` library support so you will see how this is scaled. We start by making the service stateful. It would be tempting to just code it like this:

```
export class TaskService {
  tasks: Task[];
  getTasks() {
    this.http
    .get<Task[]>('/data/tasks.json')
    .do( data => {
      this.tasks = mapTasks( data );
      localStorage.setItem('tasks', JSON.stringify(data))
    })
    .catch(err) => {
      return this.fetchLocalStorage();
    })
  }
}
```

The preceding changes we propose are bolded and entail creating a `tasks` array field and doing an assignment to the tasks field with the arriving data. This works, but it might be more than we need.

Introducing the store/feed pattern

We can do better than this, though. We can do better in the sense that we really don't need to create that last array. You might think at this point, let me get this straight; you want my service to be stateful without a backing field? Well, kind of, and it is possible using something called a `BehaviourSubject`. A `BehaviourSubject` has the following properties:

- It is able to act as an `Observer` and `Observable`, so it can push data and be subscribed to at the same time
- It can have an initial value
- It will remember the last value that it emitted

So, with the `BehaviourSubject`, we essentially kill two birds with one stone. It can remember things that were last emitted and it can push out data, making it ideal to use when connecting to other data sources such as web sockets. Let's add it first to our service:

```
export class TaskService {
  private internalStore:BehaviourSubject;

  constructor() {
    this.internalStore = new BehaviourSubject([]); // setting initial
                                                      value
  }

  get store() {
    return this.internalStore.asObservable();
  }

  private fetchTasks(){
    this.http
      .get<Task[]>('/data/tasks.json')
      .map(this.mapTasks)
      .do(data => {
        this.internalStore.next( data )
        localStorage.setItem('tasks', JSON.stringify(data))
      })
      .catch( err => {
        return this.fetchLocalStorage();
      });
  }
}
```

Here, we are instantiating the `BehaviourSubject` and as we can see its default constructor takes a parameter, an initial value. We give it an empty array. This initial value is the first thing to be presented to a subscriber. It makes sense from an application standpoint to showcase a first value while waiting for that first HTTP call to finish.

We also define a `store()` property that ensures that when we expose the `BehaviourSubject` to the world, we do so as an `Observable`. This is defensive coding. As the subject has a `next()` method on it that allows us to push values into it; we want to take that ability away from anyone that is not in our service. We do this because we want to make sure that anything added to it is handled through the public API of the `TaskService` class:

```
get store() {
  return this.internalStore.asObservable();
}
```

The last change was the addition made to the `.do()` operator:

```
// here we are emitting the data as it arrives
.do(data => {
  this.internalStore.next(data)
})
```

This will ensure that any subscribers to our service will always get the last emitted data. Try it yourself with a code like this in a component:

```
@Component({})
export class TaskComponent {
  constructor(taskService: TaskService ) {
    taskService.store.subscribe( data => {
      console.log('Subscriber 1', data);
    })

    setTimeout(() => {
      taskService.store
      .subscribe( data => console.log('Subscriber 2', data)); // will get
the latest emitted value
    }, 3000)
  }
}
```

At this point, we have made sure it doesn't matter when you start subscribing to `taskService.store`. Whether it's immediately or after 3 seconds, as the preceding code shows, we will still get the last emitted data.

Persisting data

What if we need to persist what is coming from a form in a component? Well then, we need to do the following:

- Expose an `add()` method on our service
- Do an `http.post()` call
- Poke the `getTasks()` to ensure it refetches the data

Let's start with the simpler case of adding a task from a component. We assume the user has entered all the necessary data needed to create a `Task` in the application UI.

An `addTask()` method has been invoked from the component, which in turn invokes a similar `addTask()` method on the service. We need to add the last method to our service and also in that method call an endpoint with a POST request so our task gets persisted, like this:

```
export class TaskService {
  addTask(task) {
    return this.http.post('/tasks', task);
  }
}
```

At this point, we assume the calling component is responsible for doing all sorts of CRUD operations on a component, including showing a list of tasks. By adding a task and persisting it, the mentioned list would now lack a member, which is why it makes sense to do a fresh call to `getTasks()`. So, if we had a simple service with just a `getTasks()` method, then that would just return a list of tasks, including our newly persisted task, like so:

```
@Component({})
export class TaskComponent implements OnInit {
  ngOnInit() {
    init();
  }

  private init(){
    this.taskService.getTasks().subscribe( data => this.tasks = data )
  }

  addTask(task) {
    this.taskService.addTask(task).subscribe( data => {
      this.taskService.getTasks().subscribe(data => this.tasks = data)
    });
  }
}
```

OK, so this works if we have a simplified `TaskService` that lacks our pretty store/feed pattern. There is a problem, though—we are using RxJS wrong. What do we mean by wrong? Every time we use `addTask()`, we set up a new subscription.

What you want is the following:

- One subscription to a stream of tasks
- A cleanup phase where the subscription is being unsubscribed

Let's start by tackling the first problem; one stream. We assume that we will need to use the stateful version of our `TaskService` instead. We change the component code to this:

```
@Component({})
export class TaskComponent implements OnInit{
  private subscription;

  ngOnInit() {
    this.subscription = this.taskService.store.subscribe( data =>
this.tasks = data );
  }

  addTask(task) {
    this.taskService.addTask( task ).subscribe( data => {
      // tell the store to update itself?
    });
  }
}
```

As you can see, we are now subscribing to the store property instead, but we have removed the refetch behavior inside of the `taskService.addTask()` method to read like this:

```
this.taskService.addTask(task).subscribe( data => {
  // tell the store to update itself?
})
```

We will instead place this refresh logic in the `taskService`, like so:

```
export class TaskService {
  addTask(task) {
    this.http
      .post('/tasks', task)
      .subscribe( data => { this.fetchTasks(); })
  }
}
```

Now, everything works as intended. We have one subscription to our task stream in the component and the refresh logic is being pushed back to the service by us poking the `fetchTasks()` method.

We have one more order of business. How do we deal with subscriptions, and more to the point, how do we deal with unsubscribing? Remember how we added a `subscription` member to our component? That took us halfway there. Let's implement an `OnDestroy` interface to our component and implement the contract:

```
@Component({
 template : `
  <div *ngFor="let task of tasks">
    {{ task.name }}
  </div>
  `
})
export class TaskComponent implements OnInit, implements OnDestroy{
    private subscription;
    tasks: Task[];

    ngOnInit() {
      this.subscription = this.taskService.store.subscribe( data =>
this.tasks = data );
    }

    ngOnDestroy() {
      this.subscription.unsubscribe();
    }

    addTask(task) {
      this.taskService.addTask( task );
    }
}
```

By implementing the `OnDestroy` interface, we have a way to call `unsubscribe()` on the subscription and we do that in the `ngOnDestroy()` method that the `OnDestroy` interface makes us implement. Thus, we clean up after ourselves.

The pattern of implementing the OnInit interface and the OnDestroy interface is something that you should be doing when creating a component. It is a good practice to set up subscriptions and anything else the component needs in the ngOnInit() method and conversely tear down subscriptions and other type of constructs in the ngOnDestroy() method.

There is an even better way, though, and that is using the async | async pipe. The async pipe will remove the need to save a reference to a subscription and call .unsubscribe() on it, as this is handled internally in the async pipe. We will talk more about the async pipe in the upcoming sections in this chapter, but here is what the component would look like leveraging it instead of the OnDestroy interface:

```
@Component({
  template: `
   <div *ngFor="let task of tasks | async">
     {{ task.name }}
   </div>
  `
})
export class TaskComponent implements OnInit{
   get tasks() {
     return this.taskService.store;
   }

   addTask(task) {
     this.taskService.addTask( task );
   }
}
```

Our code just removed a lot of boilerplate, and the best part is that it is still working. As long as all your data is being displayed in a component, then the async pipe is the way to go; however, if you fetch up data that is shared between other services or used as a precondition to fetching other data, then it might not be so clear-cut as to be using the async pipe.

The important thing at the end of the day is that you resort to using one of these techniques.

Refreshing our service

We are almost done describing our `TaskService`, but there is one more aspect we need to cover. Our service doesn't take into account that a third party might make changes to the endpoint database. We will see those changes if we move away from the component or reload the entire application. If we want to see those changes when they happen, we need to have some kind of behavior that tells us when data has changed. It is tempting to think of a polling solution and just refresh the data at certain intervals. This might be a painful approach, though, as the data we fetch might consist of a large object graph. Ideally, we only want to fetch what really changed and amend that to our application. Why do we care so much about this in the age of broadband connections? Here is the problem—an application should be able to be used on a mobile app and both speed as well as mobile data contracts might be an issue, so we need to consider the mobile user. Here are some things we should consider:

- The size of the data
- The polling interval

If the expected size of the data is really big, then it might be a good idea to poke an endpoint and ask it for everything that changed after a certain time; this would change the size of the payload drastically. We could also just ask for a partial object graph back. The polling interval is another thing to consider. We need to ask ourselves: how often do we really need to refetch all the data? The answer could be never.

Let's say we opt for an approach where we ask for the delta (the change after a certain time); it could look like the following:

```
constructor(){
  lastFetchedDate;
  INTERVAL_IN_SECONDS = 30;

  setInterval(() => {
    fetchTasksDelta( lastFetchedDate );
    lastFetchedDate = DateTime.now;
  }, this.INTERVAL_IN_SECONDS * 1000)
}
```

Regardless of what approach and considerations you take here, remember that not all users are on a broadband connection. It's also worth nothing that more and more of theses refresh scenarios tend to be solved with Web Sockets nowadays so you create an open connection between server and client, and the server can decide when it's time to send the client some new data. We will leave it to you, dear reader, to refactor this example using Sockets.

We now have a service which is:

- Stateless
- Able to handle offline connections
- Able to cater for other data services such as sockets
- Able to refresh its data at a certain interval

All this was made possible through the `BehaviourSubject` and `localStorage`. Don't just treat RxJS as an add-on to a `Promise`, but use its constructs and operators to craft robust services and architecture patterns.

HttpInterceptor

An interceptor is a piece of code that can be executed between your HTTP calls and the rest of the application. It can be hooked up when you are about to send a request as well as when receiving a response. So, what do we use it for? There many areas of application, but some might be:

- Adding a custom token for all outgoing requests
- Wrapping all incoming error responses in a business exception; this can also be done on the backend
- Redirecting a request somewhere else

An `HttpInterceptor` is an interface imported from `@angular/common/http`. To create an interceptor, you need to take the following steps:

1. Import and implement the `HttpInterceptor` interface
2. Register the interceptor in the root module provider
3. Write the business logic for what is to happen to the request

Creating a mock interceptor

Let's take all, the earlier mentioned steps and create a real interceptor service. Imagine that all calls to a certain endpoint are directed to a JSON file or a dictionary. Doing so will create a mock behavior where you are able to ensure that all outgoing calls are intercepted, and in their place, you answer with suitable mock data. This will allow you to develop the API at your own pace while relying on mocked data. Let's dig a little deeper into this scenario.

Let's start off by creating our service. Let's call it `MockInterceptor`. It will need to implement the `HttpInterceptor` interface like so:

```
import { HttpInterceptor } from '@angular/common/http';

export class MockInterceptor implements HttpInterceptor {
  constructor() { }

  intercept(request: HttpRequest<any>, next: HttpHandler):
Observable<HttpEvent<any>> {
  }
}
```

To fulfil the contract of the interface, we need to have the method `intercept()` that takes a request and a `next()` handler as parameters. Thereafter, we need to ensure we return an Observable of `HttpEvent` type from the `intercept()` method. We have yet to write any logic in there, so this won't actually compile. Let's add some basic code in the `intercept()` method just to make it work, like so:

```
import { HttpInterceptor } from '@angular/common/http';

export class MockInterceptor implements HttpInterceptor {
  constructor() { }

  intercept(request: HttpRequest<any>, next: HttpHandler):
Observable<HttpEvent<any>> {
    return next.handle(request);
  }
}
```

We added a call to `next.handle(request)`, which means we take the incoming request and just pass it further in the pipeline. This code doesn't do anything useful, but it does compile and does teach us that whatever we do inside the `intercept()` method, we need to call `next.handle()` with a request object.

Let's return to what we were trying to achieve in the first place—mocking an outgoing request. This means we want to replace the outgoing request with `our` request. To accomplish our mocking behavior, we need to do the following:

- Investigate our outgoing request and determine whether we want to answer with a mock or let it through
- Construct a mock response if we want to mock it
- Register our new interceptor with the `providers` for a module

Let's add some code to our `intercept()` method as follows:

```
import { HttpInterceptor } from '@angular/common/http';

export class MockInterceptor implements HttpInterceptor {
  constructor() { }

  intercept(request: HttpRequest<any>, next: HttpHandler):
Observable<HttpEvent<any>> {
    if (request.url.startsWith('/starwars') && request.method === 'GET') {
      const url = request.url;
      const newUrl = `data${url.substring('/starwars'.length)}.json`;
      const req = new HttpRequest('GET', newUrl);
      return next.handle(req);
    } else {
      return next.handle(request);
    }
  }
}
```

What we are essentially saying here is that we are trying to perform a GET request to something. `/starwars` will intercept it and instead respond with a JSON file. So, `/starwars/ships` would instead lead to us respond with `ships.json` and `/starwars/planets` would lead to `planets.json`. You get the idea; all other requests would be let through.

We have one more thing to do—tell our module this interceptor exists. We open up our module file and add the following:

```
@NgModule({
  imports: [BrowserModule, HttpClientModule]
  providers: [{
    provide: HTTP_INTERCEPTORS,
    useClass: MockInterceptor,
    multi: true }]
})
```

Some best practices

There are some best practices to follow when dealing with data services in Angular, especially when Observables are involved, and those are:

- Handle your errors. This one goes without saying and hopefully this is not something new on your radar.

- Make sure that any manually created Observables have a cleanup method.
- Unsubscribe to your streams/Observables, or else you might have resource leaks.
- Use the async pipe to manage the subscribe/unsubscribe process for you.

We have so far not discussed how to create a cleanup method when manually creating Observables, which is why we will cover that in a subsection.

The async pipe has been mentioned a couple of times in the Firebase section, but it's worth mentioning again and building on that knowledge by explaining its role in the subscribe/unsubscribe process to streams.

Async operator

The async pipe is an Angular pipe, and as such it is used in a template. It is used in conjunction with streams/Observables. It plays two roles: it helps us to type less, and secondly, it saves us the whole ceremony of having to set up and tear down a subscription.

If it did not exist, it would be tempting to type the following when trying to display data from a stream:

```
@Component({
  template: `{{ data }}`
})
export class DataComponent implements OnInit, implements OnDestroy {
  subscription;
  constructor(private service){ }

  ngOnInit() {
    this.subscription = this.service.getData()
                        .subscribe( data => this.data = data )
  }

  ngOnDestroy() {
    this.subscription.unsubscribe();
  }
}
```

As you can see, we have to subscribe and unsubscribe to the data. We also need to introduce a data property to assign it to. The async pipe saves us a few keystrokes, so we instead can type our component like this:

```
@Component({
  template: `{{ data | async }}`
})
```

```
export class DataComponent implements OnInit {
  data$;
  constructor(private service){ }

  ngOnInit() {
    this.data$ = this.service.getData();
  }
}
```

This is a lot less code. We removed:

- The `OnDestroy` interface
- The `subscription` variable
- Any call to subscribe/unsubscribe

We did need to add `{{ data | async }}`, which is a quite a small addition.

However, if what we get back is a more complicated object and we would like to display its properties, we have to type something like this in the template:

```
{{ (data | ansync)?.title }}
{{ (data | ansync)?.description }}
{{ (data | ansync)?.author }}
```

We do this as the data is not yet set, and accessing a property at that point would lead to a runtime error, hence our ? operator. Now, this looks a bit verbose, and we can fix that with the – operator, like so:

```
<div *ngIf="data | async as d">
  {{ d.title }}
  {{ d.description }}
  {{ d.author }}
</div>
```

Now it's looking a lot better. Using the async pipe will reduce a lot of boilerplate.

Being a good citizen – cleaning up after yourself

Okay, so I've told you the importance of calling `.unsubscribe()`, and you have taken my word for it at this point that if it is not called, resources won't be cleaned up. It is important to know about this mostly when you deal with streams that have a never-ending stream of data, such as scroll events, or in cases where you need to create your own Observables. I will now demonstrate a little bit of the internals of an Observable to make things clearer:

```
let stream$ = Observable.create( observer => {
  let i = 0;
  let interval = setInterval(() => {
    observer.next(i++);
  }, 2000)
})

let subscription = stream$.subscribe( data => console.log( data ));
setTimeout((
  subscription.unsubscribe();
) =>, 3000)
```

This is an example of creating our own Observable. You think you are safe now just because you called `.unsubscribe()` like you were told? Wrong. The interval will keep on ticking because you didn't tell it stop. In panic, you close the browser tab and wish the Observable away—you are safe for now. The correct approach to this is to add a cleanup function, like so:

```
let stream$ = Observable.create( observer => {
  let i = 0;
  let interval = setInterval(() => {
    observer.next(i++);
  }, 2000);

  return function cleanUp() {
    clearInterval( interval );
  }
})

let subscription = stream$.subscribe( data => console.log( data ));
setTimeout(() => subscription.unsubscribe(), 3000);
```

Upon calling `subscription.unsubscribe()`, it will call the `cleanUp()` function internally. Most of, if not all, factory methods out there used to create Observables will have their own `cleanUp()` function defined. It is important for you to know that should you venture down that rabbit hole of creating your own Observable, refer to this section, be a good citizen, and implement a `cleanUp()` function.

Summary

As we pointed out at the beginning of this chapter, it takes much more than a single chapter to cover in detail all the great things that can be done with the Angular HTTP connection functionalities, but the good news is that we have covered pretty much all the tools and classes we need.

The rest is just left to your imagination, so feel free to go the extra mile and put all of this knowledge into practice by creating brand new Twitter reader clients, newsfeed widgets, or blog engines, and assembling all kinds of components of your choice. The possibilities are endless, and you have assorted strategies to choose from, ranging from Promises to Observables. You can leverage the incredible functionalities of the Reactive Functional extensions and the tiny but powerful `Http` class.

As we have already highlighted, the sky is the limit. But, we still have a long and exciting road ahead. Now that we know how to consume asynchronous data in our components, let's discover how we can provide a broader user experience in our applications by routing users into different components. We will cover this in the next chapter.

8
Firebase

Firebase is a mobile and web application platform first developed by Firebase Inc. in 2011 and bought by Google in 2014. Since then, it has gone from a reactive database in the cloud to a whole suite of products. We will, however, focus on the database side of things, as that is the interesting part for an Angular developer. So, the best way to think of Firebase is as a backend as a service. That means that with Firebase, there is no reason to build your own REST services; you only need to connect to it.

It's worth pointing out that it is ultimately a product with paid plans, but it is definitely possible to create toy projects with it without having to pay anything.

Okay, so backend as a service, got it. That's not all, however; its real selling point is the fact that it is reactive. It is reactive in the sense that if you subscribe to a collection on the database and a client somewhere makes a change to that collection, you will be notified and can act accordingly. Does that sounds familiar? Yes, you are thinking right: it sounds like RxJS and Observables, which is why the Firebase API has been wrapped in RXJS called AngularFire2, an Angular module that you can easily install from npm and add to your project.

So, the business case for using Firebase in the first place is when you want to create collaboration applications. I'm going to be so bold as to say that it is like web sockets, but in the cloud and with an underlying database, so with not only the communication part, but data as well.

In this chapter, you will learn:

- What Firebase is
- To leverage AngularFire2 in your Angular app
- How to listen for and act on changes

- How to use CRUD operations to manipulate your Firebase data
- Why it is important to deal with authentication and authorization and how to set them up

Three-way binding versus two-way binding

We have different kinds of bindings. AngularJS made the two-way binding famous. This entails being able to change data from two different directions:

- A change in the view changes data on the controller
- A change on the controller is reflected in the view

As for three-way binding, what do we mean? Let's illustrate this with an app; it's best described through an image:

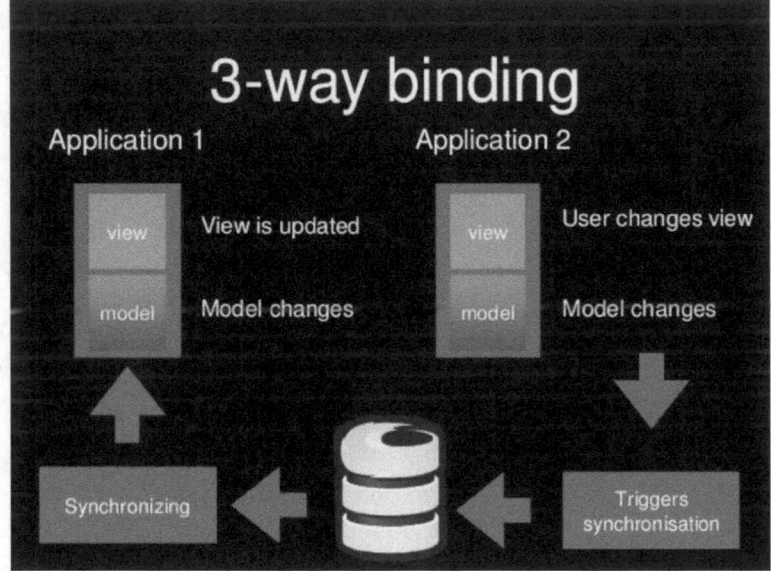

What you need to imagine here is that we developed an application that uses Firebase. We are launching said application in two different browser windows. In the first window, we make a change that is being reflected in the second browser window, for example, adding an item to a list. So, what steps take place?

What we see here is best read from right to left:

- Instance one: user changes a view
- Instance one: change propagates to the model
- This triggers synchronisation with the Firebase database instance
- The second instance is listening to the synchronisation
- The model for the second instance is being updated
- The view for the second instance is being updated

There you have it: change in one place, and see the results in two or more instances depending on how many instances you have spawned.

Some words on storage - the problem with a list

Before venturing deeper into Firebase, let's first explain why we are talking about lists in the first place. In a relational database, we would be using SQL, tables, and normal forms to define our database. This is not the case with a Firebase database, as it is made of a JSON structure, looking something like this:

```
{
  "person": {
    "age": 11,
    "name": "Charlie",
    "address": "First Street, Little Town"
  },
  "orders": {
    "someKeyHash": {
    "orderDate": "2010-01-01",
    "total": 114
  },
  "someOtherKeyHash": {
    "orderDate": "2010-02-28"
  }
}
```

Notice how the orders collection in a relational database would be an `orders` table with a lot of rows. Here, it seems to be an object; why is that?

Objects in a list - solving the deletion problem

A list normally has an index associated to every item in the list, like so:

- 0: item1
- 1: item2
- 2: item3

There's nothing wrong with that, until you start to think about what happens when many simultaneous users start to access the same data. As long as we do reads, we don't have a problem. But what happens if we attempt something else, such as deletion?

Normally when you delete things, the index gets reassigned. If we delete the preceding item2, we have a new situation that looks like this:

- 0: item1
- 1: item3

Imagine we do deletions based on the index and your data looks like this:

- 0: item1
- 1: item2
- 2: item3
- 3: item4

Now, two different users can access this data and one wants to delete index 1 and the other wants to delete index 3. We would probably employ a locking algorithm, so one user deletes index 1 a few milliseconds before user two deletes index 3. The intention of the first user was to delete item2 and the intention of the second user was to delete item4. The first user succeeds in what they set out to do, but the second one deletes an index that is out of bounds.

This means that deleting things on the index is just crazy in a multiuser database, but in the case of Firebase, it means that lists are not lists when they are stored; they are objects, looking like this:

```
{
  212sdsd: 'item 1',
  565hghh: 'item 2'
  // etc
}
```

This circumvents the deletion problem and is, therefore, the reason that lists are represented the way they are.

AngularFire2

AngularFire2 is the name of the library where the Firebase API is wrapped in Observables. That means we can somewhat anticipate what it might look like when we want to listen for changes and so on. We will come back to the change scenario in a later section in this chapter.

The official repository can be found at the following link:

`https://github.com/angular/angularfire2`

Excellent documentation on how to do CRUD and work with authentication can be found at the bottom of the page the preceding link leads to.

The core classes

There is some basic information that is good to know before venturing deeper into AngularFire2; it's about core objects and what their responsibilities are:

- `AngularFireAuth`
- `FirebaseObjectObservable`
- `FirebaseListObservable`

`AngularFireAuth` **deals with authentication.** `FirebaseObjectObservable` is the core object you want to talk to when you know that the database property you deal with is of the type object. Lastly, `FirebaseListObservable` is the object that acts like a list. From before, we know that Firebase lists aren't really lists, but that doesn't stop this object from having methods on it that a list would normally have.

The admin tools

The admin tools can be found at `https://firebase.google.com/`. Once there, in the top-right corner, click on the **GO TO CONSOLE** link. You should have a Gmail account. If you do, then you have a Firebase account as well, and you only need to set up the database. Then, you should choose to create a project; give it a title of your choice and your location.

It should look like this:

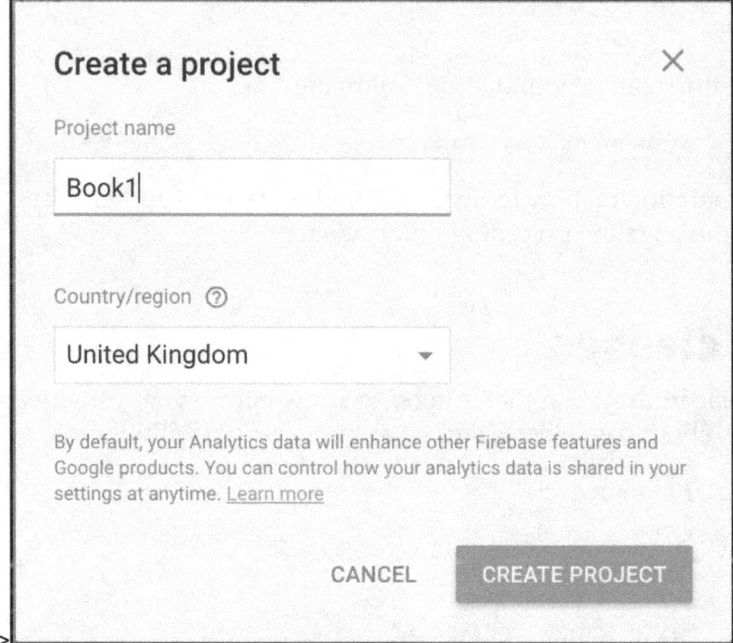

Once you've done this, you will be taken to the admin page, which looks like this:

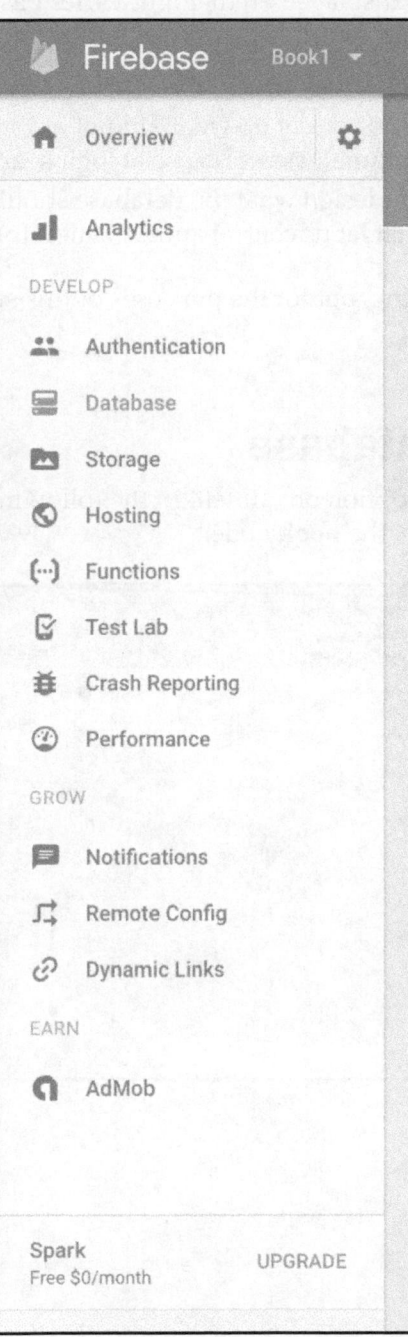

The preceding screenshot displays the left menu, and then to the right, you would have a content pane. What content is displayed on the right varies based on what you choose on the left. As you can see, you can control a lot of things. Your most important options when starting to craft your database are:

- **Authentication**: Here, you set up what kind of authentication you want: no authentication, username/password, social logins, and so on.
- **Database**: Here, you design what the database should look like. There are also some tabs in here that let us control authorization for the database collections.

The other options are interesting, but for the purposes of this section, this is something beyond our scope.

Defining your database

We go to the **Database** menu option on our left. In the following screenshot, I have already added a node to the root node, the **book** node:

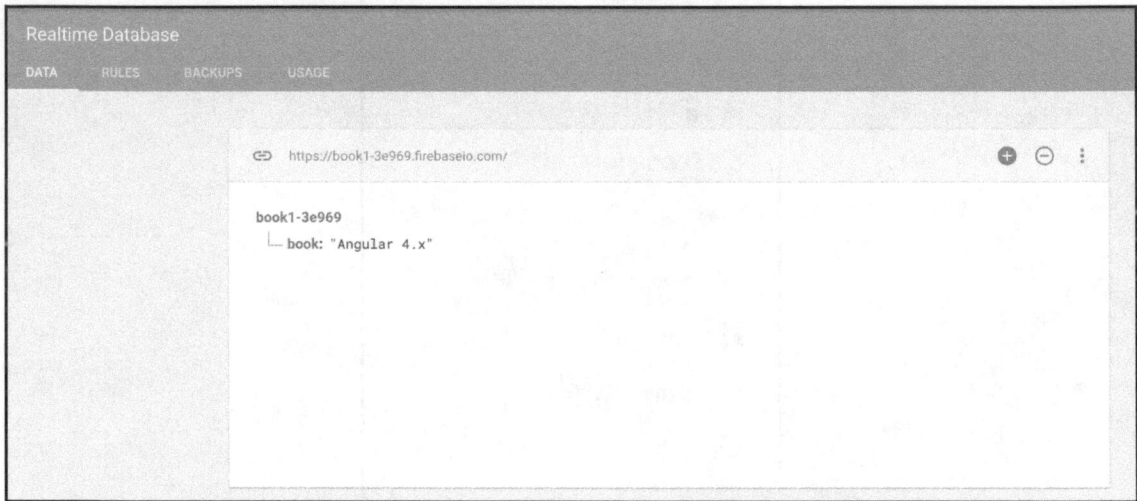

Hovering over our root element, we are presented with a + character that allows us to add a child to the root. Of course, we can also create more complex objects by clicking on a specific element and adding child nodes to them that look something like this:

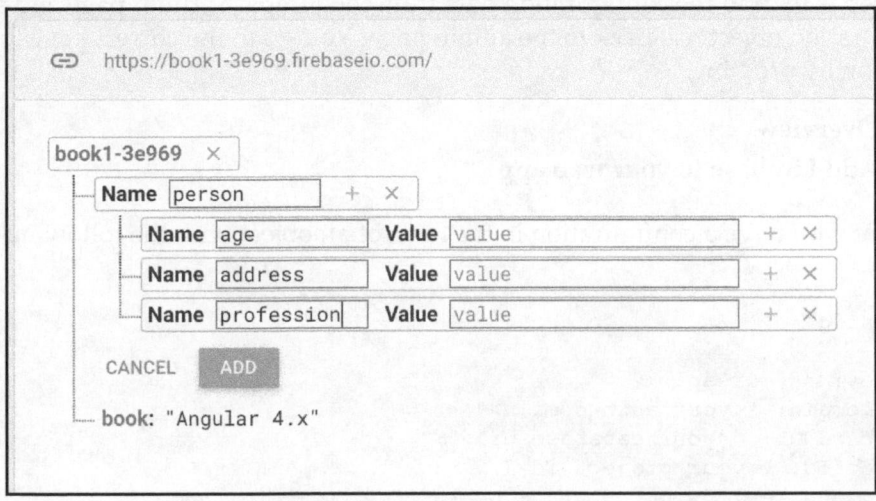

As you can see, we can quite easily build out our database and it has a JSON-like appearance.

Adding AngularFire2 to your app

The time has come to add Firebase support to our Angular application. To do that, we need to do the following:

1. Download the `npm` library for AngularFire2.
2. Import said library into our Angular application.
3. Set up our Firebase configuration so Firebase lets us retrieve the data.
4. Inject the proper Firebase service so we can access the data.
5. Present the data in a component.

The link `https://github.com/angular/angularfire2/blob/master/docs/install-and-setup.md` is the official link to set up Firebase in your Angular application. This might change over time, so it can be worth checking this page if the instructions of the book no longer seem to work after an update of the AngularFire2 library. Let's go through the steps though.

Downloading the AngularFire2 library is as simple as typing this:

```
npm install angularfire2 firebase --save
```

The next step is to grab the configuration data from the Firebase admin page and save that to a configuration object. Go back to the admin page. You go to the correct page for the configuration by pressing:

- **Overview**
- **Add Firebase to your web app**

At this point, you have a configuration in the form of an object with the following properties:

```
let config =
{
  apiKey: "<your api key>",
  authDomain: "<your auth domain>",
  databaseURL: "<your database url>",
  projectId: "<your project id>",
  storageBucket: "<your storage bucket>",
  messagingSenderId: "<your messaging senderid>"
};
```

The preceding values differ depending on your project. I can only urge you to copy the configuration from the admin page for your next step.

The next step is to scaffold an Angular application using `@angular-cli` and look up the `app.module.ts` file. In it, we will assign our config to the following variable:

```
export const environment = {
  firebase:
  {
    apiKey: "<your api key>",
    authDomain: "<your auth domain>",
    databaseURL: "<your database url>",
    projectId: "<your project id>",
    storageBucket: "<your storage bucket>",
    messagingSenderId: "<your messaging sender id>"
  }
}
```

Now we need to instruct the module to import the modules we need. Essentially, there are three modules that we can import:

- `AngularFireModule`: This is used to initialize the app
- `AngularFireDatabaseModule`: This is used to access the database; this is necessary to import
- `AngularFireAuthModule`: This is used to work with authentication; it's not necessary at first, but will definitely become so as the app grows - security anyone?

Let's import the first two, so we can work with Firebase and pull some data from it:

```
import { AngularFireModule } from 'angularfire2';
import { AngularFireDatabaseModule } from 'angularfire2/database';

@NgModule({
  imports: [
    AngularFireModule.initializeApp(environment.firebase),
    AngularFireDatabaseModule
  ]
})
```

At this point, we are done configuring the Angular module and can move on to `AppComponent`, which is where we will inject a Firebase service so we can finally pull some data from Firebase:

```
@Component({
  template : `to be defined`
})
export class AppComponent {
  constructor(private angularFireDatabase: AngularFireDatabase) {
    this.angularFireDatabase
      .object('/book')
      .valueChanges()
      .subscribe(data => {
        console.log('our book', data);
      });
  }
}
```

And there you have it: a complete Firebase setup, from downloading AngularFire2 to displaying your first data.

Protecting our app

Protecting our app is vital. It's not an if, it is a must, unless you are building a toy application. There are currently three ways to do this in Firebase:

- Authentication: This is where we verify that the user enters the correct credentials to be logged on to the application
- Authorization: This is where we set up what resources in the application the user has a right to access/modify
- Validation: This is where we ensure that only valid data is persisted in the database

Authentication - allowing access to the app

Authentication means that we identify you when you attempt to log on. If your credentials match a user in the database, then the app should let you in; otherwise, you are shown the door. Firebase has different ways of authenticating you. Currently, the following authentication methods are possible:

- Email/password
- Phone
- Google
- Facebook
- Twitter
- GitHub
- Anonymous

This is pretty much what you would expect in 2017: everything from simple authentication with email/password to OAuth.

Authorization - deciding who gets to access what data, and how

As for authorization, it is possible to set rules:

- On the whole database
- Per collection

It is also important to know that the rules are enforced in these ways:

- **Atomically**: Applies to a specific element
- **Cascading**: Applies to a specific element and all its children

The permission level is either:

- **Read**: This will make it possible to read the contents of the resource
- **Write**: This will give you the ability to modify the resource
- **Deny**: This will stop any write or read actions from being possible on the targeted resource

This calls for an example. Imagine you have the following database structure:

```
foo {
  bar: {
   child: 'value'
  }
}
```

Atomic authorization means that we need to be explicit; if we are not explicit, the default is to deny access. Let's try to enforce some rules on the preceding structure. We navigate to the rules section under the **Database** menu option. A rule is defined as a JSON object, like so:

```
rules: {
  "foo": {
    "bar": {
       ".read": true,
       ".write": false,
       "child": {}
    }
  }
}
```

This means that we have set an explicit atomic rule for `bar` and that rule is inherited by its child elements, that is, it acts in a cascading way `foo`, on the other hand, has no rule to it. This would have the following consequence if trying to access the collections:

```
// deny
this.angularFireDatabase.object('/foo');
// read allowed, write not allowed
this.angularFireDatabase.object('/foo/bar');
// read allowed, write not allowed
this.angularFireDatabase.object('/foo/bar/child');
```

This explains the types of rules that are in place. I urge you to look into this topic deeper by studying the following links:

- Securing your data in general: `https://firebase.google.com/docs/database/security/securing-data`
- Securing data per user, that is, setting different permission levels for different types of users: `https://firebase.google.com/docs/database/security/user-security`

Validation

This is quite an interesting topic. What is meant here is that we can control what data is allowed to enter our collections by setting up rules about the shape of the data. You essentially specify a set of requirements that the data must have for an insertion or update to be considered okay to perform. Just like the read/write authorization rules, we specify a rules object. Let's describe two different versions of validation so you get the hang of it:

- Incoming data must include these fields
- Incoming data must have a value within this range

The first case we can describe like so:

```
{
  "rules": {
    "order": {
      "name": {},
      "quantity"
    }
  }
}
```

Here is a code snippet showing the impact when the preceding rules are in place:

```
// will fail as 'quantity' is a must have field
angularFireDatabase.object('/order').set({ name : 'some name' });
```

In the second case, we can set up the rules like so:

```
{
  "rules": {
    "order": {
      "quantity": {
        ".validate": "newData.isNumber() && newData.val() >=0
        && newData.val() <= 100"
```

```
      }
    }
  }
}
```

The preceding specified rule states that any incoming data must be of type number, must be larger than or equal to 0, and smaller than or equal to 100.

Here is a code snippet showing the impact with this rule in place:

```
// fails validation
angularFireDatabase.object('order').set({ quantity : 101 })
```

As you can see, this makes it very easy to protect our data from unwanted input and thereby keeps the database nice and consistent.

Working with data - CRUD

Now, we have come to the exciting part: how to work with the data, read our data, add more data, and so on. In short, the term **Create, Read, Update, Delete** (**CRUD**).

So, when we work with CRUD, we need to know a little something about the structure that we are operating on. We need to know whether it is of type object or list. In terms of code, this means the following:

```
this.angularFireDatabase.object(path).<operation>
this.angularFireDatabase.list(path).<operation>
```

The preceding states that we can treat the data we look at, from the database, as either an object or list. Depending on our choice, this has an impact on what methods will be available to us, but also what the data looks like coming back. This is especially obvious if we have a list-like structure in the database and choose to treat it as an object. Assume we have the following stored structure:

```
{
  id1: { value : 1 },
  id2: { value : 2 }
}
```

If we choose to treat this as a list, we get the following response back:

```
[{
  $key: id1,
  value : 1
},
{
 $key: id2,
 value : 2
}]
```

This means we can use methods such as `push()` to add things to it.

If we choose to treat the data as an object, then it comes back as the following:

```
{
  id1: { value : 1 },
  id2: { value : 2 }
}
```

This may or may not be what you want. So remember, if it is a list, treat it as one. Firebase won't punish you with an exception if you choose `.object()` over `.list()`, but it might make the data harder to work with.

Reading data

Let's look at the read case. The following code will read the data from a property in our database:

```
let stream$ = this.angulatFireDatabase.object('/book').valueChanges();
```

As it is a stream, this means that we can get the data in one of two ways:

- Using the async pipe, which displays the observable as is, in the template
- Grabbing the data from the `subscribe()` method and assigning it to a property on your class

If we do the first scenario, it will look something like this:

```
@Component({
  template: `
    <div *ngIf="$book | async; let book;">
    {{ ( book | async )?.title }}
    </div>
  `
```

```
})
export class Component {
  book$: Observable<Book>;
    constructor(private
      angularFireDatabase: AngularFireDatabase) {
        this.book$ = this.angularFireDatabase
          .object('/book')
          .valueChanges()
          .map(this.mapBook);
    }
    private mapBook(obj): Book {
      return new Book(obj);
    }
}

class Book {
  constructor(title: string) { }
}
```

It is worth highlighting how we ask for the path in the database and transform the result
with the .map() operator:

```
this.book = this.angularFireDatabase
  .object('/book')
  .map(this.mapBook);
```

In the template, we use the async pipe and an expression to show the title of our Book entity
when it has been resolved:

```
<div *ngIf="book$ | async; let book">
  {{ book.title }}
</div>
```

If we do the second scenario, it will look something like this in code:

```
@Component({
 template: `
   <div>
     {{ book.title }}
   </div>
 `
})
export class BookComponent
{
  book:Book;

  constructor(private angularFireDatabase: AngularFireDatabase) {
    this.angularFireDatabase.object('/book')
```

```
        .map(mapBook).subscribe( data => this.book = data );
    }

    mapBook(obj): Book {
        return new Book(obj);
    }
}

class Book {
    constructor(title:string) {}
}
```

This will take away a little of the typing, but you now must remember to unsubscribe to your stream; this has not been added in the previous example. When possible, use the async pipe.

Changing data

There are two types of data changes that can happen:

- **Destructive update**: We override what is there
- **Non-destructive update**: We merge the incoming data with what is already there

The method used for the destructive update is called set() and is used in the following way:

```
this.angularFireDatabase.object('/book').set({ title : 'Moby Dick' })
```

Given that our previous data was the following:

```
{
    title: 'The grapes of wrath',
    description: 'bla bla'
}
```

It has now become:

```
{
    title: 'Moby Dick'
}
```

This is exactly what we mean by a destructive update: we get the title property overridden, but we also lose the description property as the entire object is being replaced.

If the destruction of the data was not what you had in mind, then there is a softer update you can use, which is the `update()` method. Using it is as easy as writing the following:

```
this.angularFireDatabase.object('/book').update({ publishingYear : 1931 })
```

Given that the data looked like the following before the `update()` operation:

```
{
    title: 'Grapes of wrath',
    description: 'Tom Joad and his family are forced from the farm'
}
```

It now looks like this:

```
{
    title : 'Grapes of wrath',
    description : 'Tom Joad and his family are forced from the farm...',
    publishingYear : 1931
}
```

Remember to select the appropriate update operation depending on your intention as it makes a difference.

Removing data

Removing data is simple. We need to split this up into two different parts, as they differ a bit, to remove for an object and to remove an item in a list.

There are different ways of subscribing to data in Firebase. You can either subscribe to changes, using a method called `valueChanges()`. This will give you the data you want to display. As long as you want to display data, then you are fine using this method. However, when you start to want to change specific data like removing an item in a list or in short, when you need to know the exact key value of the resource you are trying to manipulate, then you need a new function. This function is called `snapshotChanges()`. Using said function gives you a more raw version of the resource you want. In this case, you need to dig out the value that you want to display.

Let's start with the first case, that of removing an object.

Removing an object

Let's look at two different `remove()` scenarios. In the first scenario, we want to remove what our path is pointing to. Imagine we are looking at the path/book. Then, our remove code for this is very simple:

```
this.angularFireDatabase.list('/books').remove();
```

Removing an item in a list

A list in Firebase looks something like this when looking at the database from the Firebase console:

```
books {
  0 : 'tomato',
  1: 'cucumber'
}
```

Of course, there is an internal representation of each item that points to a key with a hash value. We have the following scenario; we want to delete the first item in the list. We write some code that looks like this:

```
this.angularFireDatabase.list('/books').remove(<key>)
```

It's now that we discover that we don't know what the key is for the item we want to remove. This is where we start using the method `snapshotChanges()` and try to find this out:

```
this.angularFireDatabase
  .list('/books')
  .snapshotChanges()
  .subscribe( list => {
    console.log('list',list);
  })
```

The list parameter is a list, but the list items is a complicated object that contains the key we need as well as the value that we mean to display in the UI. We realise that this is the way to go and decide on using a `map()` function on our stream to transform the it into a list of books.

First off, we amend our `book.model.ts` file to contain a key property, like so:

```
export class Book {
  title: string;
  key: string;
  constructor(json) {
    this.title = json.payload.val();
    this.key = json.key;
  }
}
```

We can see that we needed to change how we access data; our data was to be found under the `payload.val()` and our `key` was easy to retrieve. With this knowledge, we can now build a list :

```
@Component({})
export class BookComponent {
  books$:Observable<Book[]>

  constructor(private angularFireDatabase:AngularFireDatabase){
    this.books$ = this.angularFireDatabase
      .list('/books')
      .snapshotChanges()
      .map(this.mapBooks);
  }

  private mapBooks(data): Book[] {
    return data.map(json => new Book(json));
  }

  remove(key) {
    this,books$.remove(key);
  }
```

In the following code snippet, we loop all the books in the list and create a remove button for each book in the list. We also wire up each remove button to point to the `book.key`, that is, our `key`, which is what we need when communicating a remove action to Firebase:

```
<div *ngFor="let book of books | async">
  {{ book.title }}
  <button (click)="remove(book.key)">Remove</button>
</div>
```

Responding to change

Firebase's cloud database is not just a database that looks like JSON, it also pushes out the data when it changes. You can listen for when that happens. This gives you not only cloud storage, but also the opportunity to build applications in a more collaborative and real-time manner. A lot of systems out there work like this already, such as most ticketing systems, chat applications, and so on.

Imagine a system built with Firebase that, for example, books movie tickets. You would be able to see when a person books a ticket, or an incoming message in a chat system, without polling logic or refreshing the app; it would be almost child's play to build.

AngularFire2, the Angular framework on top of Firebase, uses Observables. Observables convey changes when they happen. From before, we know that we can listen to such changes by giving a subscribe method a callback, like so:

```
this.angularFireDatabase
  .list('/tickets')
  .valueChanges()
  .subscribe(tickets => {
   // this is our new ticket list
  });
```

What you can do as a developer is intercept when such a change happens, by signing up to the subscribe() method, and for example, show a CSS animation to draw the user's attention to the change, so they can respond accordingly.

Adding authentication

We can't really build an application and call it ready for release unless we at least have some proper authentication. Essentially, we can't trust just anyone with our data, only authenticated users. In Firebase, you can set authentication on the highest level for your database. Click on the **Database** menu option tab in your admin tool and then select the tab rules. That should showcase the following:

```
{
  "rules": {
    ".read": "auth != null",
    ".write": "auth != null"
  }
}
```

Let's highlight the following row:

```
".read": "auth != null"
```

In this case, this sets up the read permission for your entire database and we give it the value `auth != null`. This means that you need to be authenticated to have any kind of read access to the database. You can see in the following row we have the same value, but this time for a rule called `.write`, which governs the writing access.

This is a good default permission to have. Of course, when testing the database out, you might want to have the value `auth == null` to shut off authentication, but remember to set the value back to `auth != null`, or you will leave your database wide open.

Setting up any kind of authentication means we need to perform some steps, namely:

- Ensuring the rules are on, that is, `auth != null`
- Enabling a security method
- Adding a user or token (if it is OAuth)
- Using the `AuthService` in the application to programmatically log on the user

Simple authentication with email/password

Let's set up a simple user/password authentication. Click on the **Authentication** menu option and select the **Sign-in** method tab. Then, enable the email/password option. It should look like this:

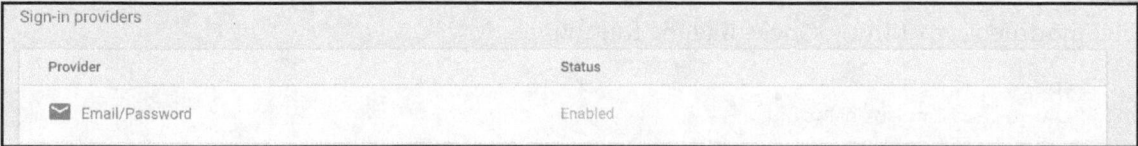

At this point, we need to add a user, a user that is allowed to access our data. So, let's set up the user. We go to the **Users** tab instead and click **ADD USER** button. It should look something like this:

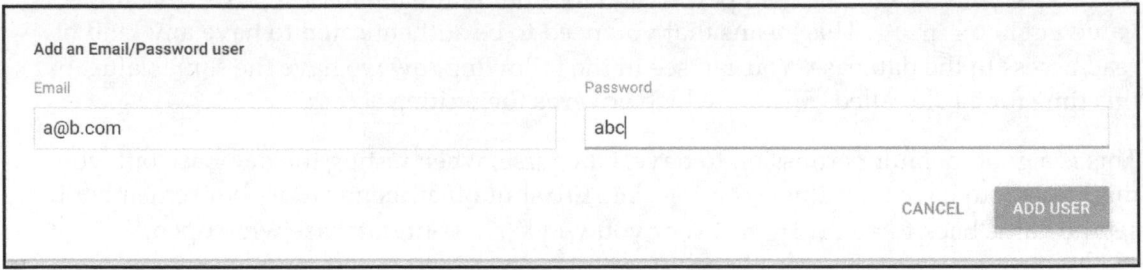

Okay, so now we have a user with an email a@b.com and password abc123. We still need to log in such a user for the database to show us the data. If we don't log in, our application will look very empty and devoid of any data. We will also get a lot of errors on the console log saying that we lack permission to look at the data.

In the previous setup of Firebase, we had only set up the database itself, not the authentication part. As Firebase is an Angular module, there are some rules we need to follow:

- Import the module and add it to the import keyword of the @NgModule
- Put the AngularFireAuth service in the providers keyword in @NgModule, so a component is able to inject it into its constructor
- Perform a programmatic login

The module side of things looks like the following:

```
import {
  AngularFireAuthModule,
  AngularFireAuth
} from 'angularfire2/auth';

@NgModule({
  imports: [
    AngularFireAuthModule
  ],
  providers: [AngularFireAuth]
})
```

Now, we are ready to inject the service into the component and perform the login:

```
import { AngularFireDatabase } from 'angularfire2/database';
import { AngularFireAuth } from 'anguarfire2/auth';

@Component({
  template : `
    <div *ngFor="let b of books$ | async">
      {{ b.title }} {{ b.author }}
    </div>
    <div *ngIf="book$ | async; let book">
      {{ book.title }} {{ book.author }}
    </div>
  `
})
export class BookComponent {
  user;
  book$: Observable<Book>;
  books$: Observable<Book[]>;

  constructor(
    private authService: AngularFireAuth,
    private angularFireDatabase: AngularFireDatabase
  ) {
    this.user = this.authService.authState;
    this.authService.auth
      .signInWithEmailAndPassword('a@b.com','abc123')
      .then(success => {
        this.book =
        this.angularFireDatabase
          .object('/book')
          .valueChanges().map(this.mapBook);

        this.books =
        this.angularFireDatabase
          .list('/books')
          .valueChanges()
          .map(this.mapBooks);
      },
      err => console.log(err)
    );
  }
}
```

Here, we do two interesting things.

First off, we assign the `authState` of the `authService` to a user. This is an Observable that, once logged in, will contain your user. We have now learned that we can show Observables with the async pipe. However, we are interested in getting two things from this user, `uid` and `email`, so we can see we are logged in as the correct user. It is tempting to write template code that looks like this:

```
<div *ngIf="user | async; let user">
  User : {{ user.uid }} {{ user.email }}
</div>
```

This creates the variable user for us that we can refer to instead. As expected, this prints out the user for us once logged in.

Now, to the second piece of our preceding code, the login call:

```
authService
.auth
.signInWithEmailAndPassword('a@b.com','abc123')
.then(success => {
  this.book = this.angularFireDatabase.object('/book')
    .map(this.mapBook);
    this.books$ = this.angularFireDatabase.list('/books')
    .map(this.mapBooks);
  },
  err => console.log(err)
)
```

Here, we talk to the `auth` property on the `authService` and we call the `signInWithEmailAndPassword(email, password)` method. We pass it the credentials. The method returns a promise and, on resolving that promise, we set our properties' book and books. If we don't do it this way and first authenticate, we will get a lot of `access not allowed` errors.

There are a ton more `signInWith...` methods, as shown here:

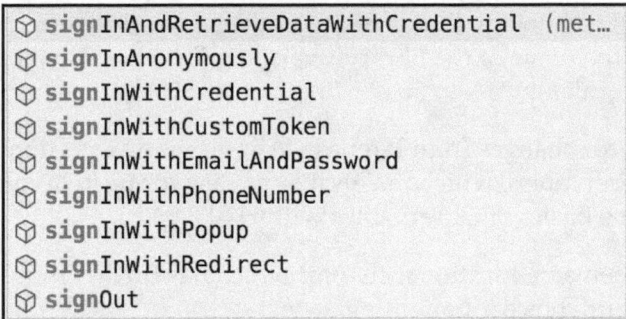

We urge you to try them out for yourself.

As for ways of authenticating, we have just scratched the surface. The following is the full range of login methods:

Try them out and see what works for you and your app.

Summary

Firebase is a powerful technology that is essentially a backend in the cloud; it has a reactive API. AngularFire2 is the name of the library wrapping Firebase. The library is especially made for use with Angular.

It is possible to listen for changes from Firebase. AngularFire2 communicates those changes through RxJS and Observables, which makes it very easy for us to involve Firebase in our apps once we grow the basics of Observables with HTTP.

Hopefully, this has been an educational chapter which has further motivated you to use RxJS in Angular as your choice for anything async.

This chapter has been about the standalone product Firebase. The point was to show that there is a very powerful piece of technology at your fingertips that expands on your newfound knowledge of RxJS.

In the next chapter, we will cover a very important aspect of building Angular applications, namely routing. Routing is a central concept that allows us to divide our application into several logical pages. We talk about logical pages instead of actual pages as we are building an SPA, which is a single page application. What is the difference, you ask? The routing component, which you will read more about in the next chapter, will help you to define components that can be routed to, as well as helping you to define viewports in your application that can be switched out. Think of your application as a passepartout or a frame. Inside the frame of your application, you can define things such as a top menu or left menu, but the painting in the middle is the part of your application that can be switched out. We call that replaceable part a page.

9
Routing

In the previous chapters, we did a great job separating concerns in our applications and adding different layers of abstraction to increase the maintainability of the app. However, we have neglected the visual side of things, as well as the user experience part.

At this moment, our UI is bloated with components and stuff scattered across a single screen, and we need to provide a better navigational experience and a logical way to change the application's state intuitively.

This is the moment where routing acquires special relevance and gives us the opportunity to build a navigational narrative for our applications, allowing us to split the different areas of interest into different pages that are interconnected by a grid of links and URLs.

However, our application is only a set of components, so how do we deploy a navigation scheme between them? The Angular router was built with componentization in mind. We will see how can we create our custom links and make components react to them in the following pages.

In this chapter, we will:

- Discover how to define routes to switch components on and off, and redirect them to other routes
- Trigger routes and load components in our views, depending on the requested route
- Handle and pass different types of parameters
- Dive into more advanced routing
- Look at different ways of securing our routes
- Uncover how to improve the response time by looking at different async strategies

Adding support for the Angular router

Having routing in your application means you want to navigate between different topics in your navigation. You usually use a top menu or left menu and press on links to get where you want. This causes the URL in the browser to change. In a **Single-Page Application** (**SPA**), this doesn't cause a page reload. To get set up with the Angular router is quite easy, but there are some things we need in place for it to be considered set up:

- Specify a base element in `index.html`
- Import the `RouterModule` and tell the root module about it
- Set up a routing dictionary
- Decide on where to place the viewport of your application, that is, decide where in the page your content should be placed
- Interact with a routing service if you want to investigate things such as routing or query parameters, or if you need to programmatically route the user to another page in your application

Specifying the base element

We need to inform Angular about the base path we want to use, so it can properly build and recognize the URLs as the user browses the website, as we will see in the next section. Our first task will be to insert a base `href` statement within our `<HEAD>` element. Append the following line of code at the end of your code statement inside the `<head>` tag:

```
//index.html

<base href="/">
```

The base tag informs the browser about the path it should follow while attempting to load external resources, such as media or CSS files, once it goes deeper into the URL hierarchy.

Importing and setting up the router module

Now, we can start playing around with all the goodies existing in the router library. First things first, we need to import the `RouterModule`, we do this in the root module of our application. So, we open a file called `app.module.ts` and insert the following line at the top of the file:

```
import { RouterModule } from '@angular/router';
```

Once we have done so, it's time to add the `RouterModule` as a dependency of the `AppModule` class.

`RouterModule` is a little bit of a different module, though; it needs to be initialized at the same time as it is added as a dependant module. It looks like the following:

```
@NgModule({
  imports: [RouterModule.forRoot(routes, <optional config>)]
})
```

We can see here that it points to variable routes that we have yet to define.

Defining the routes

The `routes` is a list of route entries that specifies what routes exist in the application and what components should respond to a specific route. It can look like this:

```
let routes = [{
  path: 'products',
  component: ProductsComponent
}, {
  path: '**',
  component: PageNotFound
}]
```

Every item in the route list is an object with a number of properties. The two most important properties are `path` and `component`. The path property is the routing path, note that you should specify the path value without a leading `/`. So, setting it to `products`, as with the preceding code, means that we define what would happen if the user navigates to `/products`. The `component` property points to the component that should respond to this route. The pointed-out components, template and data is what the user will see when navigating to the route.

The first specified route defines the path /products, and the last route item specifies **, which means it matches any path. Order matters. Had we defined the route item ** first, then products would never have been hit. The reason ** was defined last was that we wanted a route that would take care of the case when a user enters an unknown route. Rather than showing the user a blank page, we can now show them a nice page defined by the PageNotFound components template.

There are a ton more properties you can define on a route item, and also more complex routes you can set up. This will suffice for now, so we gain a basic understanding of routing setup.

Defining a viewport

Once we have come this far, it's time to define a viewport where the routed content should be rendered. Normally, we would build an application where part of the content is static and part of it can be switched out, like so:

```
//app.component.html

<body>
  <!- header content ->
  <!- router content ->
  <!- footer content ->
</body>
```

At this point, we involve the router-outlet element. It is an element that tells the router that this is where you should render the content. Update your app.component.html to look like this:

```
<body>
  <!- header content ->
  <router-outlet> </router-outlet>
  <!- footer content ->
</body>
```

Now we have the router module imported and initialized. We also have a router list defined for two routes, and we have defined where the routed content should be rendered. This is all we need for a minimal setup of the router. In the next section, we will look at a more realistic example and further expand our knowledge of the routing module and what it can help us with.

Building a practical example – setting up the router service

Let's describe the problem domain. Through the course of this book, we have been dealing with `Tasks` within the context of Pomodoro sessions. So far we have been creating all the components and other constructs that we needed in one big visual pile. It's a visual pile in the sense that everything has been visible in one page. A more natural approach to this is to imagine that we have dedicated views that we navigate between. Here are the options from a user standpoint:

- The user reaches our app and checks the current listing of the pending tasks. The user can schedule the tasks to be done in order to get the required time estimation for the next Pomodoro session.
- If desired, the user can jump onto another page and see a create task form (we will create the form, but will not implement its editing features until the next chapter).
- The user can choose any task at any time and begin the Pomodoro session required to accomplish it.
- The user can move back and forth across the pages they have already visited.

Let's take the preceding user interactions and translate what this means in terms of different views that we should support:

- There needs to be a page listing all the tasks
- There should be a page with a create task form
- Lastly, there should be a way to navigate back and forth between the pages

Building a new component for demonstration purposes

So far, we have built two well-differentiated components we can leverage to deliver a multi-page navigation. But in order to provide a better user experience, we might need a third one. We will now introduce the form component we will be exploring more thoroughly in `Chapter 10`, *Forms in Angular*, as a way to have more navigation options in our example.

We will create a component in our tasks feature folder, anticipating the form we will use in the next chapter to publish new tasks. Create the following files in the locations pointed out for each one:

```
// app/tasks/task-editor.component.ts file

import { Component } from '@angular/core';

@Component({
  selector: 'tasks-editor',
  templateUrl: 'app/tasks/task-editor.component.html'
})
export default class TaskEditorComponent {
  constructor() {}
}

// app/tasks/task-editor.component.html file

<form class="container">
  <h3>Task Editor:</h3>
  <div class="form-group">
    <input type="text"
           class="form-control"
           placeholder="Task name"
           required>
  </div>
  <div class="form-group">
    <input type="Date"
           class="form-control"
           required>
  </div>
  <div class="form-group">
    <input type="number"
           class="form-control"
           placeholder="Points required"
           min="1"
           max="4"
           required>
  </div>
  <div class="form-group">
    <input type="checkbox" name="queued">
    <label for="queued"> this task by default?</label>
  </div>
  <p>
    <input type="submit" class="btn btn-success" value="Save">
    <a href="/" class="btn btn-danger">Cancel</a>
  </p>
</form>
```

This is the most basic definition of a component. We need to expose this new component from our feature module. Finally, we need to enter the route item for this component in a route list and configure the routes. Add the following code snippet in the `app/tasks/task.module.ts` file:

```
import { TasksComponent } from './tasks.component';
import { TaskEditorComponent } from './task.editor.component';
import { TaskTooltipDirective } from './task.tooltip.directive';

@NgModule({
  declarations: [
    TasksComponent,
    TaskEditorComponent,
    TaskTooltipDirective
  ],
  exports: [
    TasksComponent,
    TaskEditorComponent,
    TaskTooltipDirective
  ]
})
export class TaskModule{}
```

Now the time has come to configure the routes. We do this in two steps:

- Creating the `routes.ts`, a module that contains our routes
- Setting up the routes in the root module

The first order of business is defining the routes:

```
// app/routes.ts file

[{
    path: '',
    component : HomeComponent
},{
  path: 'tasks',
  name: 'TasksComponent',
  component: TasksComponent
}, {
  path: 'tasks/editor',
  name: 'TaskEditorComponent',
  component: TaskEditorComponent
}, {
  path: 'timer',
  name: 'TimerComponent',
  component: TimerComponent
```

```
    }
  ]
```

The second order of business is initializing the routes. We do this in the root module. To initialize the routes, we need to call `RouteModule` and its static method, `forRoot`, and provide it with the routes list as an argument:

```
// app/app.module.ts file

import { RouterModule } from '@angular/router';
import routes from './routes';

@NgModule({
  ...
  imports: [RouterModule.forRoot(routes)]
  ...
})
```

Cleaning up the routes

At this point, we have set up the routes so they work the way they should. However, this approach doesn't scale so well. As your application grows, more and more routes will be added to the `routes.ts` file. Just like we moved the components and other constructs into their respective feature directory, so should we move the routes to where they belong. Our routing list so far consists of one route item belonging to the timer feature, two items to the task feature, and one route that points to the default route `/`.

Our cleanup work will consist of:

- Creating one dedicated `routes.ts` file per feature directory
- Calling `RouteModule.forChild` in each feature module that has routes
- Removing routes from any root module that isn't strictly application-wide, for example `** = route not found`

This means that the application structure now looks something like the following:

```
/timer
  timer.module.ts
  timer.component.ts
  routes.ts
/app
  app.module.ts
  app.component.ts
  routes.ts
```

```
/task
  task.module.ts
  task.component.ts
  routes.ts
  ...
```

After the creation of a few more files, we are ready to initialize our feature routes. Essentially, the initialization is the same for both `/timer/routes.ts` as `/task/routes.ts`. For that reason, let's look at one of the `routes.ts` files and the intended change:

```
import routes from './routes';

@NgModule({
  imports: [
    RouteModule.forChild(routes)
  ]
})
export class FeatureModule {}
```

The point here is that moving routes from `app/routes.ts` to `<feature>/routes.ts` means we set up the routes in their respective module file instead, namely `<feature>/<feature>.module.ts`. Also, we call `RouteModule.forChild`, and not `RouteModule.forRoot`, when setting up feature routes.

The router directives – RouterOutlet, RouterLink, and RouterLinkActive

We already mentioned in the *Adding support for the Angular router* section, that to set up a router there were some essential basic steps to make routing work. Let's remind ourselves of what they were:

- Define a routes list
- Initialize the `Route` module
- Add a viewport

For the intents and purposes of this practical example, we have done the top two items, what remains is to add the viewport. A directive handles the viewport for Angular; it is called the `RouterOutlet` and just needs to be placed in the template for the component that sets up routing. So essentially, by opening up `app.component.html` and adding `<router-outlet></router-outlet>`, we sort out the last bullet item on our list.

There is a lot more to routing, of course. One interesting thing, which is expected of every router, is the ability to generate clickable links given a defined route. The `routerLink` directive handles that for us and is used in the following way:

```
<a routerLink="/" routerLinkActive="active">Home</a>
```

The `routerLink` points to the route path, note the leading slash. This will look up which route item is defined in our routes list that corresponds to the route path /. After some investigation in our code, we find a route item that looks like the following:

```
[{
  path : '',
  component : HomeComponent
}]
```

Take extra notice here that when defining the route; we should not have a leading slash, but when creating a link with said route item and using the `routerLink` directive, we should have a trailing slash.

This has produced the following element:

```
<a _ngcontent-c0="" routerlink="/" routerlinkactive="active" ng-reflect-
router-link="/" ng-reflect-router-link-active="active" href="/"
class="active">Home</a>
```

That looks interesting, the key take away is that `href` is set to / and the class has been set to active.

The last bit was interesting, why would the class be set to active? That's what the `routerLinkActive="active"` does for us. It investigates whether the current route we are on corresponds to the `routerLink` element we are currently on. If so, it gets awarded the active CSS class. Consider the following markup:

```
<a routerLink="/" routerLinkActive="active" >Home</a>
<a routerLink="/tasks"routerLinkActive="active" >Tasks</a>
<a routerLink="/timer"routerLinkActive="active" >Timer</a>
```

Only one of the elements will get the active class set. If the browser URL points to /tasks, it will be the second item, instead of the first. The fact that the active class is being added gives you, as developer, the opportunity to style the active menu element, because a menu is what we are creating by defining a list of links, such as the preceding code.

Triggering routes imperatively

There are more ways to navigate than to click on an element that has the `routerLink` directive on it. We can handle navigation in code or imperatively, as it is also called. To do so, we need to inject a navigation service that has the capacity to navigate.

Let's inject the navigation service, also called the `Router`, into a component:

```
@Component({
  template : `
    <Button (click)="goToTimer()">Go to timer</Button>
  `
})
export class Component {
  constructor(private router:Router) {}

  goToTimer() {
    this.router.navigate(['/timer']);
  }
}
```

As you can see, we set up a `goToTimer` method and associate that to the click event of the button. Inside of this method, we call `router.navigate()`, which takes an array. The first item in the array is our route; note the use of the trailing slash. That is how simple it can be to navigate imperatively.

Handling parameters

We have configured pretty basic paths in our routes so far, but what if we want to build dynamic paths with support for parameters or values created at runtime? Creating (and navigating to) URLs that load specific items from our data stores is a common action we need to address on a daily basis. For instance, we might need to provide a master-detail browsing functionality, so each generated URL living in the master page contains the identifiers required to load each item once the user reaches the detail page.

We are basically tackling a double trouble here: creating URLs with dynamic parameters at runtime, and parsing the value of such parameters. No problem; the Angular router has got our back and we will see how by using a real example.

Building detail pages – using route parameters

First, let's get back to the tasks list component template. We have a router that takes us to that list of tasks, but what if we wanted to a look at specific task, and what if we wanted that task on a specific page? We can easily solve that by doing the following:

1. Update the tasks component to add a navigation capability per item that lets us navigate to a task detail view.
2. Set up routing for one task, the URL path to it will be `tasks/:id`.
3. Create a `TaskDetail` component that shows just one task.

Let's start with the first bullet point: updating `tasks.component.ts`.

It should be said that we can solve this in two ways:

- Navigate imperatively
- Build a route using `routerLink` that adds a parameter to the route

Let's try to show how to navigate imperatively first:

```
// app/tasks/tasks.component.html file

@Component({
  selector: 'tasks',
  template: `
    <div*ngFor="let task of store | async">
      {{ task.name }}
      <button (click)="navigate(task)">Go to detail</button>
    </div>
  `
})
export class TasksComponent {
  constructor(private router: Router) {}

  navigate(task:Task) {
    this.router.navigate(['/tasks',task.id]);
  }
}
```

Let's highlight the following piece of code:

```
this.router.navigate(['/tasks',task.id]);
```

This produces a link that looks like `/tasks/13` or `/tasks/99`. In this case, `13` and `99` are just made-up numbers to show what the route path might look like.

The second way of navigating is to use the `routerLink` directive. To accomplish this, our preceding template will look slightly different:

```
<div*ngFor="let task of store | async">
  {{ task.name }}
  <a [routerLink]="['/tasks/',task.id]">Go to detail</a>
</div>
```

Both these ways work, just use the one that's best for you.

Now for the second item in the list, which is to set up routing, this will match the route path described previously. We open `task/routes.ts` and add the following entry to our list:

```
[
  ...
  {
    path : '/tasks/:id',
    component : TaskDetailComponent
  }
  ...
]
```

With this route in place, we have the last item in our list to fix, which is defining the `TaskDetailComponent`. Let's start with a simple version of it:

```
import { Component } from '@angular/core';

@Component({
  selector: 'task-detail',
  template: 'task detail'
})
export class TaskDetailComponent {
}
```

With all this in place, we are able to click a task in the list and navigate to a `TaskDetailComponent`. However, we are not satisfied here. The real reason for doing this was so we can do a more detailed lookup of a task. So, we are missing a data call from the `TaskDetail` component to our `TaskService`, where we ask for just one task. Remember how our route to `TaskDetail` was `/tasks/:id`? For us to make a correct call to our `TaskService`, we need to dig out the ID parameter from the route and use that as a parameter when calling our `TaskService`. If we route to `/tasks/13`, we need to call `TaskService` with a `getTask(13)` and expect one `Task` back.

So, we have two things to do:

1. Dig out the router parameter ID from the route.
2. Add a `getTask(taskId)` method to `TaskService`.

To succeed with the first mission, we can inject something called `ActivatedRoute` and talk to its `params` property, which is an Observable. The data coming from that Observable is an object where one of the properties is our route parameter:

```
this.route
  .params
  .subscribe( params => {
    let id = params['id'];
  });
```

Okay, so this only solves half the problem. We are able to dig out the value of our ID parameter this way, but we don't do anything with it. We should be performing a data fetch as well.

If we add a `switchMap` statement, then we can get hold of the data, carry out a data call, and return the result of the data instead, like so:

```
@Component({
  template: `
    <div *ngIf="(task$ | async) as task">
      {{ task.name }}
    </div>
  `
})
export class TaskDetailComponent implements OnInit {
  task$:Observable<Task>;

  constructor(private route:ActivatedRoute) {}

  ngOnInit() {
    this.task$ = this.route
      .params
      .switchMap( params =>
        this.taskService.getTask(+params['id'])
      )
  }
}
```

The last step is to add the `getTask` method to the `TaskService`:

```
export class TaskService{
  ...
  getTask(id): Observable<Task> {
    return this.http.get(`/tasks/${id}`).map(mapTask);
  }
}
```

Filtering your data – using query parameters

So far we have been dealing with routing parameters on the format of `tasks/:id`. Links formed like that tell us that the context is tasks and to get to one particular task, we need to specify which one, by specifying its number. It's about narrowing down to the specific data we are interested in. Query parameters have a different job, they aim to either sort your data or narrow down the size of your data set:

```
// for sorting
/tasks/114?sortOrder=ascending

// for narrowing down the data set
/tasks/114?page=3&pageSize=10
```

Query parameters are recognized as everything happening after the ? character and are separated by an and (&) sign. To get to those values, we can work with the `ActivatedRoute`, just like we did with routing parameters but we look at a different collection on the `ActivatedRouter` instance:

```
constructor(private route: ActivatedRoute) {}

getData(){
  this.route.queryParamMap
  .switchMap( data => {
    let pageSize = data.get('pageSize');
    let page = data.get('page');
    return this._service.getTaskLimited(pageSize,page);
  })
```

Advanced features

So far we have covered basic routing, with route parameter as well as query parameters. The Angular router is quite capable though, and able to do much more, such as :

- Defining child routes, every component can have their own viewport
- Relative navigation
- Named outlets, the possibility to have different viewports in the same template
- Debugging, you can easily enable debugging to showcase how the routing works based on your routing list

Child routes

What is a child route? A child route is a concept where we say that a route has children. We could write the routes for a feature like this:

```
{
  path : 'products',
  component : ProductListComponent
},
{
  path : 'products/:id',
  component : ProductsDetail
},
{
  path : 'products/:id/orders',
  component : ProductsDetailOrders
}
```

What happens, though, if we want to have a products container component and in that component, we would like to have a product list or a product detail showing? For that case, we want to group our routes differently. We have clearly said that the Product container is the parent component that you should route to. So, it would be the first responder when going to the route /products. Let's start by setting up the products route. It should listen to /products URL and have the ProductsContainerComponent responding, like so:

```
{
  path: 'products',
  component : ProductsContainerComponent
}
```

Our other routes can be added as its children, like so:

```
{
  path: 'products',
  component : ProductsContainerComponent,
  children : [{
    path : '',
    component : ProductListComponent
  }, {
    path: ':id',
    component : ProductDetailComponent
  }, {
    path : ':id/orders',
    component : ProductsDetailOrders
  }]
}
```

Now, this might make more sense from an organizational viewpoint but there is a bit of a technical difference; the `ProductsContainer` will need to have its own `router-outlet` for this to work. So, a quick overview of our app so far would look like this:

```
/app . // contains router-outlet
  /products
    ProductsContainerComponent // contains router outlet
    ProductListComponent
    ProductDetailComponent
    ProductsDetailOrders
```

The main driver for doing it this way is so that we can create a container to give that some header or footer information and render replaceable content, much like we can do with the template for the app component:

```
// ProductsContainerComponent template
<!-- header -->
<router-outlet></router-outlet>
<!-- footer -->
```

In summary the benefits to a container approach is the following:

- Creating child routes means we can treat a feature landing page like a page view or a viewport, thereby we can define things such as a header, a footer, and a part of the page as a piece of content that can be replaced
- We need to write less when defining the route path, the parent's route is already assumed

Absolute versus relative navigation

There are two ways to navigate: either we use absolute routes or relative routes. An absolute route is specifying its route all the way from the route root, such as `/products/2/orders`, whereas a relative route is aware of its context. A relative route might therefore look like `/orders`, given that it is aware of it already being at `/products/2`, so the full route would read as `/products/2/orders`.

You might be fine using only absolute paths; there is an upside to using relative paths, though: it gets easier to refactor. Imagine moving a bunch of components around, and suddenly all your hardcoded paths points are wrong. You might argue that you should have created a typed version of the route, such as `routes.ProductList`, so that you only have to change in one place anyway. That might be so, and then you are in a good place. If, however, you don't employ those ways of working, relative routes are for you. So, let's have a look at an example usage:

```
this.router.navigate(['../'], { relativeTo: this.route });
```

Here, we are going one level up. Imagine we are on `/products`. This would take us back to `/`. The important part here is to include the second parameter and specify the `relativeTo: this.route` bit.

Named outlets

We can have more that one outlet directive in a component template, if you just keep adding them, like so:

```
<router-outlet></router-outlet>
<router-outlet></router-outlet>
<router-outlet></router-outlet>
<router-outlet></router-outlet>
```

We will have the content rendered out four times. That's not really why we add multiple outlets. We add more than one `router-outlet` so we can put different names on it. What is the business case for doing that, though? Imagine we wanted to show a header portion and a body portion; depending on what router portion we are on, these would differ. It can look like the following:

```
<router-outlet name="header"></router-outlet>
<router-outlet name="body"></router-outlet>
```

Now, we are able to target a specific `router-outlet` when routing. So how do we:

- Define a route that should target a specific named outlet?
- Navigate to a named outlet?
- Clear a named outlet?

The following code shows how we set up the route:

```
{ path: 'tasks',
  component: JedisShellComponent,
  children : [{
    path: '',
    component : JediHeaderComponent,
    outlet : 'header'
  },
  {
    path: '',
    component : JediComponent,
    outlet : 'body'
  }]
}
```

The preceding code shows how we set up a shell page, it's called a shell as it acts like a shell for named outlets. That means our shell component looks like this:

```
static data
<router-outlet name="header"></router-outlet>
<router-outlet name="body"></router-outlet>
some static data after the outlet
```

We also set up two child routes pointing to one named outlet each. The idea is that when we route to /tasks, the `TaskHeaderComponent` will be rendered to the header outlet and the `TaskComponent` will be rendered to the body outlet.

There is an entirely different way of using routes, namely as pop-up outlets. This means we can render content to an outlet and also take it away. To accomplish this, we need to set up the route like this:

```
{
  path : 'info',
  component : PopupComponent,
  outlet : 'popup'
}
```

This needs to go along with a named outlet being defined, like so:

```
<router-outlet name="popup"></router-outlet>
```

Starting off by surfing to a page, this `PopupComponent` will not be visible, but we can make it visible by setting up a method wherein we navigate to it, like so:

```
@Component({
  template : `
    <button (click)="openPopup()"></button>
  `
})
export class SomeComponent {
  constructor(private router: Router) {}

  openPopup(){ this.router.navigate([{ outlets: { popup : 'info' }}]) }
}
```

The interesting part here is the argument to `router.navigate` being `{ outlets : { <name-of-named-outlet> : <name-of-route> } }`.

With this kind of syntax, it becomes apparent that we can render anything in there as long as the route is correctly set up. So, let's say the routing looked like this instead:

```
{
  path : 'info',
  component : PopupComponent,
  outlet : 'popup'
},
{
  path : 'error',
  component : ErrorComponent,
  outlet : 'popup'
}
```

Now, we have two candidates that could possibly be rendered at the `popup` outlet. To render the error component, simply write the following instead:

```
this.router.navigate([{ outlets: { popup : 'error' }])
```

There is one final thing we need to cover, and that is how to remove the content of the named outlet. To do so, we amend the following to our component:

```
@Component({
  template : `
    <button (click)="openPopup()"></button>
  `
})
export class SomeComponent {
  constructor(private router: Router) {}
```

```
openPopup(){ this.router.navigate([{ outlets: { popup : 'info'} }]) }

closePopup() { this.router.navigate([{ outlets: { popup: null }}]) }
}
```

We added the `closePopup()` method, and what we do inside of there is target our named `popup` outlet and provide it with a null argument, like so:

```
this.router.navigate([ outlets: { popup: null } ])
```

Debugging

Why do we want to debug the router? Well, sometimes the route doesn't do what we think it should do; when that is the case, it is good to know more about how the routing acts and why. To enable debugging, you need to provide a configuration object that enables debugging, like so:

```
RouterModule.forRoot(routes,{ enableTracing: true })
```

Attempting to route to, say, /products from our start page will look like this:

```
▼ Router Event: NavigationStart
  NavigationStart(id: 2, url: '/products')
  ▶ NavigationStart {id: 2, url: "/products"}
▼ Router Event: RoutesRecognized
  RoutesRecognized(id: 2, url: '/products', urlAfterRedirects: '/products', state: Route(url:'', path:'') { Route(url:'products',
  path:'products') { Route(url:'', path:''), Route(url:'', path:'') } } )
  ▶ RoutesRecognized {id: 2, url: "/products", urlAfterRedirects: "/products", state: RouterStateSnapshot}
▼ Router Event: GuardsCheckStart
  GuardsCheckStart(id: 2, url: '/products', urlAfterRedirects: '/products', state: Route(url:'', path:'') { Route(url:'products',
  path:'products') { Route(url:'', path:''), Route(url:'', path:'') } } )
  ▶ GuardsCheckStart {id: 2, url: "/products", urlAfterRedirects: UrlTree, state: RouterStateSnapshot}
▼ Router Event: GuardsCheckEnd
  GuardsCheckEnd(id: 2, url: '/products', urlAfterRedirects: '/products', state: Route(url:'', path:'') { Route(url:'products',
  path:'products') { Route(url:'', path:''), Route(url:'', path:'') } } , shouldActivate: true)
  ▶ GuardsCheckEnd {id: 2, url: "/products", urlAfterRedirects: UrlTree, state: RouterStateSnapshot, shouldActivate: true}
▼ Router Event: ResolveStart
  ResolveStart(id: 2, url: '/products', urlAfterRedirects: '/products', state: Route(url:'', path:'') { Route(url:'products',
  path:'products') { Route(url:'', path:''), Route(url:'', path:'') } } )
  ▶ ResolveStart {id: 2, url: "/products", urlAfterRedirects: UrlTree, state: RouterStateSnapshot}
▼ Router Event: ResolveEnd
  ResolveEnd(id: 2, url: '/products', urlAfterRedirects: '/products', state: Route(url:'', path:'') { Route(url:'products',
  path:'products') { Route(url:'', path:''), Route(url:'', path:'') } } )
  ▶ ResolveEnd {id: 2, url: "/products", urlAfterRedirects: UrlTree, state: RouterStateSnapshot}
▼ Router Event: NavigationEnd
  NavigationEnd(id: 2, url: '/products', urlAfterRedirects: '/products')
  ▶ NavigationEnd {id: 2, url: "/products", urlAfterRedirects: "/products"}
>
```

What we can see here is that several events are triggered:

- `NavigationStart`: When the navigation starts
- `RoutesRecognized`: Parsing of the URL and recognizing the URL
- `RouteConfigLoadStart`: Triggered when reading a lazy load configuration
- `RouteConfigLoadEnd`: After the route has been lazy loaded
- `GuardsCheckStart`: Evaluating the router guard, that is, can we go to this route
- `GuardsCheckEnd`: Router guard check done
- `ResolveStart`: Attempting to fetch data that we need before routing to a path
- `ResolveEnd`: Done resolving the data it was relying on
- `NavigationCancel`: Someone or something canceled the routing
- `NavigationEnd`: Done routing

There are a lot of events that can happen. As you can see from the preceding image, our bullet list covers more events than the image showed. This is due to us not having any modules that are lazy loaded, so those events aren't triggered, and also that we haven't set up any resolve guards, for example. Also, `NavigationCancel` doesn't occur unless the routing fails for some reason. It's important what events are triggered and when, so that you know what part of the code might be wrong. We will look closely at the events, `GuardsCheckStart` and `GuardsCheckEnd`, in our next section on determining whether you are authorized to visit a specific route.

Fine-tuning our generated URLs with location strategies

As you have seen, whenever the browser navigates to a path by command of a `routerLink` or as a result of the execution of the navigate method of the `Router` object, the URL showing up in the browser's location bar conforms to the standardized URLs we are used to seeing, but it is in fact a local URL. No call to the server is ever made. The fact that the URL shows off a natural structure is because of the `pushState` method of the HTML5 history API that is executed under the folds, and allows the navigation to add and modify the browser history in a transparent fashion.

There are two main providers, both inherited from the `LocationStrategy` type, for representing and parsing state from the browser's URL:

- `PathLocationStrategy`: This is the strategy used by default by the location service, honoring the HTML5 `pushState` mode, yielding clean URLs with no hash-banged fragments (`example.com/foo/bar/baz`).
- `HashLocationStrategy`: This strategy makes use of hash fragments to represent state in the browser URL (`example.com/#foo/bar/baz`).

Regardless of the strategy chosen by default by the `Location` service, you can fall back to the old hashbang-based navigation by picking the `HashLocationStrategy` as the `LocationStrategy` type of choice.

In order to do so, go to `app.module.ts` and tell the router, from now on, any time the injector requires binding to the `LocationStrategy` type for representing or parsing state (which internally picks `PathLocationStrategy`), it should use not the default type, but use `HashLocationStrategy` instead.

You just need to provide a second argument in the `RouterModule.forRoot()` method and make sure the `useHash` is set to `true`:

```
....
@NgModule({
  imports : [
    RouterModule.forRoot(routes, { useHash : true })
  ]
})
```

Securing the routes with AuthGuard and CanActivate hook

We can use `CanActivate` in two ways:

- Restricting access to data you need to be logged in for
- Restricting access to data you need to have the correct role for

So essentially, it is about potentially both authentication and authorization. What we need to do to make this happen is:

- Create a service that needs to evaluate whether you have permission
- Add said service to the route definition

This is just any service you create, but it needs to implement the `CanActivate` interface. So, let's create it:

```
@Injectable()
export class AuthGuard implements CanActivate {
  constructor(private authService: AuthService) { }

  canActivate() {
    return this.authService.isAuthenticated();
  }
}
```

What we have done is implement the `CanActivate` interface by declaring the `canActivate()` method. We also injected an `AuthService` instance that we pretend exists. The point is that the `canActivate()` method should return `true` if navigation should continue and `false` if it should be stopped.

Now, on to the next step of adding this service to the routing config; we do that by adding to the list that the `canActivate` property holds:

```
{
  path : 'products',
  component: ProductsShell,
  canActivate: [ AuthGuard ]
}
```

Let's try this out and see how our route debug changes if we return `true` from the `canActivate()` method, or `false`:

```
Router Event: GuardsCheckEnd
  GuardsCheckEnd(id: 1, url: '/products', urlAfterRedirects: '/products', state: Route(url:'', path:'') { Route(url:'products',
  path:'products') { Route(url:'', path:''), Route(url:'', path:'') } } , shouldActivate: true)
  ▶ GuardsCheckEnd {id: 1, url: "/products", urlAfterRedirects: UrlTree, state: RouterStateSnapshot, shouldActivate: true}
```

In `GuardsCheckEnd` we see that the `shouldActivate : true` property is emitted. This is because our `canActivate` method currently returns `true`, that is, we allow the routing to happen.

Let's see what happens if we change `canActivate` to return `false`:

```
▼ Router Event: GuardsCheckEnd
    GuardsCheckEnd(id: 1, url: '/products', urlAfterRedirects: '/products', state: Route(url:'', path:'') { Route(url:'products',
    path:'products') { Route(url:'', path:''), Route(url:'', path:'') } } , shouldActivate: false)
    ▶ GuardsCheckEnd {id: 1, url: "/products", urlAfterRedirects: UrlTree, state: RouterStateSnapshot, shouldActivate: false}
▼ Router Event: NavigationCancel
    NavigationCancel(id: 1, url: '/products')
    ▶ NavigationCancel {id: 1, url: "/products", reason: ""}
>
```

Here, we can see that in the `GuardsCheckEnd` event the `shouldActivate` now has the value `false`. We can also see that the `NavigationCancel` event has been emitted. The end result is that we weren't allowed to change route based on the `canActivate()` method returning `false`. Now it is up to you to implement an authentication/authorization method and make it work for real.

Resolve<T> – fetching and resolving data before routing

The reason for using this hook is so we can delay the routing to happen after we have fetched all the necessary data. You should not have anything long-running happening though. A more real case is that you have navigated to a product route, such as `/products/114`, and want to look up in the database what that product is and provide that to the route.

You'll need the following to implement this:

- Implement the `Resolve<T>` interface
- Return a `Promise` from the `resolve()` method
- Set the service as a provider to the module
- Set the service in the resolve property of the route it is providing data to

Let's implement said service:

```
@Injectable()
export class ProductResolver implement Resolve<Product> {
  constructor(
    private http:Http,
    private service: DataService,
    private router:Router
```

```
  ) {}

  resolve(route: ActivatedRouteSnapshot) {
    let id = route.paramMap.get('id');
    return this.service.getProduct( id ).then( data => {
      if(data) {
        return data;
      }
      else {
        this.router.navigate(['/products']);
      }
    }, error => { this.router.navigate(['/errorPage']) });
  }
}


// product.service.ts
export class DataService {
  getProduct(id) {
    return http.get(`/products/${id}`)
    .map( r => r.json )
    .map(mapProduct)
    .toPromise()
  }
}
```

At this point, we have implemented the `Resolve<T>` interface and we also ensure that a `Promise` is returned from the `resolve()` method. We also have some logic saying we will redirect the user if the data we get back is not what we expect or if an error happens.

As a next step, we need to add the service to the `providers` keyword of our module:

```
@NgModule({
  ...
  providers: [ProductResolver]
  ...
})
```

For the last step, we need to add the service to the route:

```
{
  path: 'products/:id',
  resolve: [ProductResolver],
  component: ProductDetail
}
```

The CanDeactivate – handling cancel and save

Okay, so we have the following situation: the user is on a page, they have filled in a lot of data when they decide to press a navigation link that takes them away from the page. At this point, you, as a developer, want to establish the following:

- If the user has filled in all data, they should then continue with navigation
- If the user has not filled in all data, they should have the option of leaving the page anyway or remaining to complete the data entry

To support these scenarios, we need to do the following:

1. Create a service that implements the `CanDeactivate` interface.
2. Inject the target component into the service.
3. Set said service up as a provider to the module.
4. Set service as `canDeactivate` responder in the route.
5. Make the target component injectable and set it up as a provider to the module.
6. Write logic to handle the case that all fields are filled in – keep routing, if fields are missing show a confirm that lets the user decide whether to continue to route away or not.

Starting with the service, it should look like this:

```
@Injectable()
export class CanDeactivateService implements CanDeactivate {
  constructor(private component: ProductDetailComponent) {}

  canDeactivate(): boolean | Promise<boolean> {
    if( component.allFieldsAreFilledIn() ) {
      return true;
    }

    return this.showConfirm('Are you sure you want to navigate away,
                             you will loose data');
  }

  showConfirm() {
    return new Promise(resolve => resolve( confirm(message) ))
  }
}
```

Worth highlighting here is how we define the logic in the `canDeactivate` method to have a return type that is either `Boolean` or a `Promise<boolean>`. This gives us the freedom to short circuit the method early if all valid fields are filled in. If they are not, we show the user a confirm message that freezes on the confirm until the user has decided what to do.

The second step is telling the module about this service:

```
@NgModule({
  providers: [CanDeactivateService]
})
```

Now, to perform a change in the route:

```
{
  path : 'products/:id',
  component : ProductDetailComponent,
  canDeactivate : [ CanDeactivateService ]
}
```

For the next step, we are going to do something we don't usually do, namely, set up the component as an injectable; this is needed so it can be injected into the service:

```
@Component({})
@Injectable()
export class ProductDetailComponent {}
```

This means we need to add the component as a provider in the module:

```
@NgModule({
  providers: [
    CanDeactivateService, ProductDetailComponent
  ]
})
```

Async routing – improving response time

Eventually, your application will grow in size and the amount of data you put into it will also grow. The net result of this is that the application takes a long time to start initially, or certain parts of your application take a long time to start. There are ways around this, such as lazy loading and preloading.

Lazy loading

Lazy loading means we don't start with all of the application loaded initially. Parts of our application can be cordoned off into chunks that are only loaded when you ask for them. Today, this is centered around routes, this means that if you ask for a specific route you have not visited before, the module and all its constructs will be loaded. This is not something that is there by default but something you can quite easily set up.

Let's have a look at an existing module and its routes, and see how we can turn that into a lazy-loaded module. We will have to make changes in the following places :

- The routes list for our feature module
- Add a route entry in our application routes, with a specific lazy-load syntax
- Remove all references to the feature module in other modules

First, a quick look at our feature modules routing list, prior to the change:

```
// app/lazy/routes.ts
let routes = [{
  path : 'lazy',
  component : LazyComponent
}]

// app/lazy/lazy.module.ts
@NgModule({
  imports: [RouterModule.forChild(routes)]
})
export class LazyModule {}
```

Our first order of business is to change the path for the first route entry from lazy to ' ', an empty string. It sounds a bit counterintuitive, but it has an explanation.

The second thing we do is to remedy the first thing; we need to add a lazy route entry to our app module routing, like so:

```
// app/routes.ts
let routes = [{
  path: 'lazy',
  loadChildren: 'app/lazy/lazy.module#LazyModule'
}];
```

As you can see, we add the `loadChildren` property and this property expects a string as a value. This string value should point to where the module can be found, so essentially it looks like `<path to the module from the root>#<Module class name>`.

The last step is to remove all references to this module in other modules, for a very natural reason: if you haven't navigated to /lazy, a service or component and so on doesn't really exist yet, as its bundle hasn't been loaded to the application.

Finally, let's have a look at what this looks like in the debug mode. The first image will show what it looked like before we navigated to our lazy module:

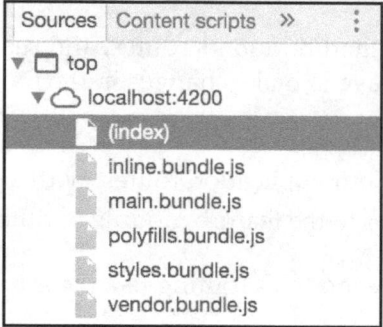

Here, we have our normal bundles that our project setup produces. Let's now navigate to our lazy route:

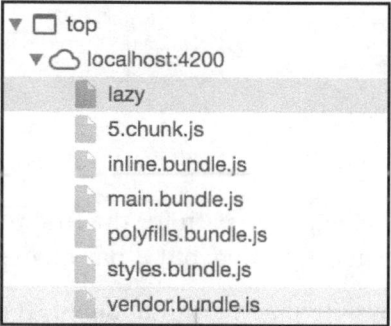

We can see that a bundle has been added called 5.chunk.js, and it contains our newly loaded module and all its constructs.

A little word of caution though, is to not place constructs in lazy-loaded modules that you think you will use elsewhere. Conversely, you can let your lazy module depend on services and constructs found in other modules, as long as those are not lazy loaded. A good practice is therefore, to make as many modules as possible lazy loaded but shared functionality can't be lazy loaded, for the above mentioned reason.

CanLoad – don't lazy load unless the user has access

Lazy loading is a great feature that can drastically reduce the loading time of your application by ensuring your application only starts with the bundles it absolutely needs. However, even if you ensure that most of your modules are lazy loaded, you need to take it a step further, especially if your application has any authentication or authorization mechanisms in place.

Consider the following, let us say that more than one of your modules needs the user to be authenticated or to have the role of admin. It would make no sense to load those modules when a user routes to their path if they are not allowed in that area anyway. To remedy this scenario, we can use a guard called CanLoad. CanLoad ensures we first validate whether it makes sense to lazy load a certain module based on a condition. You need to do the following to use this:

1. Implement the CanLoad interface and the canLoad() method, in a service.
2. Add the preceding service to the CanLoad property of your route.

The following creates a service that implements the CanLoad interface:

```
@Injectable()
export class CanLoadService implements CanLoad {
  canLoad(route: Route) {
    // replace this to check if user is authenticated/authorized
    return false;
  }
}
```

As you can see from the code, the canLoad() method returns a Boolean. In this case, we have made it return false, which means the module will not be loaded.

The second thing we needed to do was to update the route to use this service as a canLoad guard:

```
{
  path: 'lazy',
    loadChildren : 'app/lazy/lazy.module#LazyModule',
    canLoad: [CanLoadService]
}
```

If we attempt to surf to `localhost:4200/lazy`, we go nowhere as our `canLoad`, by returning `false`, tells us that we can't. Having a look at our console, we also see the following:

```
Router Event: NavigationCancel                                              platform-browser.es5.
  NavigationCancel(id: 1, url: '/lazy')                                      platform-browser.es5.
                                                                            platform-browser.es5.
  ▶NavigationCancel {id: 1, url: "/lazy", reason: "NavigationCancelingError: Cannot load children bec… guard of the route "path: 'lazy'" returned false"}
```

Here, it says it cannot load children due to the guard, so the guard is working.

Notice how everything works fine and loads like it should when you update the `CanLoadService` and `canLoad()` method to return `true`.

 Don't forget to add `CanLoadService` to the providers array of the root module.

Preloading

So far, we have been discussing eager loading and lazy loading. Eager loading, in this case, has meant that we load the entire application at once. Lazy loading has been about us identifying certain modules as modules that we only load on demand, that is, they are lazy loaded. There is, however, something in between: preloaded modules. Why do we need something in between, though? Well, imagine that we know with a good certainty that a normal user will want to access the products module within 30 seconds after logging in. It makes sense to mark the products module as a module that should be lazy loaded. It would be even better if it could be loaded in the background right after login so that it is ready to go when the user navigates to it. That is exactly what preloading does for us.

We enable preloading by issuing the following command:

```
@NgModule({
  imports: [
    RouterModule.forRoot(routes, {
      preloadingStrategy: PreloadAllModules
    })
  ]
})
```

This `PreloadAllModules` value preloads each and every lazy-loaded route, except for the ones guarded by the `canLoad` guard. This makes sense: the `canLoad` only loads if we are authenticated/authorized, or based on some other condition that we set up.

So, if we had a bunch of modules that were all set up as lazy, such as products, admin, categories, and so on, all of those would be loaded right after the initial boot based on `PreloadAllModules`. That might be good enough on a desktop. However, if you are on a mobile connection such as 3G, this might be way too heavy. At this point, we want better, more fine-grained control. What we can do is implement our own custom strategy for this. We need to do the following to do that:

1. Create a service that implements `PreloadingStrategy` and the `preload` method.
2. The `preload()` method must call the `load()` method, if it should be preloaded, or should return an empty Observable otherwise.
3. Define whether a route should be preloaded, by using the data attributed on a route, or by using a service.
4. Set the create strategy service as the value of `preloadingStrategy`.

For the first order of business, defining our service, we create it like this:

```
@Injectable()
export class PreloadingStrategyService implements PreloadingStrategy {
  preload(route: Route, load: () => Observable<any>): Observable<any> {
    if(route.data.preload) {
      return load();
    } else {
      return Observable.of(null);
    }
  }
}
```

We can see how we invoke the load method if our `route.data` contains the preload Boolean.

Now, for setting up the route correctly:

```
{
  path: 'anotherlazy',
    loadChildren: 'app/anotherlazy/anotherlazy.module#AnotherLazyModule',
    data: { preload: true }
}
```

The data property has been set to an object containing our `preload` property.

Now for the last step. Let's make the `RouterModule.forRoot()` aware that this service exists:

```
@NgModule({
  imports: [
    RouterModule.forRoot(routes, {
      preloadingStrategy: PreloadingStrategyService
    })
  ]
})
```

In short, this is a very efficient way of ensuring the user has the best possible experience without succumbing to either eager loading, or having to wait for a lazy load.

Summary

We have now uncovered the power of the Angular router and we hope you have enjoyed the journey into the intricacies of this library. One of the things that definitely shines in the Router module is the vast number of options and scenarios we can cover with such a simple but powerful implementation.

We have learned the basics of setting up routing and handling different types of parameters. We have also learned more advanced feature such as child routing. Furthermore, we have learned how to protect our routes from unauthorized access. Finally, we have shown the full power of async routing and how you can really improve response time with lazy loading and preloading.

In the next chapter, we will beef up our task-editing component to showcase the mechanisms underlying web forms in Angular and the best strategies to grab users' input with form controls.

10
Forms in Angular

Using forms, in general, is our way of collecting data from the web so we can later persist it. We have expectations of the form experience, such as:

- Easily being able to declare different kinds of input fields
- Setting up different kind of validations and displaying any validation errors to the user
- Supporting different strategies for stopping a post submission if the form contains errors

There are two approaches to handling forms: template-driven forms and reactive forms. Neither approach is considered better than the other; you just have to go with the one that suits your scenario the best. The major difference between the two approaches is who is responsible for what:

- In the template-driven approach, the template is responsible for creating elements, forms, and setting up validation rules, and synchronization happens with two-way data binding
- In the reactive approach, the `Component` class is responsible for creating the form, its elements, and setting up the validation.

In this chapter, we will:

- Learn about template-driven forms
- Bind data models and interface types for forms and input controls
- Design forms using the reactive forms approach
- Dive into the alternatives for input validation
- Build our own custom validators

Template-driven forms

Template-driven forms are one of two different ways of setting up forms with Angular. This approach is all about doing the setup in the template, which greatly resembles the approach used in AngularJS. So, if you have a background in AngularJS, this approach will be quite familiar to you.

Turning a simple form into a template-driven form

We have defined the following form, which consists of a `form` tag, two `input` fields, and a `button`, like so:

```
<form>
  <input id="name" name="name" placeholder="first name" required>
  <input id="surname" name="surname" placeholder="surname" required>
  <button>Save</button>
</form>
```

Here, we clearly have two `input` fields that are required, hence the `required` attribute for the input elements. We also have a **Save** button. The requirement we have on such a form is that it should not submit its data until all required fields are filled in. To accomplish this, we need to do two things:

- Save the input field values to an object with `[(ngModel)]`
- Only submit the form if it has no errors, by using the `ngForm` directive

We now change the form to look like this:

```
<form #formPerson="ngForm">
  <input [(ngModel)]="person.firstName" id="name" name="name"
  placeholder="first name" required>
  <input [(ngModel)]="person.surname" id="surname" name="surname"
  placeholder="surname" required>
  <button (click)="submit()" *ngIf="formPerson.form.valid">Save</button>
</form>
```

Let's talk about the changes we made. First off, we have the following piece of code:

```
<form (ngSubmit)="save()" #formPerson="ngForm">
```

We created a view reference called `formPerson` that has the value `ngForm` assigned to it. This means we have a reference to the form. The form view reference now contains a lot of interesting properties that will help us determine whether the form is ready to be submitted.

As for the second change we made, we connected the input data to `ngModel`:

```
<input [(ngModel)]="person.name" id="name" name="name"
 placeholder="first name" required>
```

 The `ngModel` allows us to create a double binding to a property. It is known as a *banana in a box*, which is really a memory rule for you to be able to remember how to type it. We create it in two steps. First we have `ngModel`, then we add the banana, the parenthesis, like this: `(ngModel)`. After that we put the banana in a box. Square brackets will serve as our box, which means we finally have `[(ngModel)]`. Remember, it's called *banana in a box*, not *box in a banana*.

Here, we ensured that the value of the input was saved down to `person.name`, by utilizing the `ngModel` directive.

Lastly, we decorated our button element using the `*ngIf` directive, like this:

```
<button *ngIf="formHero.form.valid">Save</button>
```

We used an `*ngIf` directive to be able to hide the button, should the form prove to be invalid. As you can see, we are utilizing our form view reference and its valid property. If the form is valid, then show the button; otherwise, hide it.

This is the very basics of setting up a template-driven form. Let's investigate this a little deeper by looking at:

- What CSS is being rendered, so we can render that appropriately depending on the form state
- How to detect a specific error on an input element

Input field error – from a CSS standpoint

There are different CSS classes being assigned to an input element depending on what state it is in. Let's have a look at an input element with a required attribute set, prior to us inputting any data. We expect it to tell us that something is wrong, due to the fact that the `input` field is empty and we have added a `required` attribute to it:

```
<input id="name" name="name" placeholder="first name" required ng-reflect-
required ng-reflect-name="name" ng-reflect-model class="ng-untouched ng-
pristine ng-invalid">
```

We can see that the following classes have been set:

- `ng-untouched`, which means that no one has attempted to press the **Submit** button yet
- `ng-pristine`, which essentially means that no attempts have been made to input data into this field. It would be set to `false` if you enter a character and remove the said character
- `ng-invalid`, which means that the validator is reacting and says something is wrong

Entering a character into the field, we see that `ng-pristine` disappears. Entering some characters in both fields and pressing **Submit**, we see that `ng-untouched` turns into `ng-touched`. This also causes `ng-invalid` to turn into `ng-valid`.

OK, so now we have a better understanding of what CSS turns into what, at what time, and can style our component appropriately.

Detecting an error on an input field with named references

So far, we have settled for looking at the form reference when we want to know whether our form is valid or not. We can do a lot better here, we can detect whether a specific input control has an error. An input control may have more than one validator, which means we might have more than one validation error to show as well. So how do we detect that? There are a number of steps to be taken to accomplish this:

We need to:

1. Create a view reference for each input element and also assign it the value `ngModel`.
2. Give each element a `name` attribute.

Let's update our form code and add view references and `name` attributes according to the preceding steps:

```
<form #formPerson="ngForm">
 <input #firstName="ngModel" [(ngModel)]="person.name" id="name"
  name="name" placeholder="first name" required>
 <input #surName="ngModel" [(ngModel)]="person.surname" id="surname"
  name="surname" placeholder="surname" required>
 <button *ngIf="formPerson.form.valid">Save</button>
</form>
```

Once we have done the pre-work, it is time to talk about what errors we can detect. There are two types of errors that are of interest:

- A general error, which is an error that says there is something wrong on the input control, but doesn't specify what
- A specific error, which will indicate the exact type of error, for example, the value is too short

Let's start with a general error:

```
<input #firstName="ngModel" [(ngModel)]="person.name" id="name"
 name="name" placeholder="first name" required>
{{ firstName.valid }} // an empty field sets this to false
```

We use our view reference `firstName` and query it for its valid property, which indicates whether an error exists.

Now for the other more detailed error. To detect a more detailed error we use the errors object on our view reference and output the whole object using the JSON pipe:

```
{{ firstName.errors | json }}  // outputs { required: true }
```

This means we can suddenly find out whether a specific error has been set and we can therefore decide to display a conditional text based on a certain error being present, like so:

```
<div *ngIf="firstName.errors && firstName.errors.required">
  First name is a required field
</div>
```

Other specific errors will populate the errors object, and the only thing you have to do is know what the error is called. When in doubt, output the errors object using the JSON pipe to find out what the validation error is called for a certain validator, and what validation error values go with it.

Improving the form

So far, we have covered the basic mechanisms for knowing when a form is erroneous and how to display a text based on a specific error. Let's build on that knowledge by covering some more examples. First off, we will add more validation types to our input field:

```
<input minlength="3" required #name="ngModel" name="name">
{{ name.errors | json }}
```

Now we have added `minlength` as a validation rule to our element, besides the pre-existing required rule. Required is the prioritized error, so that will show first. If we input some characters then the required error goes away. It should now display the following:

```
{"minlength": { "requiredLength": 3, "actualLength": 1 }  }
```

Just like with the required error, we can show an error text for just this error, like so:

```
<div *ngIf="name.errors && name.errors.minlength" >
  Name value is too short
</div>
```

There are some validation rules already written for us:

- `required`, which requires the value to be non empty
- `requiredTrue`, which specifically requires the value to be `true`
- `minlength`, which says the value needs to have a certain minimum length
- `maxlength`, which says the value cannot be over a certain length
- `pattern`, which forces the value to adhere to a `RegEx` pattern
- `nullValidator`, which checks the value is not null
- `compose`, which is used if you want to compose multiple validators into one, the validation rule is the result of taking the union of all validators provided

Try to see if any of those covers your scenario. You might find that some validation rules are missing. If that is the case, then this can be remedied by creating a custom validator. We will cover how to build a custom validator rule later in this chapter.

Showing errors at the right time

So far, our form has had a behavior of not showing the **Submit** button if at least one error exists. There are alternate approaches to take here. Sometimes it might be perceived as the UI being broken when a button doesn't exist or shows as disabled. This has to do with how you construct the UI in other places. A consistent approach is better. For that reason, there are different ways we could control how a form gets submitted.

Here are the main approaches:

- Show the **Submit** button when there are no errors in the form, we have covered how to do this one already. This approach may look like we forgot to design the form properly because the button seems to be missing entirely when the form has an error.
- Disable the submit button as long as there are form errors. It is nice if this is accompanied with showing validation errors to avoid any misunderstandings on why it is disabled.
- Enable the call to submit only when there are no errors, the major difference here is that the **Submit** button is clickable but the submit action won't be taking place. The drawback of this version is making the user feel like nothing is happening. This approach needs to be accompanied with showing the validation error that prevents the form from being submitted.

This is how you would code the first approach. Here, we hide the button if the form is not valid:

```
<button *ngIf="form.valid">Save</button>
```

The second approach involves setting the button to a disabled state. We can do so by binding to the `disabled` attribute:

```
<button [disabled]="form.valid">Save</button>
```

The third and final approach is to create a `Boolean` condition that needs to return `true` for the other statement to be executed:

```
<button (ngSubmit)="form.valid && submit()">Save</button>
```

Reactive forms

For reactive forms, we have a programmatic approach to how we create form elements and set up validation. We set everything up in the `Component` class and merely point out our created constructs in the template.

The key classes involved in this approach are:

- `FormGroup`, which is a grouping containing one-to-many form controls
- `FormControl`, which represents an input element

AbstractControl

Both the `FormGroup` and `FormControl` inherit from `AbstractControl`, which contains a lot of interesting properties that we can look at and use to render the UI differently, based on what status a certain thing has. For example, you might want to differ UI-wise between a form that has never been interacted with and one that has. It could also be of interest to know whether a certain control has been interacted with at all, to know what values would be part of an update. As you can imagine, there are a lot of scenarios where it is interesting to know a specific status.

The following list contains all the possible statuses:

- `controls`, a list of `FormControl` instances that you added through the constructor `new FormGroup(group)`.
- `value`, a dictionary representing a key-value pair. The key is the reference you gave the `FormControl` at creation and the value is what you entered in the input control `{ :'<reference>', <value entered> }`.
- `dirty`, once we enter something in the form it is considered dirty.
- `disabled`, the form can be disabled.
- `pristine`, a form where none of the controls have been interacted with.
- `status`, a string representation of whether it is valid or not, it says invalid if it isn't.
- `touched`, the **Submit** button has been pressed at least once.
- `untouched`, the **Submit** button has not yet been pressed.
- `enabled`, Boolean saying whether the form is enabled.
- `valid`, if there are no errors this one is `true`.
- `invalid`, the opposite of valid.

Programmatic and dynamic approach

We have a programmatic approach to how things are being done, and we have two possible approaches to this:

- We can create forms with N number of elements. This means we can generate forms that are completely dynamic in what and how many input controls, as well as forms, that should be used. A typical example is when creating a content management system where pages and their content are completely configurable from a config file or database.

- We can create deep structures. Normally we have a form and N number of elements in it, but reactive forms allow us to nest forms within forms.

Notice here how the `FormGroup` is being called a group and not a `Form`. This is because you should consider this as only a grouping and not necessarily the only one of its kind. You could easily have a structure like this:

- Person : FormGroup
  - Name : FormControl
  - Surname : FormControl
  - Age : FormControl
  - Address : FormGroup
    - City: FormControl
    - Country: FormControl

Here we have a representation of `Person` and we can see that we want to handle the input of that person's address in a form by itself, hence the hierarchy.

Turning a form into a dynamic form

The `FormGroup` is the construct that consists of many form controls. To create such a construct we need to do the following:

1. Import the reactive `Forms` module.
2. Instantiate as many `FormControls` as you need, through code.
3. Place the controls in a dictionary.
4. Assign the dictionary as input to the `FormGroup`.
5. Associate our `Form` group instance with the `[formGroup]` directive.
6. Associate each `FormControl` instance to a `[formControlName]` directive.

The first step lies in importing the module:

```
@NgModule({
  imports: [ReactiveFormsModule]
})
```

The second step is creating form controls. Let's create two different ones, one with validation and one without:

```
const control = new FormControl('some value');
const control2 = new FormControl('other value', Validators.required);
```

The third step is to create a dictionary for this:

```
const group = {};
group['ctrl1'] = control;
group['ctrl2'] = control2;
```

The fourth step is to assign the group to a `formGroup` instance:

```
const formGroup = new FormGroup(group);
```

Your full code should look something like this:

```
import { FormControl, FormGroup } from '@angular/forms';
import { Component, OnInit } from '@angular/core';

@Component({
  selector: 'dynamic',
  template: `
  dynamic
  <div [formGroup]="form">
    dynamic
    <input [formControl]="group['ctrl1']" placeholder="name">
  </div>`
})
export class DynamicComponent implements OnInit {
  form:FormGroup;
  group;
  constructor() {
    this.group = {};
    this.group['ctrl1'] = new FormControl('start value');
    this.form = new FormGroup(this.group);
  }

  ngOnInit() { }
}
```

Your form's UI should look like this. As you can see, your `start value` is set to the input control:

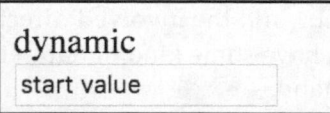

Adding controls with validation rules

Let's add a validator to a form control:

```
this.group['ctrl2'] = new FormControl('',Validators.required)
```

If you investigate the markup for this newly added form, you can see that indeed its CSS class has been set to `ng-invalid` due to its value being empty.

Now the next burning question, how do I reference individual elements so I know what errors they may or may not have? The answer is simple, under your form member, of type `FormGroup`, is a controls dictionary that contains controls. One of these controls works just like a view reference with template forms:

```
ctrl2 valid {{ form.controls['ctrl2'].valid }}
{{ form.controls['ctrl2'].errors | json }}
```

As you can see in the preceding code snippet, we can refer to an individual control through `form.controls['key']`. It has the properties valid and errors on it so we can show individual errors, like so:

```
<div *ngIf="form.controls['ctrl2'].errors.required">This field is
required</div>
```

Refactoring – making the code more dynamic

So, we have understood the basic mechanisms so far
with `FormGroup` and `FormControl` and the involved directives, but our code looks very static, so let's fix that. We need to have some kind of dataset that we loop through that creates our `Form` controls on demand:

```
this.questions = [{
  Question : 'What is Supermans real name',
  Key : '1'
},{
  Question : 'Who is Lukes father',
  Key : '2'
}];

this.questionGroup = {};
this.questions.forEach( qa => {
  this.questionGroup[qa.Key] = new FormControl('',Validators.required)
});

this.dynamicForm = new FormGroup( this.questionGroup );
```

Now for defining the UI. We have a list of questions that we use an `*ngFor` to display:

```
<form (ngSubmit)="submit()" [formGroup]="dynamicForm">
  <div *ngFor="let q of questions">
    {{ q.Question }}
    <input [formControl]="questionGroup[q.Key]" placeholder="fill in answer">
  </div>
  <button>Save</button>
</form>
```

We loop through the questions array and assign the `[formControl]` directive the appropriate control. From our question instance, we are also able to output the question itself. This looks a lot more dynamic.

Now we just have one step left, and that is accessing the values the user actually fills in:

```
submit() {
  console.log( this.dynamicForm.value ) // { "1" : "", "2" : "Darth" }
}
```

This gives us a dictionary of the form control reference along with any value the user entered in the input upon pressing **Submit**.

Updating our component form model – using setValue and patchValue

First off, let's have a little reminder of how we can create a form programmatically. We used to use the dictionary variable and pass that to the `FormGroup` constructor, but we may as well skip that variable and define the dictionary inline, as in the following code:

```
const form = new FormGroup({
  name: new FormControl(''),
  surname: new FormControl(''),
  age: new FormControl
})
```

To change any of the values in the form, we can use one of two approaches:

- `setValue()`, which will replace all values
- `patchValue()`, which will only update the mentioned controls

setValue

Using this method completely replaces all the values. As long as you mention all the values that the form was created with then you are fine, like this:

```
form.setValue({
  name: 'chris',
  surname: 'noring',
  age: 37
})
```

If however, you forget a field, you will get an error back saying you must specify a value for all fields:

```
form.setValue({
  name: 'chris',
  surname: 'noring'
})
```

If you only wanted to do a partial update then the `patchValue()` function is for you.

patchValue

Using `patchValue()` is as easy as typing the following:

```
form.patchValue({
  name: 'chris',
  surname: 'noring'
})
```

For example, if the previous values before calling `patchValue()` were as follows:

```
{
  name: 'christoffer',
  surname: 'n',
  age: 36
}
```

Then applying `form.patchValue()`, defined earlier, will cause the resulting form to contain the following:

```
{
  name: 'chris',
  surname: 'noring',
  age: 36
}
```

Upon closer inspection, we can see that the surname and name have been updated but the age property has been left alone.

Cleaning up our form creation and introducing FormBuilder

So far, we have been creating our forms like this:

```
const form = new FormGroup({
  name: new FormControl(''),
  surname: new FormControl(''),
  age: new FormControl,
  address: new FormGroup({
    city: 'London',
    country: 'UK'
  })
})
```

This, however, constitutes a lot of noise. We can use a construct called `FormBuilder` to take away a lot of that noise. To use the `FormBuilder` we need to do the following:

1. Import it from `@angular/forms`.
2. Inject it into the constructor.
3. Use the instance and call the group function on the `FormBuilder` instance.

Let's showcase this in the following code snippet:

```
import { FormBuilder } from '@angular/forms'

@Component({
})
export class FormComponent {
  formGroup: FormGroup;
  constructor(private formBuilder: FormBuilder) {
    this.formGroup = this.formBuilder.group({
      name :'',
      surname :'',
      age: 0,
      address : this.formBuilder.group({
        city: 'London',
        country : 'UK'
      })
    });
  }
}
```

This looks a lot easier to read and we don't have to deal with the `FormGroup` and `FormControl` data types explicitly, although that is what is being created implicitly.

There are three different ways of specifying a value to our element:

- `elementName : ''`, here the default value is being set to a primitive
- `elementName: { value : '', disabled: false }`, here we assign the `elementName` to an entire object, where the property value in the object is what the default value will become
- `elementName : [ 'default value', <optional validator> ]`, here we assign it a complete array with the first item in the array being the default value and the second to Nth values being the validators

Here is what the code looks like using all three approaches:

```
this.dynamicForm2 = this.formBuilder.group({
  // set to a primitive
  fullname: 'chris',
  // setting a default value
  age: { value : 37, disabled: true },
  // complex type 'address'
  address : this.formBuilder.group({
    // default value + x number of validators
    city: ['', Validators.required, Validators.minLength],
    country: [''] // default value, no validators
  })
});
```

Here, we are rendering out the mentioned field in our preceding backing code. As you can see, the key names in the group object correspond to the `formControlName` attribute in the markup:

```
<form (ngSubmit)="submit(dynamicForm2)" [formGroup]="dynamicForm2">
  <input formControlName="fullname">
  <input formControlName="age">
  <div formGroupName='address'>
    <input formControlName="city">
    <input formControlName="country">
  </div>
  <button>Save</button>
</form>
```

How do we show a specific error though? That's an easy one, it looks like this:

```
<div *ngIf="dynamicForm2.get('address').hasError('required')">
```

Note how we refer to the form by its property name on the class `dynamicForm2`, we call the `get()` method and specify the key as an argument, and lastly, we call `hasError` and ask for a specific error. In this particular case, the address property is defined in the code as consisting of city and country. Specifying an error like this would just tell us that either city or country has an error on it, or both.

Building your own custom validator

Sometimes the default validators won't cover all the scenarios that you might have in your application. Luckily, it is quite easy to write your own custom validator.

A custom validator is just a function that needs to return an object with the error specified or null. Null means we don't have an error.

Starting to define such a function is easy:

```
import { AbstractControl, ValidatorFn } from '@angular/forms';

export function minValueValidator(compareToThisValue: number): ValidatorFn
{
  return (control: AbstractControl): {[key: string]: any} => {
    const lessThan = parseInt( control.value ) < compareToThisValue;
    return lessThan ? {'minValue'</span>: {value: control.value}} : null;
  };
}
```

In this case, we are building a `minValue` validator. The outer function takes the parameter we will compare to. We return an inner function that tests the control's value to our compare value. If our condition is `true` we raise an error where we return an error structure `{ 'minValue' : { value : control.value } }`, or if it is `false` then we return null.

To use this new validator all we have to do is import it in our component file and type the following:

```
formBuilder.group({
  age : [0, minValueValidator(18)]
})
```

And to show an error message in the template, if this error is raised, we just write this:

```
<div *ngIf="form.get('age').hasError('minValue')">
  You must be at least 18
</div>
```

Watching state changes and being reactive

So far, we have seen how we can create forms programmatically using the `FormBuilder` and how we can specify all our fields and their validations in the code. We haven't really talked about why a reactive form is called *reactive*. Here is the thing, we can listen to changes on the input fields in the form when they happen and react accordingly. A suitable reaction could be to disable/enable a control, provide a visual hint, or something else. You get the idea.

How is this made possible though? It is made possible by the fact that the fields we declare have two Observables connected to them, `statusChanges` and `valueChanges`. By subscribing to those, we are able to listen to changes and make the suggested changes we mentioned earlier in this paragraph.

An interesting case for demonstrating how we can watch state changes is that of login. In a login scenario we want the user to type in their username and password, followed by pressing a button. What we should be able to support the user with in such a scenario is:

- Showing a hint if something is wrong with the entered username, it may be empty or entered in a way that is not allowed
- Disabling the login button if not all required fields are entered

We opt for showing a hint if the username is not constructed correctly. We don't want to show the hint unless the user has started to enter values.

Let's do this in steps. We first build our component, like so:

```
@Component({
  template: `
    <div class="form-group" [formGroup]="loginForm">
      <input type="text"
             class="form-control"
             placeholder="Your username">
      <p *ngIf="showUsernameHint"class="help-block">
        That does not look like a proper username
      </p>
    </div>

})
export class LoginComponent {
  loginForm: FormGroup;
  notValidCredentials: boolean = false;
  showUsernameHint: boolean = false;
  constructor(
   formBuilder: FormBuilder,
```

```
    private router: Router
  ) {
    this.loginForm = formBuilder.group({
      username: ['', Validators.compose([
      Validators.required,
      Validators.email])],
      password: ['', Validators.required]
    });
  }
}
```

Here we have set up a form with two input fields, a `username` field and a `password` field. We have also stated that these two fields are required by the way we have set up the validation rules. The next step is to set up the subscriber to the username fields so we can be notified of changes to it. The required changes are highlighted in bold:

```
@Component({
  template : `
  <div class="form-group">
    <input type="text"
           class="form-control"
           placeholder="Your username"
           [formControlName]="username">
    <p *ngIf="showUsernameHint"class="help-block">
      That does not look like a proper username
    </p>
  </div>`
})
export class LoginComponent {
  loginForm: FormGroup;
  notValidCredentials: boolean = false;
  showUsernameHint: boolean = false;
  constructor(
    formBuilder: FormBuilder,
    private router: Router
  ) {
    this.loginForm = formBuilder.group({
      username: ['', Validators.compose([
      Validators.required,
      Validators.email])],
      password: ['', Validators.required]
    });

    const username:AbstractControl = this.loginForm.get('username');
    username.valueChanges.subscribe(value => {
      this.showUsernameHint = (username.dirty &&
      value.indexOf('@') < 0);
    });
```

```
        }
    }
```

We can see here that we do this in two steps. First we create a reference to our username field by asking the `loginForm` for it, like so: `this.loginForm.controls['username']`. Then we set up a subscription to the form control reference `username:FormControl` by calling `username.subscribe(...)`. Inside of the `.subscribe()` we evaluate whether to set the `this.showUsernameHint` variable to `true` or `false`. The logic reads that if an @ character is missing and the user has started typing, then show the visual hint. Setting the hint to `true` will trigger the template to show the hint text, like so:

```
<p *ngIf="showUsernameHint"class="help-block">
  That does not look like a proper username
</p>
```

Of course, there is more to creating a login component, such as sending the username and password to an endpoint and rerouting the user to a suitable page, and so on, but this code shows off the reactive nature. Hopefully, this has clearly conveyed how you can take advantage of the reactive nature of forms and respond accordingly.

Summary

In this section, we have learned that Angular provides you with two different flavors for creating forms, template-driven and reactive forms, and that neither approach can be said to be better than the other. We have also covered what different types of validations exist and we now know how to create our own validations.

In the next chapter, we will take a look at how we can skin our application to look more beautiful with the help of the framework Angular Material. Angular Material comes with a lot of components and styling ready for you to use in your next project. So, let's give your Angular project the love it deserves.

11
Angular Material

When you develop an application, you need a clear strategy on how to create your UI. The strategy should include using good, contrasting colors; having a consistent look and feel; it should work well on different devices, as well as browsers; and many more requirements. In short, there are a lot of requirements on an application being built for the web platform today when it comes to UI and UX. It is no wonder that most developers consider UI/UX to be a daunting task and therefore turn to UI frameworks that do a lot of the heavy lifting. There are some frameworks that are used more than others, namely:

- Twitter Bootstrap
- Foundation
- HTML5 Quickstart

There is, however, a new kid on the block, or should we say, a new design language, Material Design. This chapter will try to explain what Material Design is and will look at what frameworks implement the principles of Material Design, and we will especially focus on Angular Material, made especially for Angular.

In this chapter, we will:

- Learn about what Material Design is and a little bit of its history
- Learn more about known implementations
- Delve deeper into Angular Material and what parts it consists of
- Build an Angular application with Angular Material

Material Design

Material Design is a design language that was developed by Google in 2014. Google states that its new design language is based on paper and ink. The creators of Material Design tried to explain the goal they were trying to reach, with the following quote:

> *"We challenged ourselves to create a visual language for our users that synthesises the classic principles of good design with the innovation and possibility of technology and science."*

They explain further the goals as:

- Develop a single underlying system that allows for a unified experience across platforms and device sizes
- Mobile precepts are fundamental, but touch, voice, mouse, and keyboard are all first-class input methods

It is clear that the design language wants to have one take, and one take only on how the UI and user interaction should look and feel, across devices. Also, that input plays a large role on the overall experience of a UI.

Material Design rests on three principles:

- Material is the metaphor
- Bold, graphic, intentional
- Motion provides meaning

All in all, it can be said that there is a lot of theory behind the design language, and there is good documentation on the topic should you wish to delve further in, such as at the official documentation site, `https://material.io/`.

Now, all of this is probably very interesting if you are a designer and care about graphical theory. It is our guess that you who is reading this book is a developer and that you are asking yourself a question right now. So what, why should I care?

Well, every time Google sets out to build something, it becomes big. Not everything remains over time, but there is sufficient muscle behind this, and Google have paved the way by using this on a lot of their own products such as Firebase, Gmail, Google Plus, and so on.

Of course, by itself a design language isn't that interesting, at least not for a developer, which brings us to our next section on the fact that there does exist a number of implementations based on the design principles laid out by Material Design. More on this in the coming section.

Known implementations

For a developer, design is there to make sense of your code and give the user a nice experience, both visually and from a usability standpoint. Currently, three major implementations exist of Material Design.

Those are:

- Materialize, `http://materializecss.com/about.html`. 24,000+ stars on GitHub tells you that this is very well used. It works to be used as a standalone, but there are also bindings to frameworks such as AngularJS and React. It offers navigation elements, components, and much more, a good choice.
- AngularJS Material, `https://material.angularjs.org/latest/`, is Google's own implementation meant for AngularJS. It is quite capable and comes with themes, navigation elements, components, and of course directives.
- Angular Material, `https://material.angular.io/`, is Google's own implementation and is built for Angular specifically. We will focus on this one throughout the rest of this chapter.

If you are an Angular developer, then AngularJS Material or Materialize are both valid options, as the latter has AngularJS bindings, found at `https://krescruz.github.io/angular-materialize/`. Materialize can be used by many other application frameworks and is the most generic choice of the three. Angular Material is made for Angular alone.

Now the time has come to look at Angular Material in detail.

Angular Material

The library was developed to implement Material Design for the new Angular. It's still a work in progress, but it continues to evolve. There are, however, enough components in place for it to be adopted already. You should know that it is still in Beta, so a certain amount of caution is good if you consider adopting it. The official documentation can be found at `https://material.angular.io` and the repository can be found at `https://github.com/angular/material2`. It is a quite popular library with 10,000+ stars.

Angular Material promotes itself with the following bullet points:

- **Sprint from zero to app**: The intention is to make it very easy for you as an app developer to hit the ground running. The goal is for there to be a minimum amount of effort in setting it up.
- **Fast and consistent**: This is to say that performance has been a major focus point and also that it is guaranteed to work well on all major browsers.
- **Versatile**: This puts focus on two major points, there should be a multitude of themes that should be easy to customize and there is also great support for localization and internationalization.
- **Optimized for Angular**: The very fact that it is built by the Angular team itself means the support for Angular is a big priority.

The framework consists of the following parts:

- **Components**: This means that there are a ton of constructs in place to help you be successful, such as different kinds of input, buttons, layout, navigation, modals, and different ways to show tabular data.
- **Themes**: The library comes with themes preinstalled, but it's also easy to refer to external themes. There is also a theming guide, if you have your heart set on creating a custom theme, at `https://material.angular.io/guide/theming`.
- **Icons**: Material Design comes with over 900 icons so you are likely to find just the icon you need. For a full display of what those are, go to `https://material.io/icons/`.
- **Gestures**: Not everything in a UI is a button click. As Material Design supports mobile, it thereby supports mobile gestures through the use of the library HammerJs.

Installation

I know you are probably itching to try it out, so let's delay no further. First off, we need to install it. Let's start out by ensuring we have an Angular project ready to install it on, by telling the Angular CLI to scaffold a project for us, like so:

```
ng new AngularMaterialDemo
```

Now it is time to install the necessary dependencies for Angular Material:

```
npm install --save @angular/material @angular/cdk
```

Now let us also install support for animations. It isn't strictly necessary for it to work but we want some cool animations, right?

The following is needed to install it:

```
npm install @angular/animations
```

Thereby, we are done installing Angular Material and are ready to use it in our app. As we have learned from previous chapters, to use external Angular modules, we need to import them. Once that is done, we can start using the constructs that these modules publicly export. In reality, there are many modules to import, depending on what we need, for example, every control has its own module but animation has only one.

Our first Angular Material app

By now you have already scaffolded an Angular application, using the Angular CLI. You have installed the necessary node modules and are eagerly waiting to use the constructs in Angular Material. We expect two things from our Angular Material application, some nice rendering as well as some nice animations to go with it. To start using a UI control such as a button or a checkbox, we need to import its corresponding module. To get the UI rendering and the animation behavior, we need to add the necessary modules and select a theme to use.

Let's start out with the module we need, which is the BrowserAnimationsModule. To start using it, we import it and register it with our root module, like so:

```
import {
  BrowserAnimationsModule
} from '@angular/platform-browser/animations';

@NgModule({
  imports: [ BrowserAnimationsModule ]
})
export class AppModule {}
```

At this point, we haven't really added UI elements to use, so let's do that as the next order of business. Our first example will be about buttons. To use an Angular Material button we need to add the MatButtonModule to our root module:

```
import {
  BrowserAnimationsModule
} from '@angular/platform-browser/animations';
import { MatButtonModule } from '@angular/material';

@NgModule({
```

```
    imports: [
      BrowserAnimationsModule,
      MatButtonModule
    ]
  })
  export class AppModule {}
```

We need one more thing, namely a theme. If we don't add a theme we will get a boring button that just looks grey. If we, however, have a theme, we will get all the nice animations that have come to be associated with Material Design.

To add a theme, we need to add an entry to our `styles.css` file. This file is used to set CSS styles for the whole application. So let's add the necessary row to `styles.css`:

```
@import "~@angular/material/prebuilt-themes/indigo-pink.css";
```

The tilde operator ~ informs webpack, the underlying engine that fuels Angular CLI, that such a path should be treated as an aliased path handled by webpack, and not just a regular field path or URL

Now we are ready to use our first Angular Material UI element. Our choice for this is a Material Design button. To use it, we need to add the `mat-button` attribute to an element that we want Material Design rendering and behavior on.

We start in our root module, `app.module.ts`, adding the following entries:

```
@Component({
  template : `
    <button mat-button>Click me!</button>
  `
})
```

In the template, an ordinary button becomes a Material Design button by us adding the `mat-button` attribute. `mat-button` is a directive that gives our button a new look as well as associated animations. Clicking the button now should give off a nice animation.

This demonstrates how simple it is to get started with Angular Material, but there is more, much more. Let's talk about most of the components in the upcoming section.

Component overview

Angular Material consists of a lot of components of differing types, those are:

- **Form controls**: By form controls, we mean any type of controls that we use to collect data from a form, such as autocomplete, checkbox, normal input, radio button, select list, and so on.
- **Navigation**: By navigation, we mean things like a menu, a sidenav, or a toolbar.
- **Layout**: By layout, we mean how we can place the data on the page, such as using a list, a card, or tabs.
- **Buttons**: Those are what they sound like, buttons you can push. But there are a number of different ones you can use, such as icon buttons, raised buttons, and more.
- **Popups and modals**: These are specific windows that block any user interaction until you have interacted with the popup or modal.
- **Data table**: This is simply to show data in a tabular way. What kind of table you need depends on whether your data is massive and needs pagination, or if it needs to be sorted, or both.

Buttons

So far, our app has only consisted of a simple button, which we declared in the following way:

```
<button mat-button>simple button</button>
```

There are, however, a lot more button types, namely:

- `mat-button`, this is a normal looking button
- `mat-raised-button`, this is a raised button that is displayed with a shadow, to indicate its raised state
- `mat-icon-button`, this button is meant to be used with an icon
- `mat-fab`, this is a rounded button
- `mat-button-toggle`, this is a button that indicates if it has been pressed or not, having pressed/not pressed as states

The markup for the buttons is as follows:

```
<button mat-button>Normal button</button>
<button mat-raised-button>Raised button</button>
<button mat-fab>Fab button</button>
<button mat-icon-button>
    <mat-icon class="mat-icon material-icons" role="img"
     aria-hidden="true">home</mat-icon>
    Icon button
</button>
<mat-button-toggle>Button toggle</mat-button-toggle>
```

It's worth noting that we need to import the `MatButtonToggleModule` to be able to use the `mat-button-toggle` button. The buttons look like the following:

To use these buttons, we need to make sure we import and register the modules they belong to. Let's update our root module to look like the following:

```
import { BrowserModule } from '@angular/platform-browser';
import { NgModule } from '@angular/core';
import { BrowserAnimationsModule } from '@angular/platform-browser/animations';
import {
  MatButtonModule,
  MatIconModule,
  MatButtonToggleModule
} from '@angular/material';
import { AppComponent } from './app.component';

@NgModule({
  declarations: [
    AppComponent
  ],
  imports: [
    BrowserModule,
    BrowserAnimationsModule,
    MatButtonModule,
    MatIconModule,
    MatButtonToggleModule
  ],
```

```
    bootstrap: [AppComponent]
})
export class AppModule { }
```

We can see that we need to register `MatIconModule` to support the use of the `mat-icon` directive, and we also need to register the `MatButtonToggleModule` to use the `<mat-button-toggle>` UI element, a toggle button.

Form controls

Form controls are about collecting input data in different ways so that you might persist the data by calling an endpoint over HTTP.

There are quite a few controls in Material Design of varying types, namely:

- **Autocomplete**: This control enables the user to start typing in an input field and be presented with a list of suggestions while typing. This helps to narrow down the possible values that the input can take.
- **Checkbox**: This is a classic checkbox representing a state that is either checked or unchecked.
- **Date picker**: This is a control that enables the user to select a date in the calendar.
- **Input**: This is a classic input control. Material Design enhances the control with meaningful animation so you can clearly see when you are typing or not.
- **Radio button**: This is a classic radio button, and just like with the input control, Material Design's take on this one is to add animations and transitions while editing to create a better user experience.
- **Select**: This is a classic select list where the user is prompted to select one or more items from the list.
- **Slider**: The slider enables you to increase or decrease the value by pulling a slider button to either the right or the left.
- **Slide toggle**: This is just a checkbox, but a nicer rendition of it where a slider is being slid to the left or to the right.

Input

The input field is a classic input field, in that you can set different validation rules on it. You can however quite easily add the ability to show errors on the input field in a nice and reactive way.

To accomplish this, we will need to:

- Associate a `formControl` with our input field
- Define our input as a `MatInput` and add a validation rule
- Define a `mat-error` element and a rule for when it should be shown

For the first bullet, we do the following:

```
<mat-form-field>
  <input matInput placeholder="Name" [formControl]="nameInput">
</mat-form-field>
```

This sets up an input control for us and a reference to a `formControl` so we can listen to changes on the input. This needs to be accompanied with us adding a reference in the code to the `app.component.ts` file, like so:

```
nameInput:FormControl;

constructor() {
  this.nameInput = new FormControl();
}
```

We then need to add the `matInput` directive to the input and add a validation rule, so it looks like this:

```
<mat-form-field>
  <input [formControl]="nameInput" required matInput >
</mat-form-field>
```

Lastly, we add the `mat-error` element and wrap the `mat-input-container` in a form element. We need to remember at this point to include the `FormsModule` in our root module as well. We also need to set up a rule for when the `mat-error` element should be shown, using `*ngIf`:

```
<form name="person-form">
  <mat-input-container>
    <input [formControl]="nameInput" required matInput >
    <mat-error *ngIf="nameInput.hasError('required')">
      Name field is required
    </mat-error>
  </mat-input-container>
</form>
```

The previous markup sets up the input element and the validation rules of when to show, but as mentioned, we need to include the `FormsModule` in our root module as a last step, so let's show what that looks like:

```
import {FormsModule} from '@angular/forms';

@NgModule({
  imports: [FormsModule]
})
export class AppModule {}
```

This all comes together to look like the following:

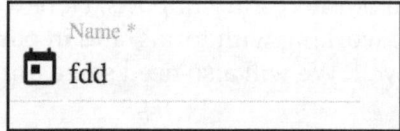

When the validation error has been triggered, it then looks like so:

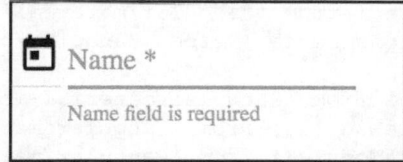

We have gone through a subset of all the form controls that Angular Material consists of, namely the autocomplete, the checkbox, the date picker, and lastly a normal input showcasing a validation error. There are other form controls such as radio button, select, slider, and slide toggle that we encourage you to explore at your own pace.

Autocomplete

The idea with autocomplete is to help the user narrow down what possible values an input field can have. In a normal input field, you would just type something and hope a validation would tell you if what you input is incorrect. With autocomplete, you are presented with a list as you type. The list is narrowed down as you type, and at any point you can decide to stop typing and instead select an item from the list. This is a time saver as you don't have to type the entire item's name, and it also enhances correctness as the user is being made to select from a list, rather than to type in the whole thing.

With this being the complete behavior of autocorrect, it means that we need to provide it with a list of possible answers and also an input box in which to receive the input.

We need to set up this control in five steps:

1. Import and register all the necessary modules with our root module.
2. Define a `mat-form-field`, containing an input control.
3. Define a `mat-autocomplete` control, this is the list of possible options.
4. Link the two controls through a view reference.
5. Add a filter that filters down the autocomplete control when the user types.

Let's start with the first step, all our necessary imports. Here we need the autocomplete functionality, but as we will be working with forms, and in particular reactive forms, we are going to need that module as well. We will also need some forms to support the input fields we mean to use:

```
import { BrowserModule } from '@angular/platform-browser';
import { NgModule } from '@angular/core';
import { AppComponent } from './app.component';
import { MatButtonModule } from '@angular/material';
import { BrowserAnimationsModule } from '@angular/platform-
browser/animations';
import { MatIconModule } from '@angular/material/icon';
import { MatButtonToggleModule } from '@angular/material/button-toggle';
import { MatAutocompleteModule } from '@angular/material';
import { ReactiveFormsModule } from '@angular/forms';
import { MatFormFieldModule } from '@angular/material/form-field';
import { MatInputModule } from '@angular/material/input';

@NgModule({
  declarations: [
    AppComponent
  ],
  imports: [
    BrowserModule,
    BrowserAnimationsModule,
    MatButtonModule,
    MatIconModule,
    MatButtonToggleModule,
    MatAutocompleteModule,
    ReactiveFormsModule,
    MatFormFieldModule,
    MatInputModule
  ],
  providers: [],
  bootstrap: [AppComponent]
```

```
})
export class AppModule { }
```

Now we are ready to add some markup to the `app.component.html` file template:

```
<mat-form-field>
  <input type="text" matInput placeholder="jedis" [formControl]="myControl"
>
</mat-form-field>
```

At this point, we have defined the input control and added the `matInput` directive. We have also added a `formControl` reference. We add that so we can later on listen to changes to our input as they happen. Changes to an input are interesting because we are able to react to them and filter our list, which is essentially what autocomplete does. The next order of business is to define a list of values that we need to suggest to the user once they start typing, so let's do that next:

```
<mat-autocomplete #auto="matAutocomplete">
  <mat-option *ngFor="let jedi of jedis" [value]="jedi">
  {{ jedi }}
  </mat-option>
</mat-autocomplete>
```

We have our list, but we lack any connection between the input field and our suggestion list. Before we fix that, we first need to look at our component class and add some code to it to support the previous markup:

```
export class AppComponent {
  myControl: FormControl;
  jedis = [
    'Luke',
    'Yoda',
    'Darth Vader',
    'Palpatine',
    'Dooku',
    'Darth Maul'
  ];
  constructor() {
    this.myControl = new FormControl();
  }
}
```

So far we have defined `matInput` and `mat-autocomplete` separately, now it's time to connect the two. We do that by adding a view reference to `mat-autocomplete` that `matInput` can refer to, like so:

```
<mat-autocomplete #auto="matAutocomplete">
```

```
    <mat-option *ngFor="let jedi of jedis"
      [value]="jedi">
    {{ jedi }}
    </mat-option>
  </mat-autocomplete>
```

And to refer to it in `matInput`, we introduce the `MatAutocomplete` directive, like so:

```
<form action="">
  <mat-input-container name="container">
    <mat-form-field hintLabel="Max 30 characters">
      <input name="input"
        type="text"
        #input
        matInput
        placeholder="type the name of the jedi"
        [formControl]="jediControl"
        [matAutocomplete]= "auto">
      <mat-hint align="end">{{input.value?.length || 0}}/30</mat-hint>
    </mat-form-field>
  </mat-input-container>
</form>
```

As you can see, `matAutocomplete` points to the `auto` view reference, thereby the list is triggered when we set focus to the input field and start typing.

We have added another useful thing in the preceding code, namely that of hints. Adding hints to your input is a great way to convey to the user what should be entered in the input field. Adding the attribute `hintLabel`, we are able to tell the user what should go into the input field. You can even take it a step further by introducing a tip on how they are doing while they are typing by using the `mat-hint` element. Let's zoom in on the preceding code that accomplished what we just described:

```
<mat-form-field hintLabel="Max 30 characters">
  <input name="input"
    type="text"
    #input
    matInput
    placeholder="type the name of the jedi"
    [formControl]="jediControl"
    [matAutocomplete]= "auto">
  <mat-hint align="end">{{input.value?.length || 0}}/30</mat-hint>
</mat-form-field>
```

Try to make use of the `hintLabel` and `mat-hint` element where applicable, it will help your users greatly.

If you typed everything in correctly, you should have something that looks like this in the UI:

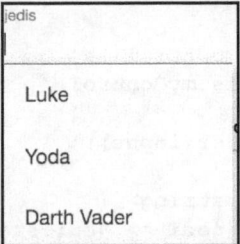

Looks great! The list is displayed when you put the input in focus. However, you notice that the list is not really being filtered down as you type. This is because we haven't picked up on the event when you type into the input control. So let us do that next.

Listening to input changing means we listen to our form control and its `valueChanges` property, like so:

```
myControl.valueChanges
```

If you look closely, you can see that this is an Observable. This means that we can use operators to filter out content we don't want. Our definition for wanted content is `jedis`, that starts with the text we entered in the input box. This means we can flesh it out to look something like this:

```
import { Component } from '@angular/core';
import { FormControl } from "@angular/forms";
import { Observable } from "rxjs/Observable";
import 'rxjs/add/operator/map';

@Component({
  selector: 'app-root',
  templateUrl: './app.component.html',
    styleUrls: ['./app.component.css']
})
export class AppComponent {
  title = 'app';
  myControl: FormControl;
  jedis = [
    'Luke',
    'Yoda',
    'Darth Vader',
```

```
      'Palpatine',
      'Dooku',
      'Darth Maul'
    ];

    filteredJedis$: Observable<string[]>;

    constructor() {
      this.myControl = new FormControl();
      this.filteredJedis$ = this.myControl
        .valueChanges
        .map(input => this.filter(input));
    }
    filter(key: string): Array<string> {
      return this.jedis.filter(jedi => jedi.startsWith(key));
    }
  }
```

Now we just need to change our template so the mat-option looks
at filteredJedis instead of the jedis array, like so:

```
<mat-autocomplete #auto="matAutocomplete">
  <mat-option *ngFor="let jedi of filteredJedis$ | async"
    [value]="jedi">
   {{ jedi }}
  </mat-option>
</mat-autocomplete>
```

Testing this out, we see that it seems to work.

Checkbox

This is the classic checkbox that holds checked, unchecked, and undetermined statuses. It is
quite simple to use but you need to import some modules to use it, like so:

```
import { MatCheckboxModule } from @angular/material/checkbox;

@NgModule({
  imports: [MatCheckboxModule]
})
```

The markup should look like this:

```
<mat-checkbox [checked]="propertyOnTheComponent" >Check me<mat-checkbox>
```

So essentially, just add `<mat-checkbox>` as an element name and make sure to bind the `checked` attribute to a property on our component.

Date picker

As usual with a date picker, you can do a lot more with it than just selecting a date from a pop-up calendar. You can disable date ranges, format the date, show it on a yearly and monthly basis, and so on. We will only explore how to get up and running with it, but we encourage you to explore the documentation for this control at `https://material.angular.io/components/datepicker/overview`.

First off we, need to import the necessary modules:

```
import {
  MatDatepickerModule,
  MatNativeDateModule
} from '@angular/material';

@NgModule({
  imports: [MatDatepickerModule, MatNativeDateModule]
})
```

For the markup, we need to do the following:

- Define an input with a `matInput` directive. The selected date will be placed here.
- Define a `<mat-datepicker>` element. This is the pop-up calendar.
- Create a connection between the two controls.

For the first bullet point, we declare it in the markup, like so:

```
<mat-form-field>
  <input matInput placeholder="Choose a date">
</mat-form-field>
```

We can see that we point out a `formControl` instance called input in our component by the use of the `formControl` directive. We also add the `matInput` directive to give our input field that nice material look and feel.

For the second task, we define the `<mat-datepicker>` element, like so:

```
<mat-datepicker></mat-datepicker>
```

Now we need to make the connection between them and, just like we did with the autocomplete control, we define a view reference, `picker`, in the `<mat-datepicker>` element, and refer to that in the input element by assigning the view reference to the `matDatepicker` directive, so it looks like the following:

```
<div>
  <mat-form-field>
    <input matInput [matDatepicker]="picker">
    <mat-datepicker-toggle matSuffix [for]="picker">
    </mat-datepicker-toggle>
    <mat-datepicker #picker></mat-datepicker>
  </mat-form-field>
</div>
```

So, in summary, we added a view reference to the `mat-datepicker` element, and referred to said reference by assigning it to the `[matDatePicker]` directive in the input element.

We also added a button that will toggle the visibility of the calendar. We made that possible by using the `<mat-datepicker-toggle>` element and assigning it the `picker` view reference:

```
<mat-datepicker-toggle matSuffix [for]="picker"></mat-datepicker-toggle>
```

Finally, your creation should now look like the following:

Navigation

Navigation is how we get around in the application. There are different ways for us to do that, such as clicking a link or clicking on a menu item for example. Angular Material offers three components for this:

- **Menu**: This is a pop-out list where you get to choose from many different menu options
- **Sidenav**: This component acts like a menu docked to the left or the right of the page and presents itself as an overlay over the application while dimming the application content
- **Toolbar**: This is typical toolbar that is a way for the user to reach commonly used actions

In this section, we will show a full example of using the menu, but we encourage you to keep exploring by learning to use the sidenav (https://material.angular.io/components/sidenav/overview), as well as the toolbar component (https://material.angular.io/components/toolbar/overview).

Menu

The menu component is what it sounds like, it's made for you to easily present a menu to the user. It uses three major directives, mat-menu, mat-menu-item, and lastly, MatMenuTriggerFor. There is only one mat-menu per menu and as many mat-menu-items as you need. The MatMenuTriggerFor is used to trigger the menu, you usually attach this one to a button.

Making the menu work can be divided into three steps:

1. Define a mat-menu control.
2. Add as many mat-menu-items as you need.
3. Add a trigger to a button by adding the MatMenuTriggerFor directive.

Before we do any of that, we need to import the MatMenuModule to be able to use the constructs previously mentioned, so let's do that:

```
import {MatMenuModule} from '@angular/material';

@NgModule({
  imports: [MatMenuModule]
})
```

Now we are ready to define our menu, like so:

```
<mat-menu>
</mat-menu>
```

Thereafter, we add as many items as we need:

```
<mat-menu>
  <button mat-menu-item >Item1</button>
  <button mat-menu-item >Item2</button>
</mat-menu>
```

Lastly, we add a trigger by adding a button that will trigger it and the `matMenuTriggerFor` directive, like so:

```
<button [matMenuTriggerFor]="menu">Trigger menu</button>
<mat-menu #menu>
  <button mat-menu-item >Item1</button>
  <button mat-menu-item >Item1</button>
</mat-menu>
```

Note how `matMenuTriggerFor` points to the `menu` view reference.

Your finished result should look something like this:

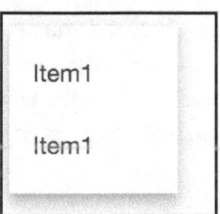

Not all menus are this simple of course. Sooner or later you will encounter a scenario where you need a menu to be nested. Material UI easily supports this. The overall approach to supporting this lies in defining a `mat-menu` definition for each menu you need and then connecting them. Then you need to define what action leads to what submenu being triggered. Sounds hard? It's really not. Let's begin with our top-level menu, our root menu. Let's give the menu items some meaningful names, like so:

```
<button [matMenuTriggerFor]="menu">Trigger menu</button>
<mat-menu #menu>
  <button mat-menu-item >File</button>
  <button mat-menu-item >Export</button>
</mat-menu>
```

At this point, we have two menu items and the last one, `wxport`, begs for some suboptions. Imagine we are dealing with tabular data in a program, it would make sense to support exporting that data to either CSV or PDF. Let's add a submenu for just that, like so:

```
<button [matMenuTriggerFor]="rootMenu">Trigger menu</button>
<mat-menu #rootMenu>
  <button mat-menu-item>File</button>
  <button mat-menu-item>Export</button>
</mat-menu>

<mat-menu #subMenu>
  <button mat-menu-item>CSV</button>
  <button mat-menu-item>PDF</button>
</mat-menu>
```

OK, so now we have two different menus, but we need to add the connection where a `rootMenu` item triggers the `subMenu` to show. Let's add that by again using the `matMenutriggerFor` directive, like so:

```
<button [matMenuTriggerFor]="rootMenu">Trigger menu</button>
<mat-menu #rootMenu>
  <button mat-menu-item >File</button>
  <button mat-menu-item [matMenuTriggerFor]="subMenu">Export</button>
</mat-menu>

<mat-menu #subMenu>
  <button mat-menu-item>CSV</button>
  <button mat-menu-item>PDF</button>
</mat-menu>
```

This should render a menu that looks like the following:

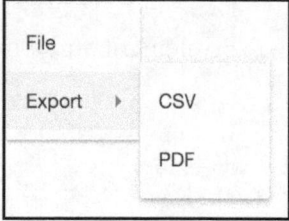

There are more things you can do with a menu than just rendering a few menu items and have them triggered by a button. Other things to consider and try out are making it more professional looking by adding an icon or catering to accessibility. Now that you know the basics of how to create a simple menu as well as nested ones, go and explore.

Layout

Layout is about defining how we place the content on our page. Angular Material gives us different components for this purpose, namely:

- **List**: This is a way to present your content as a list of items. The list can be enriched with links, icons, and can even be multiline.
- **Grid list**: This is a control that helps you arrange your content in blocks. You need to define the number of columns, and the component will make sure to fill out the visual space.
- **Card**: This is a component that wraps content and adds a box shadow. You can define a header for it as well.
- **Tabs**: This lets you divide up your content between different tabs.
- **Stepper**: This is a component that divides up your component in wizard-like steps.
- **Expansion panel**: This component works pretty much like an accordion, in that it enables you to lay out your components in a list-like way with a title for each item. Each item can be expanded, and only one item can be expanded at a time.

In this section, we will cover the list and grid list components. We urge you to explore the card component, https://material.angular.io/components/card/overview, the tabs component, https://material.angular.io/components/tabs/overview, the stepper, https://material.angular.io/components/stepper/overview, and the expansion panel, https://material.angular.io/components/expansion/overview, at your own volition.

List

The list control is built up by a mat-list element and a number of mat-list-items. The markup for this looks like:

```
<mat-list>
  <mat-list-item>Item1</mat-list-item>
  <mat-list-item>Item1</mat-list-item>
</mat-list>
```

That's it, that is all there is to it. For your effort, you are awarded with a list that looks like this:

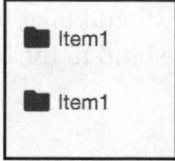

A list can, of course, be a lot more complicated, containing links, icons, and more. A more interesting example may look like this:

I think you get the idea, there are list items and I can put pretty much put anything I want in them. To read more about the capabilities, here is the link to the list documentation: `https://material.angular.io/components/list/overview`.

Grid list

The grid list is used to display your content in a list of rows and columns, while ensuring that it fills out the viewport. This is a very nice component if you want maximum freedom of deciding how to display content. This is a separate module called `MatGridListModule`. We need to add this to our list of imported modules, like so:

```
import { MatGridListModule } from '@angular/material';

@NgModule({
  imports: [MatGridListModule]
})
```

The component consists of a `mat-grid-list` element and a number of `mat-grid-tile` elements.

Let's add the `mat-grid-list` element first:

```
<mat-grid-list cols=4 rowHeight="300px">
</mat-grid-list>
```

Worth noting is how we set the number of columns and the height of each row. Now it's time to add the content. We do that by adding a number of mat-grid-tile instances, like so:

```
<mat-grid-list cols=4 rowHeight="300px">
  <mat-grid-tile *ngFor="let tile of tiles"
    [colspan]="tile.cols"
    [rowspan]="tile.rows"
    [style.background]="tile.color">
    {{ tile.text }}
  </mat-grid-tile>
</mat-grid-list>
```

Here we are defining an *ngFor to point to our list of tiles. We also bind to [colspan], that decides how much column space it should take, [rowspan], that determines how many rows it should take, and lastly, we bind to the background property in our style.

The component looks like this:

```
tiles = [
  {text: 'One', cols: 3, rows: 1, color: 'lightblue'},
  {text: 'Two', cols: 1, rows: 2, color: 'lightgreen'},
  {text: 'Three', cols: 1, rows: 1, color: 'lightpink'},
  {text: 'Four', cols: 2, rows: 1, color: '#DDBDF1'},
];
```

We encourage you to explore the card and tabs component to learn more about the remaining layout components.

Popups and modals

There are different ways that we can capture the user's attention. One way is to show a dialog over the content of the page and prompt the user to act. Another way is to display information about a part of the page when the user hovers over that particular part.

Angular Material offers three different components for this:

- **Dialog**: This is simply a modal dialog displaying itself on top of the content.
- **Tooltip**: This displays a piece of text when you hover over a specified area.
- **Snackbar**: This shows an information message at the bottom of a page. The information message is only visible for a short amount of time. It is meant to convey to the user that something has happened as a result of an action, such as saving a form.

Dialog

The dialog component is quite powerful as it helps us create a modal. It can be customized to your heart's content and is a bit tricky to set up. But don't worry, we will guide you through the process. What we need to do is:

1. Import the dialog module.
2. Create a component that is our dialog.
3. Create a component and a button that will trigger the module.
4. Add our dialog to the `entryComponents` property of our module.

First off, we import the necessary module, like so:

```
import { MatDialogModule } from '@angular/material';

@NgModule({
  imports: [MatDialogModule]
})
```

Next up, we create a component that will hold our dialog. It is a normal component with a template and a backing class, but it does need to inject a `MatDialogRef`. It should look something like this:

```
import { MatDialogRef } from "@angular/material";
import { Component } from "@angular/core";

@Component({
  selector: 'my-dialog',
  template: `
  <h1 mat-dialog-title>Perform action?</h1>
  <mat-dialog-content>Save changes to Jedi?</mat-dialog-content>
  <mat-dialog-actions>
   <button mat-button [mat-dialog-close]="true">Yes</button>
   <button mat-button mat-dialog-close>No</button>
  </mat-dialog-actions>
  `
})
export class DialogComponent {
 constructor(public dialogRef: MatDialogRef<DialogComponent>) {
   console.log('dialog opened');
 }
}
```

What we have done here is define the following general structure in the template:

```
<h1 mat-dialog-title>Save changes to Jedi?</h1>
<mat-dialog-content>
</mat-dialog-content>
<mat-dialog-actions>
  <button mat-button [mat-dialog-close]>Yes</button>
  <button mat-button mat-dialog-close >No</button>
</mat-dialog-actions>
```

At a quick glance, we define a title, a content, and an action field, where buttons are defined. To send different values back we use `[mat-dialog-close]` and assign a value to it.

As for the code part, we inject an instance of `MatDialogRef` that is typed to `MyDialog`, which is the very component we are in.

The third thing we need to do is to set up a host component, in which there is a button that, when clicked, will launch a dialog. So let's do that with the following code:

```
import { Component } from "@angular/core";
import { MatDialog } from "@angular/material/dialog";
import { DialogComponent } from "./dialog.component";

@Component({
  selector: 'dialog-example',
  template: `
  <button (click)="openDialog()">Open Dialog</button>
  `
})
export class DialogExampleComponent {
  selectedOption;
  constructor(private dialog: MatDialog) { }
  openDialog() {
    let dialogRef = this.dialog.open(DialogComponent);
    dialogRef.afterClosed().subscribe(result => {
      // do something with 'result'
    });
  }
}
```

We do two things here, we call `dialog.open()` with a type, which is our dialog component. Furthermore, by listening to the Observable we get back when calling `dialogRef.afterClosed()`, we are able to inspect the result coming back from the dialog. At this point there isn't much of a result to look at but in the next section we will look at a more advanced dialog example where we use this method.

Lastly, we need to go to our `app.module.ts` file and add our `DialogComponent` dialog to the `entryComponents` array, like so:

```
@NgModule({
  entryComponents: [DialogComponent]
})
```

So, adding things to the `entryComponents` array in an Angular module is a completely new concept to us, what does it actually do? When we add a component to that list we tell the compiler that this component needs to be compiled and needs a `ComponentFactory` so we can create it on the fly. Thus, the criteria for putting any component in here is that we want to load a component dynamically or by type. This is exactly the case with our `DialogComponent`. It doesn't actually exist before we call `this.dialog.open(DialogComponent)`. At that point, it runs a method under the hood called `ViewContainerRef.createComponent()`. In short, we need to instantiate the `DialogComponent` every time we wish to open it. So, don't forget about `entryComponents` or it won't work. You can read more on `entryComponents` at `https://angular.io/guide/ngmodule-faq#what-is-an-entry-component`.

Your dialog will end up looking something like this:

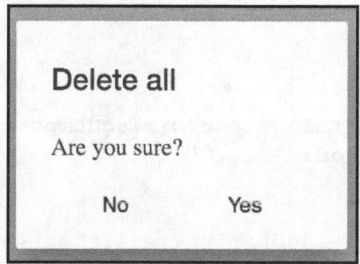

A more advanced example – sending data to and from your dialog

Previously, we introduced a simple dialog example where we learned to open the dialog and close it. That barely scratched the surface. What is really interesting is how we would send data to the dialog so it comes prebooted with some data, and also how we would send data we gather inside of the dialog back to the host component that opened it. We will look at both these scenarios.

The business case for sending data to the dialog, so it starts with some data, is so that we can, for example, show an existing record and make updates to it in the dialog.

By adding a second argument to the method `dialog.open()` we are able to send data to the dialog component that it can display:

```typescript
// jedi.model.ts
interface Jedi {
  name: string;
}

import { Component } from "@angular/core";
import { MatDialog } from "@angular/material/dialog";
import { DialogComponent } from "./dialog.component";

@Component({
 selector: 'dialog-example',
   template: `
   <button (click)="openDialog()">Open Dialog</button>
   `
})
export class DialogExampleComponent {
 selectedOption;
 jedi: Jedi;

 constructor(private dialog: MatDialog) {
   this.jedi = { name: 'Luke' };
 }

 openDialog() {
   let dialogRef = this.dialog.open(DialogComponent, {
     data: { jedi: this.jedi }
   });

   dialogRef.afterClosed().subscribe(result => {
     console.log(result);
   });
 }
}
```

On the dialog component side of things, we need to tell it about the data we are sending in. We do that by injecting MAT_DIALOG_DATA, the needed changes are in bold:

```typescript
import { MatDialogRef, MAT_DIALOG_DATA } from "@angular/material";
import { Component, Inject } from "@angular/core";

@Component({
  selector: 'my-dialog',
  template: `
  <h1 mat-dialog-title>Save changes to jedi?</h1>
    <mat-dialog-content>
```

```
            <input matInput [(ngModel)]="data.jedi.name" />
        </mat-dialog-content>
        <mat-dialog-actions>
          <button mat-button (click)="saveAndClose()">Yes</button>
          <button mat-button mat-dialog-close>No</button>
        </mat-dialog-actions>
      `,
})
export class DialogComponent {
  constructor(
    public dialogRef: MatDialogRef<DialogComponent>,
    @Inject(MAT_DIALOG_DATA) public data: any
  ) {
    console.log('dialog opened');
  }

  saveAndClose() {
    this.dialogRef.close('save');
  }
}
```

Now, because we have sent the data bound `jedi` instance from the `host` class, any changes we do to it in the `Dialog` class will be reflected in the `host` class. That takes care of sending data from the `host` class to the dialog, but what if we want to send data from dialog back? We can easily accomplish that by sending a parameter in the `dialogRef.close()` method call, like so:

```
export class DialogComponent {
  constructor(
    public dialogRef: MatDialogRef<DialogComponent>,
    @Inject(MAT_DIALOG_DATA) public data: any
  ) {
    console.log('dialog opened');
  }

  saveAndClose() {
    this.dialogRef.close('save');
  }
}
```

To do something with that data, we simply subscribe to the Observable we get from calling `afterClose()`. This is illustrated in bold as follows:

```
import { Component } from "@angular/core";
import { MatDialog } from "@angular/material/dialog";
import { DialogComponent } from "./dialog.component";
```

```
@Component({
  selector: 'dialog-example',
  template: `
<button (click)="openDialog()">Open Dialog</button>
`
})
export class DialogExampleComponent {
  selectedOption;
  jedi: Jedi;
  constructor(private dialog: MatDialog) {
    this.jedi = { name: 'Luke' };
  }

  openDialog() {
    let dialogRef = this.dialog.open(DialogComponent, {
      data: { jedi: this.jedi }
    });

    dialogRef
      .afterClosed()
      .subscribe(result => {
      // will print 'save' if we pressed 'Yes' button
      console.log(result);
    });
}}
```

Data table

There are different ways we can show the data. Showing it in rows and columns is an efficient way of getting a quick overview. You might, however, need to sort the data by column to quickly zoom in on the interesting data. Also, the amount of data might be so great that it needs to be shown in parts, by page. Angular Material addresses these issues by offering the following components:

- **Table**: This lays out the data in rows and columns, with headers
- **Sort table**: This allows you to sort your data
- **Paginator**: This allows you to slice up your data in pages while allowing you to navigate between pages

It should be said that in most cases when trying to add a table to your app, it is expected that a table can be sorted and that the data can be paged so as not to completely overwhelm the user. Let's therefore have a look at how to achieve all of this step by step.

Table

The table component is able to let us present our data in columns and rows. We need to do the following to get a table component up and running:

1. Import and register the `MatTableModule` in our root module.
2. Construct the data that we mean to display.
3. Define the markup for our table.

The first order of business is to import the necessary module, and that is easily done with the following code:

```
import {MatTableModule} from '@angular/material';

@NgModule({
  imports: [MatTableModule]
})
```

At this point, we start constructing our data and create an instance of the `MatTableDataSource` class. The code is as follows:

```
// app/jedi.model.ts
export class interface Jedi {
  name: string;
  side: string;
}

// app/table.example.component.ts
@Component({
  selector: 'example-table',
  template : `
<div>
  <mat-table #table [dataSource]="tableSource" matSort>
    // header 'Name'
    <ng-container matColumnDef="name">
      <mat-header-cell *matHeaderCellDef mat-sort-header> Name
      </mat-header-cell>
      <mat-cell *matCellDef="let element"> {{element.name}}
      </mat-cell>
    </ng-container>
    // header 'Side'
    <ng-container matColumnDef="side">
      <mat-header-cell *matHeaderCellDef mat-sort-header> Side
      </mat-header-cell>
      <mat-cell *matCellDef="let element"> {{element.side}}
      </mat-cell>
    </ng-container>
```

```
        <mat-header-row *matHeaderRowDef="displayedColumns"></mat-header-row>
        <mat-row *matRowDef="let row; columns: displayedColumns;"></mat-row>
      </mat-table>
      <mat-paginator #paginator [pageSize]="2" [pageSizeOptions]="[1, 5, 10]">
      </mat-paginator>
  </div>
  `
})
export class ExampleTableComponent {
 jediSource: Array<Jedi>;
 tableSource: MatTableDataSource<Jedi>;
 displayedColumns: string[];

 constructor() {
   this.displayedColumns = ['name', 'side'];
   this.jediSource = [{
     name: 'Yoda',
     side: 'Good'
   }, {
     name: 'Darth',
     side: 'Evil'
   }, {
     name: 'Palpatine',
     side: 'Evil'
   }];

   this.tableSource = new MatTableDataSource<Jedi>(this.jediSource);
 }
}
```

Noteworthy here is how we construct a `MatTableDataSource` instance out of an array of objects. We will use this instance in the markup and point it out as the data source. The next thing to do is construct the markup needed to support this table. The code for that is as follows:

```
<mat-table #table [dataSource]="tableSource">
  // header 'Name'
  <ng-container matColumnDef="name">
    <mat-header-cell *matHeaderCellDef> Name </mat-header-cell>
    <mat-cell *matCellDef="let element"> {{element.name}} </mat-cell>
  </ng-container>

  // header 'Side'
  <ng-container matColumnDef="side">
    <mat-header-cell *matHeaderCellDef> Side </mat-header-cell>
    <mat-cell *matCellDef="let element"> {{element.side}} </mat-cell>
  </ng-container>
```

```
        <mat-header-row *matHeaderRowDef="displayedColumns"></mat-header-row>
        <mat-row *matRowDef="let row; columns: displayedColumns;"></mat-row>
</mat-table>
```

We have pointed out several points of interest in the previous code. Columns for the table are constructed by creating an `ng-container` element containing in turn a `mat-header-cell`, where the title is defined, and a `mat-cell` where we say what data should go in there. The `mat-header-row` element, further down in the code, enables us to point out the order in which the columns should appear. We can see in our previous code snippet how this is just an array of strings. Finally, with the `mat-row` element, we simple display all the rows of our table. The end result should look like this:

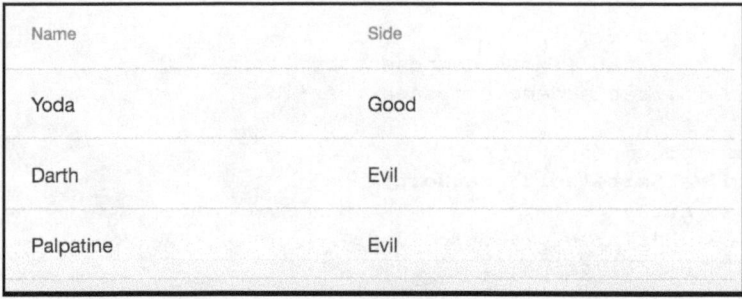

Sorting

The previous figure constitutes a nice looking table, but it lacks a pretty standard functionality, namely that of sorting. We expect that by clicking the header it will sort into ascending and descending respectively, and that it is able to recognize common data types such as strings and integers, and sort those correctly. The good news is that this is very easy to achieve. We need to do the following to ensure that our table can be sorted:

1. Import and register the `MatSortModule`.
2. Create a `ViewChild` of type `MatSort` and assign it to the `dataSources` sort property.
3. Add the directive `matSortHeader` to the headers that should be able to be sorted.

We complete the first step by adding the following code to the root module:

```
import { MatSortModule } from '@angular/material/sort';
@NgModule({
  imports: [MatSortModule]
})
```

Thereafter, we go into our component and add the `MatSort` `ViewChild` and assign it to the sort property, as described previously:

```
import { Component, ViewChild } from '@angular/core';
import { MatTableDataSource, MatSort } from "@angular/material";

@Component({
  selector: 'table-demo',
  templateUrl: './table.demo.component.html',
  styleUrls: ['./table.demo.component.css']
})
export class AppComponent {
  @ViewChild(MatSort) sort: MatSort;
  jediSource: Array<Jedi>;
  tableSource: MatTableDataSource<Jedi>;
  displayedColumns: string[];

  constructor() {
    this.displayedColumns = ['name', 'side'];
    this.jediSource = [{
      name: 'Yoda',
      side: 'Good'
    }, {
      name: 'Darth',
      side: 'Evil'
    },
    {
      name: 'Palpatine',
      side: 'Evil'
    }];

    this.tableSource = new MatTableDataSource<Jedi>(this.jediSource);
  }

  ngAfterViewInit() {
    this.tableSource.sort = this.sort;
  }
```

At this point, we need to fix the markup and then sorting should work. The changes we need to make to the markup are to simply apply the `matSort` directive to the whole table and `mat-sort-header` to each header that should be possible to sort. The code for the markup is now as follows:

```
<mat-table #table [dataSource]="tableSource" matSort>
  // header 'Name'
  <ng-container matColumnDef="name">
    <mat-header-cell *matHeaderCellDef mat-sort-header> Name </mat-header-
cell>
    <mat-cell *matCellDef="let element"> {{element.name}} </mat-cell>
  </ng-container>

  // header 'Side'
  <ng-container matColumnDef="side">
    <mat-header-cell *matHeaderCellDef mat-sort-header> Side </mat-header-
cell>
    <mat-cell *matCellDef="let element"> {{element.side}} </mat-cell>
  </ng-container>

  <mat-header-row *matHeaderRowDef="displayedColumns"></mat-header-row>
  <mat-row *matRowDef="let row; columns: displayedColumns;"></mat-row>
</mat-table>
```

The UI should now indicate with an arrow by the column **Name**, the direction in which the data is being sorted, as the following image indicates:

Name ↓	Side
Yoda	Good
Palpatine	Evil
Darth	Evil

Pagination

Our table so far is starting to look quite good. It can even be sorted, besides from displaying data. We are aware though that in most cases the data for a table is usually quite long, which leads to the user either having to scroll or browse the data page by page. We can solve the latter option with the help of the pagination element. To use it, we need to do the following:

1. Import and register the `MatPaginatorModule`.
2. Assign a `paginator` `ViewChild` instance to the data source's paginator property.
3. Add a `mat-paginator` element to the markup.

Starting with the first item on our list, we need to add the following code to our root module:

```
import {MatPaginatorModule} from '@angular/material/paginator';

@NgModule({
  imports: [MatPaginatorModule]
})
```

Thereafter, we need to add assign the `paginator` property to our `tableSource.paginator`, as described previously. The code for that looks like the following:

```
import { Component, ViewChild } from '@angular/core';
import { MatTableDataSource, MatSort } from "@angular/material";

@Component({
  selector: 'table-demo',
  template: `
  <mat-table #table [dataSource]="tableSource" matSort>
    // header 'Name'
    <ng-container matColumnDef="name">
      <mat-header-cell *matHeaderCellDef mat-sort-header> Name
      </mat-header-cell>
      <mat-cell *matCellDef="let element"> {{element.name}}
      </mat-cell>
    </ng-container>

    // header 'Side'
    <ng-container matColumnDef="side">
      <mat-header-cell *matHeaderCellDef mat-sort-header> Side
      </mat-header-cell>
      <mat-cell *matCellDef="let element"> {{element.side}}
```

```
          </mat-cell>
        </ng-container>

        <mat-header-row *matHeaderRowDef="displayedColumns"></mat-header-row>
        <mat-row *matRowDef="let row; columns: displayedColumns;"></mat-row>
      </mat-table>
    `,
  styleUrls: ['./table.demo.component.css']
})
export class AppComponent {
  @ViewChild(MatSort) sort: MatSort;
  @ViewChild(MatPaginator) paginator: MatPaginator;
  jediSource: Array<Jedi>;
  tableSource: MatTableDataSource<Jedi>;
  displayedColumns: string[];

  constructor() {
    this.displayedColumns = ['name', 'side'];
    this.jediSource = [{
      name: 'Yoda',
      side: 'Good'
    }, {
      name: 'Darth',
      side: 'Evil'
    },
    {
      name: 'Palpatine',
      side: 'Evil'
    }];

    this.tableSource = new MatTableDataSource<Jedi>(this.jediSource);
  }

  ngAfterViewInit() {
    this.tableSource.sort = this.sort;
    this.tableSource.paginator = paginator;
  }
}
```

Our remaining part is just to change the markup, which should have the following alterations (changes in bold):

```
<div>
  <mat-table #table [dataSource]="tableSource" matSort>
    // header 'Name'
    <ng-container matColumnDef="name">
      <mat-header-cell *matHeaderCellDef mat-sort-header> Name
      </mat-header-cell>
      <mat-cell *matCellDef="let element"> {{element.name}}
```

```
        </mat-cell>
      </ng-container>
      // header 'Side'
      <ng-container matColumnDef="side">
        <mat-header-cell *matHeaderCellDef mat-sort-header> Side
        </mat-header-cell>
        <mat-cell *matCellDef="let element"> {{element.side}} </mat-cell>
      </ng-container>
      <mat-header-row *matHeaderRowDef="displayedColumns"></mat-header-row>
      <mat-row *matRowDef="let row; columns: displayedColumns;"></mat-row>
    </mat-table>
    <mat-paginator #paginator [pageSize]="2" [pageSizeOptions]="[1, 5, 10]">
    </mat-paginator>
  </div>
```

Here, we clearly show that the only addition to our markup was the `mat-paginator` element at the bottom. Here, we specify our view reference, but also the page size as well as what pages we should be able to switch to, should we want to.

Summary

We set about trying to explain what Material Design is, a design language with paper and ink in mind. Thereafter, we mentioned the most well-known implementations of Material Design.

Next up, we put most of our focus on Angular Material, the Material Design implementation meant for Angular, and how it consists of different components. We went hands-on in explaining how to install it, set it up, and even how to use different form controls and input buttons.

Time was also spent covering other aspects of the components, such as layout, navigation, modals, and tabular data. Hopefully, you will have read this chapter and found that you now have a grasp of Material Design in general and Angular Material in particular, and can determine whether it is a good match for your next Angular app.

12
Animating Components with Angular

Nowadays, animations are one of the cornerstones of modern user experience design. Far from just representing visual eye candy to beautify the UI, they have become an important part of the visual narrative. Animations pave the road to convey messages in a non-intrusive way, becoming a cheap but powerful tool for informing the user about the underlying processes and events that happen while we interact with our application. The moment an animation pattern becomes widespread and the audience embraces it as a modern standard, we gain access to a priceless tool for enhancing our application's user experience. Animations are language-agnostic, not necessarily bound to a single device or environment (web, desktop, or mobile), and pleasing to the eye of the beholder, when used wisely. In other words, animations are here to stay and Angular 2 has a strong commitment to this aspect of modern visual development.

With all modern browsers embracing the newer features of CSS3 for animation handling, Angular 2 offers support for implementing imperative animation scripting through an incredibly simple but powerful API. This chapter will cover several approaches to implementing animation effects, moving from leveraging plain vanilla CSS for applying class-based animations, to implementing script routines where Angular takes full responsibility for handling DOM transitions.

In this chapter we cover the following topics:

- Creating animations with plain vanilla CSS
- Leveraging class-named animation with the `ngClass` directive to better handle transitions
- Looking at Angular's built-in CSS hooks for defining styles for each transition state

- Introducing animation triggers and declaratively attaching those animations to elements in your template
- Animating components with the **AnimationBuilder** API
- Designing directives that handle animation

Creating animations with plain vanilla CSS

The inception of CSS-based animation was an important milestone in modern web design. Before that, we used to rely on JavaScript to accommodate animations in our web applications by manipulating DOM elements through complex and cumbersome scripts based on intervals, timeouts, and loops of all sorts. Unfortunately, this was neither maintainable nor scalable.

Then, modern browsers embraced the functionalities brought about by the recent CSS transform, transition, keyframes, and animation properties. This became a game changer in the context of web interaction design. While support for these techniques in browsers, such as **Microsoft Internet Explorer**, is far from optimal, the rest of the browsers that are available (including Microsoft's very own Edge) provide full support for these CSS APIs.

MSIE provides support for these animation techniques only as of version 10.

We assume that you have a broad understanding of how CSS animation works with regard to building keyframe-driven or transition-based animations, since providing coverage to these techniques is obviously beyond of the scope of this book. As a recap, we can highlight the fact that CSS-based animation is usually implemented by either of these approaches, or even a combination of both:

- Transition properties that will act as observers of either all, or just a subset, of the CSS properties applied to the DOM elements impacted by the selector. Whenever any of these CSS properties is changed, the DOM element will not take the new value right away, but will experience a steady transition into its new state.
- Named keyframe animations, where we define different steps of the evolution of one, or several, CSS properties under a unique name, which will populate later on an animation property of a given selector, being one able to set additional parameters, such as the delay, the duration of the animation tweening, or the number of iterations that the animation is meant to feature.

As we can see in the two aforementioned scenarios, the use of a CSS selector populated with animation settings is the starting point for all things related to animation, and that is what we will do now. Let's build a fancy pulse animation to emulate a heartbeat-style effect in the bitmap that decorates our Pomodoro timer.

We will use a keyframe-based animation this time, so we will begin by building the actual CSS routine in a separate style sheet. The entire animation is based on a simple interpolation where we take an object, scale it up by 10 percent, and scale it back down again to its initial state. This keyframe-based tweening is then named and wrapped in a CSS class named `pulse`, which will execute the animation in an infinite loop where each iteration takes 1 second to complete.

All the CSS rules for implementing this animation will live in an external stylesheet, part of the timer widget component, within the `timer feature` folder:

```
// app/timer/timer.widget.component.css

@keyframes pulse {
  0% {
    transform: scale3d(1, 1, 1);
  }
  50% {
    transform: scale3d(1.1, 1.1, 1.1);
  }
  100% {
    transform: scale3d(1, 1, 1);
  }
}

.pulse {
  animation: pulse 1s infinite;
}

.task {
  background: red;
  width: 30px;
  height: 30px;
  border-radius: 50%;
}
```

From this point on, any DOM element annotated with this class name will visually beat like a heart. This visual effect is actually a good hint that the element is undertaking some kind of action, so applying it to the main icon bitmap in our timer widget when the countdown is on will help convey the feeling that an activity is currently taking place in a lively fashion.

Thankfully, we have a good way to apply such an effect only when the countdown is active. We use the `isPaused` binding in the `TimerWidgetComponent` template. Binding its value to the `NgClass` directive in order to render the class name only when the component is not paused will do the trick, so just open the timer widget code unit file and add a reference to the stylesheet we just created and apply the directive as described previously:

```
// app/timer/timer.widget.component.ts

import { Component } from "@angular/core";

@Component({
  selector: 'timer-widget',
  styleUrls: ['timer.widget.component.css'],
  template: `
  <div class="text-center">
    <div class="task" [ngClass]="{ pulse: !isPaused }"></div>
    <h3><small>{{ taskName }}</small></h3>
    <h1> {{ minutes }}:{{ seconds | number: '2.0' }} </h1>
    <p>
      <button (click)="togglePause()" class="btn btn-danger">
      Toggle
      </button>
    </p>
  </div>`
})
export class TimerWidgetComponent {
  taskName: string = 'task';
  minutes = 10;
  seconds = 20;
  isPaused = true;

  togglePause() {
    this.isPaused = !this.isPaused;
  }
}
```

And that's it! Run our Pomodoro app and click on the `Timer` link at the top to reach the timer component page and check the visual effect live after starting the countdown. Stop it and resume it again to see the effect applied only when the countdown is active.

Introducing Angular animations

The idea with an animation trigger is that you can show animations when a certain property changes from one state to the next. To define a trigger, we first need to install and import the library we need, specifically, BrowserAnimationsModule, so let's do that.

We install the library by typing the following command:

```
npm install @angular/animations --save
```

Let's now import and set up the module with BrowsersAnimationsModule:

```
import { BrowserAnimationsModule } from '@angular/platform-
browser/animations';

@NgModule({
  imports: [BrowserAnimationsModule]
})
```

After this, it's time to import a bunch of constructs that we need to set up the trigger itself:

```
import {
  trigger,
  state,
  style,
  animate,
  transition
} from '@angular/animations';
```

The imported constructs have the following functionality:

- trigger: This defines the property in the component that the animation targets; it needs a name as the first argument and an array of states and transitions as the second argument
- state: This defines the property value and what CSS properties it should have; you need to define one of these for each value that the property can assume
- transition: This defines how the animation should play out when you go from one property value to another
- animate: This carries out the defined animation when we move from one state value to the next

Our first trigger

Let's have a quick look on what an animation trigger can look like, and then explain the parts:

```
animations: [
  trigger('sizeAnimation', [
    state('small', style({
      transform:'scale(1)',
      backgroundColor: 'green'
    })),
    state('large', style({
      transform: '(1.4)',
      backgroundColor: 'red'
    })),
    transition('small => large', animate('100ms ease-in')),
    transition('large => small', animate('100ms ease-out'))
  ])
]
```

The `animations` array is something we add to the components object, such as template or `styleUrls`. Inside of the `animations` array are a number of trigger definitions. A `trigger` takes a name and an array of items, like so:

```
trigger('name', [ ... items ])
```

Those items are either a state definition or a transition. With this knowledge, it is easier to understand what we are looking at. For now, we have chosen to call the trigger `animationName`. It defines two states and two transitions. A state says that a value has been changed to this state and we react accordingly by executing a style, which is why the code should be read as the following:

```
state(
  'when I change to this value',
  style({ /*apply these style changes*/ }))
```

 Note that style properties are camel cased and not kebab cased, for example, write `backgroundColor` and not `background-color`, like you might be used to in CSS.

Looking at our example, we are saying the following:

- If someone triggers `sizeAnimation` and the value is set to `small` then apply this transform: `scale(1)` and `backgroundColor: 'green'`
- If someone triggers `sizeAnimation` and the value is set to `large` then apply this transform: `scale(1.4)` and `backgroundColor: 'red'`

The two remaining items are two calls to `transition`. This instructs the animation on how to apply the animation in a smooth way. You can read a transition definition in the following way:

```
transition(' when I go from this state > to this state ', animate( 100ms
ease-in))
```

So, when we go from one state to the next, we apply an easing function and also define for how long the animation should execute. Let's look back at our code:

```
transition('small => large', animate('100ms ease-in')),
transition('large => small',animate('100ms ease-out'))
```

We interpret it in the following way:

- When we go from the value `small` to `large`, carry out the animation for `100ms` and use the `ease-in` function
- When we go from the value `large` to `small`, carry out the animation for `100ms` and use the `ease-out` function

Connecting the parts

Now that we have dissected our `trigger` statement completely, we have one last thing to do, and that is to connect the trigger to a property it needs to look at. So, let's add a little more code to the template:

```
@Component({
  selector: 'example',
  template: `
  <button (click)="makeBigger()">Make bigger</button>
  <button (click)="makeSmaller()">Make smaller</button>
  <p class="animate" [@sizeAnimation]="state">some text</p>
  `
  ,
  animations: [
    trigger('sizeAnimation', [
      state('small', style({
```

```
        transform:'scale(1)',
        backgroundColor: 'green'})),
      state('large', style({
        transform: 'scale(1.4)',
        backgroundColor : 'red'
      })),
      transition('small => large', animate('100ms ease-in')),
      transition('large => small',animate('100ms ease-out'))
    ])
  ],
  styles: [`
    .animate {
      background: green;
      width: 100px;
    }
  `]
})
export class ExampleComponent {
  state: string;
  makeBigger() {
    this.state = 'large';
  }

  makeSmaller() {
    this.state = 'small';
  }
}
```

Now, they key thing to look at is the `[@animationName]='state'`; this is where we say that the trigger should look at the component `state` property and we already know what values `state` should have for an animation to be triggered.

The wildcard state

There can be more than just the two states that we defined for our trigger. In some cases, it makes more sense to apply transitions regardless of what state value we come from. For those cases, there is the wildcard state. Using the wildcard state is easy. You go to your transition definition and replace a state value with *, like so:

```
transition('* => larger')
```

This means regardless of what state we were in before, a transition will happen when our `state` property assumes a `larger` value.

The void state

The void state is different from the wildcard state. Void is the same thing as saying that if an element didn't exist before, then it has the void value. Upon exiting, it assumes a value. The definition of a transition call, therefore, looks like this:

```
transition(' void => *')
```

Let's make this more real by adding some code to our template:

```
<button (click)="abraCadabra()">Abracadabra</button>
<button (click)="poof()">Poof</button>

<p class="elem" [@flyInOut]="state" *ngIf="showMe">
  Show me
</p>
```

Here, we have added one button set to call `abraCadabra()` to show the element and one button that calls `poof()`, which will hide the element. Let's now add some code to the component:

```
trigger('flyInOut', [
  state('in', style({transform: 'translateX(0)'})),
  transition('void => *', [
    style({transform: 'translateX(-100%)'}),
    animate(500)
  ]),
  transition('* => void', [
    animate(500, style({transform: 'translateX(200%)'}))
  ])
])
```

This trigger definition says the following, if an element goes from not existing to existing, `void => *`, then animate from `-100%` to x position 0. When going from existing to non-existing, then move it out of the picture by moving it to x position `200%`.

Now for the final bit, our component code:

```
abraCadabra() {
  this.state = 'in';
  this.showMe = true;
}

poof() {
  this.showMe = false;
}
```

Here we can see that calling the `abraCadabra()` method will trigger the state `'in'` and setting the Boolean `showMe` to `true` will trigger the transition `void => *`. This explains the main purpose of the `void` state, which is to be used when prior elements don't exist.

Animation callbacks

There are occasions when you might want to know when you are kicking off an animation as well as knowing when the animation finishes. There is good news to be had here; we can find this out and execute whatever code we need for those occasions.

What we need to do is listen to the `start` and `done` properties of our trigger, like so:

```
[@sizeAnimation.start]=animationStarted($event)
[@sizeAnimation.done]="animationDone($event)"
[@sizeAnimation]="state"
```

And, of course, we need add code to our component so it looks like this:

```
animationStarted() {
  // animation started, execute code
}

animationDone() {
  // animation ended, execute code
}
```

Animating components with the AnimationBuilder

So far, we have covered how to do animations with pure CSS or by defining a trigger that we can hook up to our markup. There is another more programmatic approach to animation. This approach uses a service called `AnimationBuilder`. There are some key factors involved in making this approach work, namely:

- `AnimationBuilder`: This is a service we inject; it has a single method, `build`, that when called creates an instance of an `AnimationFactory`

- `AnimationFactory`: This is the result of calling `build()` on an `AnimationBuilder` instance; it has been given a number of styling transformations and one or more animations
- `AnimationPlayer`: The player needs an element on which to apply the animation instruction

Let's cover these bullets so we understand what happens, when, and to what element. First things first, we need to inject the `AnimationBuilder` to a component's constructor and also inject an `elementRef` instance so we have a target for our animation, like so:

```
import { AnimationBuilder } from '@angular/animations';

@Component({})
export class Component {
  constructor(
    private animationBuilder:AnimationBuilder,
    private elementRef: ElementRef
  ) {
  }
}
```

At this point, we have access to an instance of the `animationBuilder` and are ready to set up our style transformations and an animation, so let's do that next:

```
ngOnInit() {
  const animationFactory = this.animationBuilder.build([
    style({ width : '0px' }), // set starter value
    animate(1000, style({ width: '100px' }))  // animate to this new value
  ])
}
```

Here, we have defined a transformation that sets the width to `0px` initially, and an animation setting the width to `100px` over 1 second. We have also assigned the result of calling `animationBuilder.build()` to a variable animation that is of type `AnimationFactory`. The next step is to create an instance of an animation player and decide what element to apply this animation to:

```
const elem = this.elementRef.nativeElement.querySelector('.text');
const animationPlayer = animationFactory.create(elem);
```

We do two things here; first, we point out an element in our template where we want the animation to be applied to. Next, we create an instance of an animation player by calling `animation.create( elem )` with our element as input. What's missing now is to create the element in the UI so our `querySelector()` can find it. We need to create an element with the CSS class text, which is just what we do in the following code:

```
@Component({
  template : `
    <p class="text">Animate this text</p>
  `
})
export class ExampleComponent {}
```

The very last step is to call the `play()` method on our animation player instance:

```
animationPlayer.play();
```

Enjoy the animation as it plays in the browser. You can easily extend the animation by adding more properties to our `style({})` method call, like so:

```
ngOnInit() {
  const animation = this.builder.build([
    style({
      width : '0px',
      height : '0px'
    }),   // set starter values
    animate(1000, style({
      width: '100px',
      height: '40px'
    }))
  ])
}
```

In summary, `AnimationBuilder` is a powerful way to create reusable animations that you can easily apply to an element of your choice.

Creating a reusable animation directive

So far, we have seen how we can create an `AnimationBuilder` and how we can use it to programmatically create and apply animations at will. One way of making it reusable is to wrap it inside a directive. Creating a directive is quite a simple feat that we have done a few times already; the thing we need to keep in mind is that our directive will be applied to an element and this element is the thing that will be animated by our animation. Let's summarize what we need to do in a list:

1. Create a directive.
2. Inject `AnimationBuilder`.
3. Create our animation.
4. Create an animation player.
5. Play the animation.

This list of things is very similar to when we explained how the `AnimationBuilder` worked, and it should be; after all, the directive is the only new thing here. Let's define our directive and the animation; there really isn't much to it:

```
@Directive({
  selector : '[highlight]'
})
export class HighlightDirective implements OnInit {
  constructor(
    private elementRef: ElementRef,
    private animationBuilder: AnimationBuilder
  ) {}

  ngOnInit() {
    const animation = this.animationBuilder.build([
      style({ width: '0px' }),
      animate(1000, style({ width : '100px' }))
    ]);
    const player = animation.create( this.elementRef.nativeElement );
    player.play();
  }
}
```

This is all we need. Now we can just apply our directive to any element, like so:

```
<p highlight>animate me</p>
```

Summary

We have only scratched the surface of dealing with animations. To read up on everything you can do, we suggest looking at the official documentation at `https://angular.io/guide/animations`.

In this chapter, we started looking at how to define vanilla CSS animations. Then, we explained animation triggers and how you can declaratively attach a defined animation to an element. Then, we looked at how to programmatically define animations and attach them to an element at will. The very last thing we did was to package our programmatic animations in a directive. There is a lot more to learn about animations, but now you should have a basic understanding of what APIs exist and when to use them. Go out there and make your app full of life, but remember, less is more.

13
Unit Testing in Angular

The hard work of the previous chapters has materialized into a working application we can be proud of. But how can we ensure a painless maintainability in the future? A comprehensive automated testing layer will become our lifeline once our application begins to scale up and we have to mitigate the impact of bugs, caused by new functionalities colliding with the already existing ones.

Testing (and more specifically, unit testing) is meant to be carried out by the developer as the project is being developed. However, we will cover all the intricacies of testing Angular modules in brief in this chapter, now that the project is at a mature stage.

In this chapter, you will see how to implement testing tools to perform proper unit testing of your application classes and components.

In this chapter, we will:

- Look at the importance of testing and, more specifically, unit testing
- Build a test spec testing a pipe
- Design unit tests for components, with or without dependencies
- Put our routes to the test
- Implement tests for services, mocking dependencies, and stubs
- Intercept XHR requests and provide mocked responses for refined control
- Discover how to test directives as components with no view
- Introduce other concepts and tools such as Karma, code coverage tools, and **end-to-end** (**E2E**) testing

Why do we need tests?

What is a unit test? If you're familiar already with unit testing and test-driven development, you can safely skip to the next section. If not, let's say that unit tests are part of an engineering philosophy that takes a stand for efficient and agile development processes, by adding an additional layer of automated testing to the code, before it is developed. The core concept is that each piece of code is delivered with its own test, and both pieces of code are built by the developer who is working on that code. First, we design the test against the module we want to deliver, checking the accuracy of its output and behavior. Since the module is still not implemented, the test will fail. Hence, our job is to build the module in such a way that it passes its own test.

Unit testing is quite controversial. While there is a common agreement about how beneficial test-driven development for ensuring code quality and maintenance over time is, not everybody undertakes unit testing in their daily practice. Why is that? Well, building tests while we develop our code can feel like a burden sometimes, particularly when the test winds up being bigger in size than the piece of functionality it aims to test.

However, the arguments favoring testing outnumber the arguments against it:

- Building tests contributes to better code design. Our code must conform to the test requirements and not the other way around. In that sense, if we try to test an existing piece of code and we find ourselves blocked at some point, chances are that the piece of code we aim to test is not well designed and shows off a convoluted interface that requires some rethinking. On the other hand, building testable modules can help with early detection of side effects on other modules.

- Refactoring tested code is the lifeline against introducing bugs in later stages. Any development is meant to evolve with time, and on every refactor the risk of introducing a bug, that will only pop up in another part of our application, is high. Unit tests are a good way to ensure that we catch bugs at an early stage, either when introducing new features or when updating existing ones.

- Building tests is a good way to document our code APIs and functionalities. And this becomes a priceless resource when someone not acquainted with the code base takes over the development endeavor.

These are only a few arguments, but you can find countless resources on the web about the benefits of testing your code. If you do not feel convinced yet, give it a try. Otherwise, let's continue with our journey and see the overall form of a test.

The anatomy of a unit test

There are many different ways to test a piece of code, but in this chapter we will look at the anatomy of a test, what it is made up of. The first thing we need, for testing any code, is a test framework. The test framework should provide utility functions for building test suites, containing one or several test specs each. So what are these concepts?

- **Test suite**: A suite creates a logical grouping for a bunch of tests. A suite can, for example, be all the tests for a product page.
- **Test spec**: This is another name for a unit test.

The following shows what a test file can look like where we are using a test suite and placing a number of related tests inside. The chosen framework for this is Jasmine. In Jasmine, the `describe()` function helps us to define a test suite. The `describe()` method takes a name as the first parameter and a function as the second parameter. Inside of the `describe()` function are a number of invocations to the `it()` method. The `it()` function is our unit test; it takes the name of the test as the first parameter and a function as the second parameter:

```
// Test suite
describe('A math library', () => {
  // Test spec
  it('add(1,1,) should return 2', () => {
    // Test spec implementation goes here
  });
});
```

Each test spec checks out a specific functionality of the feature described in the suite description argument and declares one or several expectations in its body. Each expectation takes a value, which we call the expected value, and is compared against an actual value by means of a matcher function, which checks whether expected and actual values match accordingly. This is what we call an assertion, and the test framework will pass or fail the spec depending on the result of such assertions. The code is as follows:

```
// Test suite
describe('A math library', () => {
  // Test spec
  it('add(1,1) should return 2', () => {
    // Test assertion
    expect(add(1,1,)).toBe(2);
  });

  it('subtract(2,1)', () =>{
    //Test assertion
```

```
    expect(subtract(2,1)).toBe(1);
  })
});
```

In the previous example, `add(1,1)` will return the actual value that is supposed to match the expected value declared in the `toBe()` matcher function.

Worth noting from the previous example is the addition of a second test that tests our `subtract()` function. We can clearly see that this test deals with yet another mathematical operation, thus it makes sense to group both these tests under one suite.

So far, we have learned about test suites and how to group tests according to their function. Furthermore, we have learned about invoking the code you want to test and asserting that it does what you think it does. There are, however, more concepts to a unit test worth knowing about, namely setup and tear-down functionality. A setup functionality is something that sets up your code before the test is run usually. It's a way to keep your code cleaner so you can focus on just invoking the code and asserting. A tear-down functionality is the opposite of a setup functionality and is dedicated to tearing down what you set up initially; essentially it's a way to clean up after the test. Let's see how this can look in practice with a code example, using the Jasmine framework. In Jasmine, the `beforeEach()` method is used for setup functionality; it runs before every unit test. The `afterEach()` method is used to run tear-down logic. The code is as follows:

```
describe('a Product service', () => {
  let productService;

  beforeEach(() => {
    productService = new ProductService();
  });

  it('should return data', () => {
    let actual = productService.getData();
    assert(actual.length).toBe(1);
  });

  afterEach(() => {
    productService = null;
  });
});
```

We can see in the preceding code how the `beforeEach()` function is responsible for instantiating the `productService`, which means the test only has to care about invoking production code and asserting the outcome. This makes the test look cleaner. It should be said, though, in reality, tests tend to have a lot of setup going on and having a `beforeEach()` function can really make the tests look cleaner; above all, it tends to make it easier to add new tests, which is great. What you want at the end of the day is well-tested code; the easier it is to write and maintain such code, the better for your software.

Introduction to testing in Angular

In the section *The anatomy of a unit test*, we gained familiarity with unit testing and its general concepts, such as test suites, test specs, and assertions. Armed with that knowledge, it is now time to venture into unit testing with Angular. Before we start writing tests for Angular, though, we will first give an introduction to the tooling that exists within the Angular CLI to make unit testing a nice experience. When venturing into unit testing in Angular, it's important to know what major parts it consists of. In Angular these are:

- Jasmine, the testing framework
- Angular testing utilities
- Karma, a test runner for running unit tests, among other things
- Protractor, Angular's framework for E2E testing

Configuration and setting up

In terms of configuration, when using the Angular CLI, you don't have to do anything to make it work. You can, as soon as you scaffold a project, run your first test and it will work. As you venture deeper into unit testing in Angular, you will need to be aware of a few concepts that leverage your ability to test different constructs, such as components and directives. The Angular CLI is using Karma as the test runner. What we need to know about Karma is that it uses a `karma.conf.js` file, a configuration file, in which a lot of things are specified, such as:

- The various plugins that enhance your test runner.
- Where to find the tests to run? It should be said that there is usually a files property in this file specifying where to find the application and the tests. For the Angular CLI, however, this specification is found in another file called `src/tscconfig-spec.json`.

- Setup of your selected coverage tool, a tool that measures to what degree your tests cover the production code.
- Reporters, report every executed test in a console window, to a browser, or through some other means.
- Browsers to run your tests in: for example, Chrome or PhantomJS.

Using the Angular CLI, you most likely won't need to change or edit this file yourself. It is good to know that it exists and what it does for you.

Angular testing utilities

The Angular testing utilities help to create a testing environment that makes writing tests for your various constructs really easy. It consists of the `TestBed` class and various helper functions, found under the `@angular/core/testing` namespace. We will learn what these are and how they can help us to test various constructs as this chapter progresses. We will shortly introduce the most commonly used concepts so that you are familiar with them as we present them more deeply further on:

- The `TestBed` class is the most important concept and creates its own testing module. In reality, when you test out a construct to detach it from the module it resides in and reattach it to the testing module created by the `TestBed`.
  The `TestBed` class has a `configureTestModule()` helper method that we use to set up the test module as needed. The `TestBed` can also instantiate components.
- `ComponentFixture` is a class wrapping the component instance. This means that it has some functionality on it and it has a member that is the component instance itself.
- The `DebugElement`, much like the `ComponentFixture`, acts as a wrapper. It, however, wraps the DOM element and not the component instance. It's a bit more than that though, as it has an injector on it that allows us to access the services that have been injected into a component. More on this topic later.

This was a brief overview to our testing environment, the frameworks and libraries used, as well as some important concepts that we will use heavily in the upcoming sections.

Introduction to component testing

Our usual method of operation for doing anything Angular by now, is to use the Angular CLI. Working with tests is no different. The Angular CLI lets us create tests, debug them, and run them; it also gives us an understanding of how well our tests cover the code and its many scenarios. Let's have a quick look at how we can get going with some unit testing using the Angular CLI, and try to understand what is given to us by default.

If you want to code along with this chapter, you can either take an old Angular project and add tests to it or create a new standalone project, if you want to focus on practice testing only. The choice is yours.

If you opt for creating a new project, then type the following to scaffold it:

```
ng new AngularTestDemo
// go make coffee :)
cd AngularTestDemo
ng serve
```

The Angular CLI comes with testing already set up, so the only thing we need to do is follow in its footsteps and add more tests, but let's first examine what we've got and learn some neat commands to make it easier to work with testing.

The first thing we want to do is the following:

- Investigate the tests that the Angular CLI has given us
- Run the tests

By looking in the scaffolded `directory/app`, we see the following:

```
app.component.ts
app.component.spec.ts
```

We see a component being declared, together with a unit test. This means we get tests with our components, which is very good news as it saves us a bit of typing.

Let's have a look at the test that was given to us:

```
import { TestBed, async } from '@angular/core/testing';
import { AppComponent } from './app.component';

describe('AppComponent', () => {
  beforeEach(async(() => {
    TestBed.configureTestingModule({
      declarations: [
        AppComponent
```

```
      ],
    }).compileComponents();
  }));

  it('should create the app', async(() => {
    const fixture = TestBed.createComponent(AppComponent);
    const app = fixture.debugElement.componentInstance;
    expect(app).toBeTruthy();
  }));

  it(`should have as title 'app works!'`, async(() => {
    const fixture = TestBed.createComponent(AppComponent);
    const app = fixture.debugElement.componentInstance;
    expect(app.title).toEqual('app works!');
  }));

  it('should render title in a h1 tag', async(() => {
    const fixture = TestBed.createComponent(AppComponent);
    fixture.detectChanges();
    const compiled = fixture.debugElement.nativeElement;
    const actual = compiled.querySelector('h1').textContent;
    expect(actual).toContain('app works!');
  }));
});
```

That's a lot of code, but we will break it down. We see the testing setup, at the beginning of the file, with three different tests being written. Let's have a look at the setup phase first:

```
beforeEach(async(() => {
  TestBed.configureTestingModule({
    declarations: [
      AppComponent
    ],
  }).compileComponents();
}));
```

Here we are calling `beforeEach()`, as we normally do in a Jasmine test, to run code before each test actually happens. Inside of the `beforeEach()`, we call the `TestBed.configureTestingModule()` method, with an object as an argument. The object resembles the object that we give the `NgModule` as an argument. This means we can take our knowledge of `NgModule` and how to set up Angular modules and apply that to how to set up testing modules, because it is really one and the same. Looking at the code, we can see that we specify a declarations array with the `AppComponent` as an item in that array. For `NgModule`, this means that the `AppComponent` belongs to that module. Lastly, we call the `compileComponents()` method and the setup is done.

So what does the `compileComponents()` do? As per its name, it compiles components that are configured in the testing module. In the compilation process, it also inlines external CSS files as well as external templates. By calling `compileComponents()`, we also close down the possibility to further configure the testing module instance.

The second part of our test files are the tests. Look at the first test:

```
it('should create the app', async(() => {
&gt;   const fixture = TestBed.createComponent(AppComponent);
    const app = fixture.componentInstance;
    expect(app).toBeTruthy();
}));
```

We see that we call `TestBed.createComponent(AppComponent)`, this returns an object of type `ComponentFixture<AppComponent>`. We are able to interact with this object further by calling:

```
const app = fixture.debugElement.componentInstance;
```

This gives us a component instance, which is what we get when we instantiate an object from the following class:

```
@Component({})
export class AppComponent {
    title: string;
}
```

The first test just wants to verify that we are able to create a component and the `expect` condition tests just that, that `expect(app)` is truthy, meaning is it declared; and in truth it is.

For the second test, we actually try to investigate whether our component contains the properties and values we think; so the test looks like this:

```
it(`should have as title 'app works!'`, async(() => {
    const fixture = TestBed.createComponent(AppComponent);
    const app = fixture.debugElement.componentInstance;
    expect(app.title).toEqual('app works!');
}));
```

Now, this test creates a component but it also calls `fixture.detectChanges`, which tells Angular to force change detection. This will make sure that the code in the constructor and any `ngInit()`, if it exists, is executed.

With a component specification we expect that the `title` property should get set when the component is created, like this:

```
@Component({})
export class AppComponent {
  title: string = 'app works!'
}
```

That is exactly what the second test is testing:

```
expect(app.title).toEqual('app works!');
```

Let's see how this works by extending our `app.component.ts` with one more field:

```
@Component({})
export class AppComponent {
  title: string;
  description: string;
  constructor() {
    this.title = 'app works'
    this.description ='description';
  }
}
```

We added the description field and also initialized it with a value; we will test whether this value is set to our property. Therefore, we need to add an extra `expect` condition in our test, so the test now looks like this:

```
it(`should have as title 'app works!'`, async(() => {
    const fixture = TestBed.createComponent(AppComponent);
    const app = fixture.debugElement.componentInstance;
    expect(app.title).toEqual('app works!');
    expect(app.description).toEqual('description');
})));
```

As you can see, we have an extra `expect` condition and the test passes as it should. Don't take our word for it though; let's run our test runner using a node command. We do that by typing:

```
npm test
```

This will execute the test runner and it should look something like this:

This means that we understand how to extend our component and test for it. As a bonus, we now also know how to run our tests. Let's have a look at the third test. It is a bit different as it tests the template:

```
it('should render title in a h1 tag', async(() => {
  const fixture = TestBed.createComponent(AppComponent);
  fixture.detectChanges();
  const compiled = fixture.debugElement.nativeElement;
  expect(compiled.querySelector('h1').textContent).toContain('app works!');
}));
```

Instead of talking to `fixture.debugElement.componentInstance`, we now talk to `fixture.debugElement.nativeElement`. This will allow us to verify that the expected HTML markup is what we think it is. When we have access to the `nativeElement`, we can use the `querySelector` and find the elements we defined in our template and verify their content.

We've gained quite a lot of insight just by looking at the test we were given. We now know the following:

- We set up the test by calling `TestBed.configureTestingModule()` and pass it an object that looks like the object we pass to `NgModule`
- We call `TestBed.createComponent(<Component>)` to get a reference to a component
- We call `debugElement.componentInstance` on our component reference to get to the actual component and we can test for the existence and values of properties that should exist on our component object
- We call `debugElement.nativeElement` to get a reference to the `nativeElement` and can now start verifying the resulting HTML
- We also learned how to run our tests in the browser by typing `npm test`

`fixture.debugElement.nativeElement` points to the HTML element itself. When we use the `querySelector()` method, we are in fact using a method available in the Web API; it's not an Angular method.

Component testing with dependencies

We have learned a lot already, but let's face it, no component that we build will be as simple as the one we wrote in the preceding section. There will almost certainly be at least one dependency, looking like this:

```
@Component({})
export class ExampleComponent {
  constructor(dependency:Dependency) {}
}
```

We have different ways of dealing with testing such a situation. One thing is clear though: if we are testing the component, then we should not test the service as well. This means that when we set up such a test, the dependency should not be the real thing. There are different ways of dealing with that when it comes to unit testing; no solution is strictly better than the other:

- Using a stub means that we tell the dependency injector to inject a stub that we provide, instead of the real thing
- Injecting the real thing, but attaching a spy, to the method that we call in our component

Regardless of the approach, we ensure that the test is not performing a side effect such as talking to a filesystem or attempting to communicate via HTTP; we are, using this approach, isolated.

Using a stub to replace the dependency

Using a stub means that we completely replace what was there before. It is as simple to do as instructing the TestBed in the following way:

```
TestBed.configureTestingModule({
  declarations: [ExampleComponent]
  providers: [{
    provide: DependencyService,
    useClass: DependencyServiceStub
  }]
});
```

We define a providers array like we do with the NgModule, and we give it a list item that points out the definition we intend to replace and we give it the replacement instead; that is our stub.

Let's now build our DependencyStub to look like this:

```
class DependencyServiceStub {
  getData() { return 'stub'; }
}
```

Just like with an `@NgModule`, we are able to override the definition of our dependency with our own stub. Imagine our component looks like the following:

```
import { Component } from '@angular/core';
import { DependencyService } from "./dependency.service";

@Component({
  selector: 'example',
  template: `
<div>{{ title }}</div>
  `
})
export class ExampleComponent {
  title: string;

  constructor(private dependency: DependencyService) {
    this.title = this.dependency.getData();
  }
}
```

Here we pass an instance of the dependency in the constructor. With our testing module correctly set up, with our stub, we can now write a test that looks like this:

```
it(`should have as title 'stub'`, async(() => {
  const fixture = TestBed.createComponent(AppComponent);
  const app = fixture.debugElement.componentInstance;
  expect(app.title).toEqual('stub');
}));
```

The test looks normal, but at the point when the dependency would be called in the component code, our stub takes its place and responds instead. Our dependency should be overridden, and as you can see, the `expect(app.title).toEqual('stub')` assumes the stub will answer, which it does.

Spying on the dependency method

The previously-mentioned approach, using a stub, is not the only way to isolate ourselves in a unit test. We don't have to replace the entire dependency, only the parts that our component is using. Replacing certain parts means that we point out specific methods on the dependency and assign a spy to them. A spy is an interesting construct; it has the ability to answer what you want it to answer, but you can also see how many times it is being called and with what argument/s, so a spy gives you a lot more information about what is going on. Let's have a look at how we would set a spy up:

```
beforeEach(() => {
  TestBed.configureTestingModule({
    declarations: [ExampleComponent],
    providers: [DependencyService]
  });

  dependency = TestBed.get(DependencyService);

  spy = spyOn( dependency,'getData');
  fixture = TestBed.createComponent(ExampleComponent);
})
```

Now as you can see, the actual dependency is injected into the component. After that, we grab a reference to the component, our fixture variable. This is followed by us using the `TestBed.get('Dependency')` to get hold of the dependency inside of the component. At this point, we attach a spy to its `getData()` method through the `spyOn( dependency,'getData')` call.

This is not enough, however; we have yet to instruct the spy what to respond with when being called. Let us do just that:

```
spyOn(dependency, 'getData').and.returnValue('spy value');
```

We can now write our test as usual:

```
it('test our spy dependency', () => {
  var component = fixture.debugElement.componentInstance;
  expect(component.title).toBe('spy value');
});
```

This works as expected, and our spy responds as it should. Remember how we said that spies were capable of more than just responding with a value, that you could also check whether they were invoked and with what? To showcase this, we need to improve our tests a little bit and check for this extended functionality, like so:

```
it('test our spy dependency', () => {
  var component = fixture.debugElement.componentInstance;
  expect(spy.calls.any()).toBeTruthy();
})
```

You can also check for the number of times it was called, with `spy.callCount`, or whether it was called with some specific arguments: `spy.mostRecentCalls.args` or `spy.toHaveBeenCalledWith('arg1', 'arg2')`. Remember if you use a spy, make sure it pays for itself by you needing to do checks like these; otherwise, you might as well use a stub.

> Spies are a feature of the Jasmine framework, not Angular. The interested reader is urged to research this topic further at `http://tobyho.com/2011/12/15/jasmine-spy-cheatsheet/`.

Async services

Very few services are nice and well-behaved, in the sense that they are synchronous. A lot of the time, your service will be asynchronous and the return from it is most likely an observable or a promise. If you are using RxJS with the `Http` service or `HttpClient`, it will be an observable, but if using the `fetch` API, it will be a promise. These are two good options for dealing with HTTP, but the Angular team added the RxJS library to Angular to make your life as a developer easier. Ultimately it's up to you, but we recommend going with RxJS.

Angular has two constructs ready to tackle the asynchronous scenario when testing:

- `async()` and `whenStable()`: This code ensures that any promises are immediately resolved; it can look more synchronous though
- `fakeAsync()` and `tick()`: This code does what the async does but it looks more synchronous when used

Let's describe the `async()` and `whenStable()` approaches. Our service has now grown up and is doing something asynchronous when we call it like a timeout or a HTTP call. Regardless of which, the answer doesn't reach us straightaway. By using `async()` in combination with `whenStable()`, we can, however, ensure that any promises are immediately resolved. Imagine our service now looks like this:

```
export class AsyncDependencyService {
  getData(): Promise<string> {
    return new Promise((resolve, reject) => {
      setTimeout(() => { resolve('data') }, 3000);
    })
  }
}
```

We need to change our spy setup to return a promise instead of returning a static string, like so:

```
spy = spyOn(dependency,'getData')
.and.returnValue(Promise.resolve('spy data'));
```

We do need to change inside of our component, like so:

```
import { Component, OnInit } from '@angular/core';
import { AsyncDependencyService } from "./async.dependency.service";

@Component({
  selector: 'async-example',
  template: `
  <div>{{ title }}</div>
  `
})
export class AsyncExampleComponent {
  title: string;

  constructor(private service: AsyncDependencyService) {
    this.service.getData().then(data => this.title = data);
  }
}
```

At this point, it's time to update our tests. We need to do two more things. We need to tell our test method to use the `async()` function, like so:

```
it('async test', async() => {
  // the test body
})
```

We also need to call `fixture.whenStable()` to make sure that the promise will have had ample time to resolve, like so:

```
import { TestBed } from "@angular/core/testing";
import { AsyncExampleComponent } from "./async.example.component";
import { AsyncDependencyService } from "./async.dependency.service";

describe('test an component with an async service', () => {
  let fixture;
  beforeEach(() => {
    TestBed.configureTestingModule({
      declarations: [AsyncExampleComponent],
      providers: [AsyncDependencyService]
    });

    fixture = TestBed.createComponent(AsyncExampleComponent);
  });

  it('should contain async data', async () => {
    const component = fixture.componentInstance;
    fixture.whenStable.then(() => {
      fixture.detectChanges();
      expect(component.title).toBe('async data');
    });
  });
});
```

This version of doing it works as it should, but feels a bit clunky. There is another approach using `fakeAsync()` and `tick()`. Essentially, `fakeAsync()` replaces the `async()` call and we get rid of `whenStable()`. The big benefit, however, is that we no longer need to place our assertion statements inside of the promise's `then()` callback. This gives us synchronous-looking code. Back to `fakeAsync()`, we need to make a call to `tick()`, which can only be called within a `fakeAsync()` call, like so:

```
it('async test', fakeAsync() => {
  let component = fixture.componentInstance;
  fixture.detectChanges();
  fixture.tick();
  expect(component.title).toBe('spy data');
});
```

As you can see, this looks a lot cleaner; which version you want to use for async testing is up to you.

Testing pipes

A pipe is basically a class that implements the `PipeTransform` interface, thus exposing a `transform()` method that is usually synchronous. Pipes are therefore very easy to test. We will begin by testing a simple pipe, creating, as we mentioned, a test spec right next to its code unit file. The code is as follows:

```
import { Pipe, PipeTransform } from '@angular/core';

@Pipe({
  name: 'formattedpipe'
})
export class FormattedPipe implements PipeTransform {
  transform(value: any, ...args: any[]): any {
      return "banana" + value;
    }
}
```

Our code is very simple; we take a value and add banana to it. Writing a test for it is equally simple. The only thing we need to do is to import the pipe and verify two things:

- That it has a transform method
- That it produces the expected results

The following code writes a test for each of the bullet points listed earlier:

```
import FormattedTimePipe from './formatted-time.pipe';
import { TestBed } from '@angular/core/testing';

describe('A formatted time pipe' , () => {
  let fixture;

  beforeEach(() => {
    fixture = new FormattedTimePipe();
  })

  // Specs with assertions
  it('should expose a transform() method', () => {
    expect(typeof formattedTimePipe.transform).toEqual('function');
  });
```

```
it('should produce expected result', () => {
  expect(fixture.transform( 'val' )).toBe('bananaval');
})
});
```

In our `beforeEach()` method, we set up the fixture by instantiating the pipe class. In the first test, we ensure that the `transform()` method exists. This is followed by our second test that asserts that the `transform()` method produces the expected result.

Mocking HTTP responses with HttpClientTestingController

It is super simple to get started with mocking HTTP, once you understand how to. Let's first have a look at the service we mean to test:

```
import { HttpClient } from '@angular/common/http';
import { Injectable } from '@angular/core';

@Injectable()
export class JediService {
  apiUrl: string = 'something';
  constructor(private http: HttpClient) {}
  getJedis() {
    return this.http.get(`/api/jedis`);
  }
}
```

There are two important players when it comes to testing our service:

- `HttpTestingController`, we can instruct this class to listen for specific URLs and how to respond when it is being called
- Our service, this is the service we want to test; the only thing we really want to do with it is to invoke it

As with all tests, we have a setup phase. Here we need to import the module, `HttpClientTestingModule`, that contains our `HttpTestingController`. We also need to tell it to provide us with our service, like so:

```
import {
  HttpClientTestingModule,
  HttpTestingController
} from '@angular/common/http/testing';
import { JediService } from './jedi.service';
```

```
describe('testing our service', () => {
 beforeEach(() => {
   TestBed.configureTestingModule({
     imports: [HttpClientTestingModule],
     providers: [JediService]
   });
 });
});
```

The next step is to set up the test, and by set up we mean that we need to get an instance of our service as well as `HttpTestingController`. We also need to instruct the latter what type of API calls to expect and give it suitable mock data to respond with:

```
it('testing getJedis() and expect a list of jedis back', () => {
  // get an instance of a Jedi service and HttpTestingController
  const jediService = TestBed.get(JediService);
  const http = TestBed.get(HttpTestingController);

  // define our mock data
  const expected = [{ name: 'Luke' }, { name: 'Darth Vader' }];
  let actual = [];
  // we actively call getJedis() on jediService,
  // we will set that response to our 'actual' variable
  jediService.getJedis().subscribe( data => {
    expect(data).toEqual(expected);
  });

  /*
  when someone calls URL /api/jedis
  we will resolve that asynchronous operation
  with .flush() while also answering with
  'expected' variable as response data
  */
  http.expectOne('/api/jedis').flush(expected);
});
```

We have provided inline comments for the preceding code snippet, but just to describe what happens one more time ,we have three phases to our test:

1. **Arrange**: This is where we grab an instance of the `JediService` as well as an instance of the `HttpTestingController`. We also define our mock data by setting the `expected` variable.
2. **Act**: We carry out the test by calling `jediService.getJedis()`. This is an observable so we need to subscribe to its content.
3. **Assert**: We resolve the asynchronous code by calling `flush(expected)` and we assert that we get the right data back by carrying out our assertion `expect(actual).toEqual(expected)`.

As you can see, faking calls to the HTTP is quite easy. Let's show the entire unit test code:

```
import {
  HttpTestingController,
  HttpClientTestingModule
} from '@angular/common/http/testing/';
import { TestBed } from '@angular/core/testing';

import { JediService } from './jedi-service';

describe('a jedi service', () => {
  beforeEach(() => TestBed.configureTestingModule({
    imports: [HttpClientTestingModule],
    providers: [JediService]
  }));

  it('should list the jedis', () => {
    const jediService = TestBed.get(JediService);
    const http = TestBed.get(HttpTestingController);

    // fake response
    const expected = [{ name: 'Luke' }, { name: 'Darth Vader' }];
    let actual = [];

    jediService.getJedis().subscribe( data => {
      expect(data).toEqual(expected);
    });

    http.expectOne('/api/jedis').flush(expected);
  });
});
```

Input and outputs

So far, we have tested components in the sense that we have tested simple properties on the component and also how to tackle dependencies, synchronous as well as asynchronous, but there is more to a component than that. A component can also have input and outputs that should be tested as well. Because our context is Jedis, we know Jedis normally have ways to either the light side or the dark side. Imagine that our component is used within the context of a Jedi management system; we want to have the ability to turn a Jedi dark as well as bring it back to the light side again. What we are talking about is, of course, a toggle functionality.

Imagine, therefore, that we have a component that looks like this:

```
@Component({
  selector : 'jedi-detail'
  template : `
    <div class="jedi"
      (click)="switchSide.emit(jedi)">
      {{ jedi.name }} {{ jedi.side }}
    </div>
  `
})
export class JediComponent {
  @Input() jedi:Jedi;
  @Output() switchSide = new EventEmitter<Jedi>();
}
```

Testing such a component should be done in two ways:

- We should verify that our input binding gets correctly set
- We should verify that our output binding triggers properly and that what it emits is received

Starting with the @Input, a test for it would look like the following:

```
describe('A Jedi detail component', () => {
  it('should display the jedi name Luke when input is assigned a Jedi
object', () => {
    const component = fixture.debugElement.componentInstance;
    component.jedi = new Jedi(1, 'Luke', 'Light');
    fixture.detectChanges();
    expect(component.jedi.name).toBe('Luke');
  });
});
```

Worth noting here is our call to `fixture.detectChanges()`, this ensures that the binding happens in the component.

Let's now have a look at how to test `@Output`. What we need to do is to trigger it somehow. We need to click the div defined in our template. To receive the value the `switchSide` property emits, we need to subscribe to it, so we need to do two things:

- Find the `div` element and trigger a click on it
- Subscribe to the emission of the data and verify that we receive our `jedi` object

As for getting a reference to the div, it is quite easily done, like so:

```
const elem = fixture.debugElement.query(By.css('.jedi'));
elem.triggerEventHandler('click', null);
```

For the second part, we need to subscribe to the `switchSide` Observable and capture the data, like so:

```
it('should invoke switchSide with the correct Jedi instance, () => {
  let selectedJedi;
  // emitting data
  component.switchSide.subscribe(data => {
    expect(data.name).toBe('Luke');
  });
  const elem = fixture.debugElement.query(By.css('.jedi'));
  elem.triggerEventHandler('click', null);
})
```

With this code, we are able to trigger an outputs emit indirectly, through the click event and listen to the output, through a subscribe.

Testing routing

Just like components, routes play an important role in the way our applications deliver an efficient user experience. As such, testing routes becomes paramount to ensuring a flawless performance. There are different things we can do with routing and we need to test for the different scenarios. These scenarios are:

- Ensuring that the navigation targets the right route address
- Ensuring that the correct parameters are made available so you can fetch the correct data for the component, or filter the dataset the component needs
- Ensuring that a certain route ends up loading the intended component

Testing navigation

Let's have a look at the first bullet point. To load a specific route, we can call a `navigateToUrl(url)` method on the `Router` class. A good test is to ensure that such a method is being called when a certain state happens in a component. There could, for example, be a create component page, that after saving should navigate back to a list page, or a missing route parameter should lead to us back to a home page. There is more than one good reason for programatically navigating inside of a component. Let's look at some code in a component, where such a navigation takes place:

```
@Component({})
export class ExampleComponent {
  constructor(private router: Router) {}

  back() {
    this.router.navigateByUrl('/list');
  }
}
```

Here we can see that invoking the `back()` method will perform a navigation. Writing a test for this is quite simple. The test should test whether the `navigateToUrl()` method is being called. Our approach will consist of stubbing the router service in combination with adding a spy to the `navigateToUrl()` method itself. First off, we define a stub and then we instruct our testing module to use the said stub. We also ensure that we create an instance of the component so that we may later invoke the `back()` method on it, like so:

```
describe('Testing routing in a component using a Stub', () => {
  let component, fixture;

  class RouterStub {
    navigateByUrl() {}
  }

  beforeEach(() => {
    TestBed.configureTestingModule({
      declarations: [ExampleRoutingComponent],
      providers: [{
        // replace 'Router' with our Stub
        provide: Router, useClass: RouterStub
      }]
    }).compileComponents();
  })

  beforeEach(() => {
    fixture = TestBed.createComponent(Component);
    component = fixture.debugElement.componentInstance;
```

```
  })
  // ... test to be defined here
}
```

The next thing we need to do is to define our test and inject the router instance. Once we have done so, we can set a spy on the `navigateToUrl()` method:

```
import { inject } from '@angular/core/testing';

it('test back() method', inject([Router], router: Router) => {
  const spy = spyOn(router, 'navigateByUrl');
  // ... more to come here
})
```

Now at this point, what we want the test to test for is whether the method is called at all. Writing such a test can be seen as defensive. As important as it is to test for correctness, it is also important to write tests to make sure that another developer, or yourself, doesn't remove a behavior that should work. So let's add some verification logic that ensures that our spy is being called:

```
import { inject } from '@angular/core/testing';

it('test back() method', inject([Router], (router: Router)) => {
  const spy = spyOn(router, 'navigateByUrl');
  // invoking  our back method that should call the spy in turn
  component.back();
  expect(spy.calls.any()).toBe(true);
}))
```

The entire test is now replacing the original router service for a stub. We are attaching a spy to the `navigateByUrl()` method on the stub and we are lastly asserting that spy is called as intended, when we invoke the `back()` method on the component:

```
describe('Testing routing in a component', () => {
  class RouterStub {
    navigateByUrl() {}
  }

  beforeEach(() => {
    TestBed.configureTestingModule({
      providers: [{
        provide: Router, useClass: RouterStub
      }]
    }).compileComponents();
  });

  beforeEach(() => {
```

```
    fixture = TestBed.createComponent(Component);
    component = fixture.debugElement.componentInstance;
  });

  it('should call navigateToUrl with argument /list', () => {
    spyOn(router, 'navigateByUrl');
    /*
    invoking our back() method
    that should call the spy in turn
    */
    component.back();
    expect(router.navigateByUrl).toHaveBeenCalledWithArgs('/list');
  })
})
```

Testing routes by URL

So far, we have tested routing by placing a spy on the navigation method and in the case with routing parameters, we had to build a mock for an Observable. There is another approach, though, and that is to let the routing happen and afterwards investigate where we ended up. Let's say we have the following scenario: we are at a list component and want to navigate to a detail component. After navigation has taken place, we want to investigate what state we are in. Let us first define our list component:

```
import { Router } from '@angular/router';
import { Component, OnInit } from '@angular/core';

@Component({
  selector: 'list-component',
  template : ``
})
export class ListComponent {
  constructor(private router: Router) {}
  goToDetail() {
    this.router.navigateByUrl('detail/1');
  }
}
```

As you can see, we have a `goToDetail()` method that, if invoked, will navigate you to a new route. For this to work, however, we need to have had routing set up properly in the module file, like so:

```
const appRoutes: Routes = [
  { path: 'detail/:id', component: DetailComponent }
];
```

```
@NgModule({
  ...
  imports: [
    BrowserModule,
    FormsModule,
    HttpClientModule,
    RouterModule.forRoot(appRoutes),
    TestModule
  ],
  ...
})
export class AppModule { }
```

The important part here is the definition of `appRoutes` and calling `RouterModule.forRoot()` in the imports array.

The time has come to define the test for this. We need to interact with a module called `RouterTestingModule` and we need to provide that module with the routes it should contain. `RouterTestingModule` is a very qualified stub version of the routing, so in that sense, there isn't much difference in principle from creating your own stub. Look at it this way though, you can create your own stub, but as you use more and more advanced functionality, using an advanced stub quickly pays off.

We will start off by instructing our `RouterTestingModule` that it should load the `DetailComponent` when the `detail/:id` route is being hit. This doesn't really differ from how we would set up the routing from our `root` module. The benefit is that we only need to set up the routes we need for our test, rather than every single route in the app:

```
beforeEach(() => {
  TestBed.configureTestingModule({
    imports: [
      RouterTestingModule.withRoutes([{
        path: 'detail/:id',
        component: DetailComponent
      }])
    ],
    declarations: [ListComponent, DetailComponent]
  });
});
```

After we have done the setup, we need to grab a copy of the component in our test so that we can invoke the method that navigates us away from the list component. Your test should look like the following:

```
it('should navigate to /detail/1 when invoking gotoDetail()', async() => {

  let fixture = TestBed.createComponent(ListComponent);
  let router = TestBed.get(Router);
  let component = fixture.debugElement.componentInstance;

  fixture.whenStable().then(() => {
    expect(router.url).toBe('/detail/1');
  });
  component.goToDetail();
})
```

The important part here is the invocation of the method that makes us navigate:

```
component.goToDetail();
```

And the assertion where we verify that our router has indeed changed state:

```
expect(router.url).toBe('/detail/1');
```

Testing route parameters

You will have some component that does routing and some components that are being routed to. Sometimes components that are being routed to have a parameter, and typically their route looks something like this: `/jedis/:id`. The component then has the mission of digging out the ID parameter and doing a lookup on the specific Jedi that matches this ID. So, a call to a service will be made and the response should populate a suitable parameter in our component that we then can show in the template. Such a component will typically look like this, in its entirety:

```
import { ActivatedRoute, Router } from '@angular/router';
import { Component, OnInit } from '@angular/core';
import { Observable } from 'rxjs/Rx';

import { Jedi } from './jedi.model';
import { JediService } from './jedi.service';

@Component({
  selector: 'detail-component',
  templateUrl: 'detail.component.html'
})
```

```
export class ExampleRoutingParamsComponent{
  jedi: Jedi;
  constructor(
    private router: Router,
    private route: ActivatedRoute,
    private jediService : JediService
  ) {
    route.paramMap.subscribe( p => {
      const id = p.get('id');
      jediService.getJedi( id ).subscribe( data => this.jedi = data );
    });
  }
}
```

Worth highlighting is how we get hold of the parameter in the router. We interact with the `ActivatedRouter` instance, that we named as `route` and its `paramMap` property, which is an observable, like so:

```
route.paramMap.subscribe( p => {
  const id = p.get('id');
  jediService.getJedi(id).subscribe( data => this.jedi = data )
})
```

So what do we want to test for? We would like to know that if a certain route contains an ID parameter, then our `jedi` property should be properly populated, through our service. We don't want to do an actual HTTP call, so our `JediService` will need to be mocked somehow and there is another thing complicating it, namely that `route.paramMap` will need to be mocked as well and that thing is an observable.

This means we need a way to create a stub of an observable. This might sound a bit daunting but it really isn't; thanks to a `Subject`, we can make this quite easy for ourselves. A `subject` has the nice ability of being something we can subscribe to, but we can also pass it values. With that knowledge, let's start to create our `ActivatedRouteStub`:

```
import { convertToParamMap } from '@angular/router';

class ActivatedRouteStub {
  private subject: Subject<any>;

  constructor() {
    this.subject = new Subject();
  }

  sendParameters( params : {}) {
    this.subject.next(convertToParamMap(params)); // emitting data
  }
```

```
  get paramMap() {
    return this.subject.asObservable();
  }
}
```

Now, let's explain this code, we add the `sendValue()` method so it can pass the value we give it to the subject. We expose the `paramMap` property, as an observable, so we can listen to the subject when it emits any values. How does this correlate to our test though? Well, calling `sendValue` on the stub is something we want to do in the setup phase, that is inside of a `beforeEach()`. This is a way for us to simulate reaching our component through routing while passing a parameter. In the test itself, we want to listen for when a router parameter is being sent to us so we can pass it on to our `jediService`. So, let's start sketching on the test. We will build the test in two steps:

1. The first step is to support the mocking of the `ActivatedRoute` by passing the `ActivatedRouteStub`.
2. The second step is to set up the mocking of the `jediService`, ensuring that all HTTP calls are intercepted, and that we are able to respond with mock data when an HTTP call occurs.

For the first step, we set up the test as we have done so far by calling `TestBed.configureTestingModule()` and passing it an object. We mentioned that we built a stub for an activated route already and we need to make sure that we provide this instead of the real `ActivatedRoute`. This looks like the following code:

```
describe('A detail component', () => {
  let fixture, component, activatedRoute;

  beforeEach(() => {
    TestBed.configureTestingModule({
      providers: [{
        provide: ActivatedRoute,
        useClass: ActivatedRouteStub
      },
      JediService
      ]
    })
  })
})
```

This means that when our component gets the `ActivatedRoute` dependency injected in its constructor, it will instead inject `ActivatedRouteStub`, like so:

```
@Component({})
export class ExampleRoutingParamsComponent {
  // will inject ActivatedRouteStub
  constructor(activatedRoute: ActivatedRoute) {}
}
```

Moving on with our test, we need to do three things:

- Instantiate the component
- Feed a route parameter to our `ActivatedRouteStub` so that a routing parameter is emitted
- Subscribe to the `ActivatedRouteStub` so we can assert that a parameter is indeed emitted

Let's add these to our test code:

```
beforeEach(() => {
  fixture = TestBed.createComponent(ExampleRoutingParamsComponent);
  component = fixture.debugElement.componentInstance;
  activatedRoute = TestBed.get(ActivatedRoute);
})
```

Now we have set up the fixture, the component, and our `activatedRouteStub`. The next step is to feed the `activatedRouteStub` the actual routing parameter, and to set up a `subscribe` of the `activatedRouteStub` so we know when we receive a new routing parameter. We do this inside the test itself, instead of the `beforeEach()` method, like so:

```
it('should execute the ExampleRoutingParamsComponent', () => {
  // listen for the router parameter
  activatedRoute.paramMap.subscribe(para => {
    const id = para.get('id');
    // assert that the correct routing parameter is being emitted
    expect(id).toBe(1);
  });
  // send the route parameter
  activatedRoute.sendParameters({ id : 1 });
})
```

So what does this mean for our component? How much of our component have we tested at this stage? Let's have a look at our `DetailComponent` and highlight the code covered by our test so far:

```
@Component({})
export class ExampleRoutingParamsComponent {
  constructor( activatedRoute: ActivatedRoute ) {
    activatedRoute.paramMap.subscribe( paramMap => {
      const id = paramMap.get('id');
      // TODO call service with id parameter
    })
  }
}
```

As you can see, we have, in the test, covered the mocking of the `activatedRoute` and managed to subscribe to it. What is missing on both the component and test is to account for there being a call to a service that in turn calls HTTP. Let's start with adding that code to the component, like so:

```
@Component({})
export class ExampleRoutingParamsComponent implements OnInit {
  jedi: Jedi;
  constructor(
    private activatedRoute: ActivatedRoute,
    private jediService: JediService ) {}

  ngOnInit() {
    this.activatedRoute.paramMap.subscribe(route => {
      const id = route.get('id')
      this.jediService.getJedi(id).subscribe(data => this.jedi = data);
    });
  }
}
```

In the code, we added the `Jedi` field as well as a call to `this.jediService.getJedi()`. We subscribed to the result and assigned the result of the operation to the `Jedi` field. Adding testing support for this part is something we have already covered in the previous section on mocking the HTTP. It's good to repeat this, so let's add the necessary code to the unit test, like so:

```
it('should call the Http service with link /api/jedis/1', () => {
  .. rest of the test remains the same

  const jediService = TestBed.get(JediService);
  const http = TestBed.get(HttpTestingController);
  // fake response
  const expected = { name: 'Luke', id: 1 };
```

```
      let actual = {};
      http.expectOne('/api/jedis/1').flush(expected);

      ... rest of the test remains the same
    })
```

What we did here is to get a copy of our `JediService` by asking for it from the `TestBed.get()` method. Furthermore, we asked for an instance of the `HttpTestingController`. We move on by defining the expected data that we want to respond with, and we instruct the instance of the `HttpTestingController` that it should expect a call to `/api/jedis/1`, and when that happens then the expected data should be returned. So now we have a test that covers both the scenario of testing for the `ActivatedRoute` parameters, as well as the HTTP call. The full code of the test looks like the following:

```
import { Subject } from 'rxjs/Rx';
import { ActivatedRoute, convertToParamMap } from '@angular/router';
import { TestBed } from '@angular/core/testing';
import {
  HttpClientTestingModule,
  HttpTestingController
} from "@angular/common/http/testing";

import { JediService } from './jedi-service';
import { ExampleRoutingParamsComponent } from
'./example.routing.params.component';

class ActivatedRouteStub {
  subject: Subject<any>;
  constructor() {
    this.subject = new Subject();
  }

  sendParameters(params: {}) {
    const paramMap = convertToParamMap(params);
    this.subject.next( paramMap );
  }

  get paramMap() {
    return this.subject.asObservable();
  }
}

describe('A detail component', () => {
  let activatedRoute, fixture, component;

  beforeEach(async() => {
```

```
  TestBed.configureTestingModule({
    imports: [HttpClientTestingModule ],
    declarations: [ ExampleRoutingParamsComponent ],
    providers: [
      { provide: ActivatedRoute, useClass: ActivatedRouteStub },
      JediService
    ]
  });
})

beforeEach(() => {
  fixture = TestBed.createComponent(ExampleRoutingParamsComponent);
  component = fixture.componentInstance;
  activatedRoute = TestBed.get(ActivatedRoute);
});

it('should call the Http service with the route /api/jedis/1 and should
display the jedi name corresponding to the id number in the route', async()
=> {
  activatedRoute.paramMap.subscribe((para) => {
    const id = para.get('id');
    expect(id).toBe(1);
  });

  activatedRoute.sendParameters({ id : 1 });

  const http = TestBed.get(HttpTestingController);
  // fake response
  const expected = { name: 'Luke', id: 1 };
  let actual = {};

  http.expectOne('/api/jedis/1').flush(expected);
  fixture.detectChanges();

  fixture.whenStable().then(() => {
    expect(component.jedi.name).toBe('Luke');
  });
});
});
```

So what have we learned from testing route parameters? It is a bit more cumbersome as we need to create our `ActivatedRouteStub`, but all in all, it is quite straightforward.

Testing directives

The last leg of our journey into the world of unit testing Angular elements will cover directives. Directives will usually be quite straightforward in their overall shape, being pretty much components with no view attached. The fact that directives usually work with components gives us a very good idea of how to proceed when testing them.

A directive can be simple in the sense that it has no external dependencies. It looks something like this:

```
@Directive({
  selector: 'some-directive'
})
export class SomeDirective {
  someMethod() {}
}
```

Testing is easy, you just need to instantiate an object from the `SomeDirective` class. However, it is likely that your directive will have dependencies and in those cases, we need to test the directive implicitly through it being attached to the component. Let's have a look at such an example. Let's first define the directive, like so:

```
import {
  Directive,
  ElementRef,
  HostListener
} from '@angular/core';

@Directive({ selector: '[banana]' })
export class BananaDirective {
  constructor(private elementRef: ElementRef) { }

  @HostListener('mouseover') onMouseOver() {
    this.elementRef.nativeElement.style.color = 'yellow';
  }

  @HostListener('mouseout') onMouseOut() {
      this.elementRef.nativeElement.style.color = 'inherit';
  }
}
```

What you see here is a simple directive that shifts the font color to yellow if we hover over it. We need to attach it to a component. Let us define an element next, like so:

```
import { Component } from '@angular/core';

@Component({
  selector: 'banana',
  template: `
  <p class="banana" banana>hover me</p>
  `
})
export class BananaComponent {}
```

Here we can see that we added the element as an attribute to the p-tag that we defined in the components template.

Next, let's go over to our test. We now know how to write tests, and especially how to test elements, so the following test code should come as no surprise:

```
import { By } from '@angular/platform-browser';
import { TestBed } from "@angular/core/testing";
import { BananaComponent } from './banana.component';
import { BananaDirective } from './banana.directive';

describe('A banana directive', () => {
  beforeEach(() => {
    TestBed.configureTestingModule({
      declarations: [BananaDirective, BananaComponent]
    }).compileComponents();
  });

  it('should set color property to yellow when mouseover event happens', ()
=> {
    const fixture = TestBed.createComponent(BananaComponent);
    const element = fixture.debugElement.query(By.css('.banana'));
    element.triggerEventHandler('mouseover', null);
    fixture.detectChanges();

    expect(element.nativeElement.style.color).toBe('yellow');
  });
})
```

In the `beforeEach()` method, we talk to `TestBed` to configure our testing module and tell it about the `BananaDirective` as well as the `BananaComponent`, with this code:

```
beforeEach(() => {
  TestBed.configureTestingModule({
    declarations: [ BananaDirective, BananaComponent ]
  }).compileComponents();
});
```

In the test itself, we use `TestBed` yet again to create a component. Thereafter, we find our element by its CSS class. We find the element so that we are able to trigger an event, a `mouseover`. Triggering a `mouseover` event will trigger code in the directive that will make the font color yellow. With the event triggered, then we are able to assert the element's font color with this line:

```
expect(element.nativeElement.style.color).toBe('yellow');
```

Now, this is how simple it can be to test a directive, even if it has dependencies. The key takeaway is that if that is the case, you need an element to place the directive on, and that you implicitly test the directive through the element.

The road ahead

This last test example wraps up our journey into unit testing with Angular, but keep in mind that we have barely scratched the surface. Testing web applications in general, and Angular applications in particular, poses a myriad of scenarios that usually need a specific approach. Remember that if a specific test requires a cumbersome and convoluted solution, we are probably facing a good case for a module redesign instead.

Where should we go from here? There are several paths to compound our knowledge of web application testing in Angular and enable us to become great testing ninjas.

Introducing code coverage reports in your test stack

How can we know how far our tests go on testing the application? Are we sure we are not leaving any piece of code untested and if so, is it relevant? How can we detect the pieces of code that fall outside the scope of our current tests so we can better assess whether they are worth testing or not?

These concerns can be easily addressed by introducing code coverage reporting in our application tests stack. A code coverage tool aims to track down the scope of our unit testing layer and produce an educated report informing you of the overall reach of your test specs and what pieces of code still remain uncovered.

There are several tools for implementing code coverage analysis in our applications, the most popular ones at this time being Blanket (`http://blanketjs.org`) and Istanbul (`https://gotwarlost.github.io/istanbul`). In both cases, the installation process is pretty quick and easy.

Implementing E2E tests

In this chapter, we saw how we could test certain parts of the UI by evaluating the state of the DOM. This gives us a good idea of how things would look from the end user's point of view, but ultimately this is just an educated guess.

End-to-end (E2E) testing is a methodology for testing web applications using an automated agent that will programmatically follow the end user's flow from start to finish. Contrary to what unit testing poses, the nuances of the code implementation are not relevant here since E2E testing entails testing our application from start to finish from the user's endpoint. This approach allows us to test the application in an integrated way. While unit testing focuses on the reliability of each particular piece of the puzzle, E2E testing assesses the integrity of the puzzle as a whole, finding integration issues between components that are frequently overlooked by unit tests.

For the previous incarnation of the Angular framework, the Angular team built a powerful tool named Protractor (`http://www.protractortest.org/`), which is defined as follows:

> *"An end to end test runner which simulates user interactions that will help you verify the health of your Angular application."*

The tests syntax will become pretty familiar since it also uses Jasmine for putting together test specs. Unfortunately, E2E sits outside the scope of this book, but there are several resources you can rely on to expand your knowledge on the subject. In that sense, we recommend the book *Angular Test-Driven Development*, *Packt Publishing*, which provides broad insights on the use of Protractor to create E2E test suites for our Angular applications.

Summary

We are at the end of our journey, and it's definitely been a long but exciting one. In this chapter, you saw the importance of introducing unit testing in our Angular applications, the basic shape of a unit test, and the process of setting up Jasmine for our tests. You also saw how to code powerful tests for our components, directives, pipes, routes, and services. We also discussed new challenges in your path for mastering Angular. It is fair to say that there is still a long road ahead, and it is definitely an exciting one.

The end of this chapter is also the end of this book, but the experience continues beyond its boundaries. Angular is still a pretty young framework, and as such, all the great things that it will bring to the community are yet to be created. Hopefully, you will be one of those creators. If so, please let the authors know.

Thanks for taking the time to read this book.

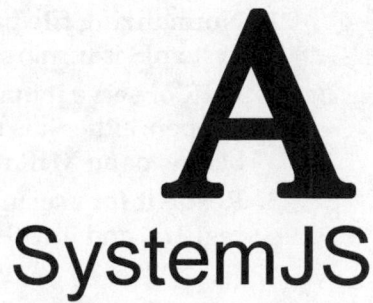

A
SystemJS

SystemJS is a module loader found at the following GitHub link `https://github.com/SystemJS/SystemJS`.

It is built on top of the original ES6 module loader polyfill. It's meant to solve the basic problem of loading modules in the browser, which currently doesn't work unless the browser gets some help from a library, such as SystemJS.

In this appendix, we will cover:

- The SystemJS itself
- A practical SystemJS example with the quickstart repository for Angular

SystemJS introduction

SystemJS loads the files from top to bottom, and thereafter instantiates from bottom to top. What does that mean, though? Well, it means that if you have a file you need to load called `Module1` that has a dependency on `Module2`, then `Module1` will be loaded first. So much for loading, then we have the part on executing the code that takes the reverse direction. In this case it will execute `Module2`, to get an instance of it and pass it to `Module1`.

A typical usage of SystemJS will look like the following:

```
System.import('./file.js').then( file => // do something )
```

There are different steps that SystemJS undertakes when processing a script:

1. **Normalizing file paths**: Paths can be relative, absolute, and aliased, and SystemJS is turning all those into one format
2. **XHR or serve it up**: When a module is asked for them, one of two things can happen; either it is loaded from the internal registry if it's already been preloaded before, or an XHR request is made for it
3. **Ready it for use**: In this last step, the module will be executed, added to the registry, and it will resolve its promise

A flying start with the quickstart repository

To get started with the `quickstart` repository, you need to grab a copy of that project by using the following command:

```
git clone https://github.com/angular/quickstart.git quickstart
```

This will copy down all the needed files from GitHub and place them in a directory called `quickstart`. Now, navigate into that directory:

```
cd quickstart
```

The project will have specified a bunch of libraries it is dependent on. You need to install these. That is accomplished by typing:

```
npm install
```

Lastly, we need to serve up the application, that is, display it in a browser. That is done by typing the following command:

```
npm start
```

Worth mentioning is that this repository uses SystemJS as a module loader and for bootstrapping our Angular application.

Understanding the parts

Being given a GitHub repository or using a scaffolder tool is great. You get started quickly, and you will feel productive almost instantly. There is a *but* to this, though. If something goes wrong, how do we fix it? To be able to do that, we need to have a better understanding of what's going on under the hood.

The essential concepts that makes out any Angular project set up with SystemJS

These are the concepts making up the core of your application. They will be there for every project:

- Starter web page
- **Node Package Manager** (**npm**)
- SystemJS
- TypeScript setup and TypeScript definition files
- Linting

Let's discuss these concepts to give an introduction to the set up.

All web projects will need a starter web page.

Node.js is JavaScript on the server side. In the context of an *Angular build*, Node.js is used to pull in a lot of libraries (from npm) to help with tasks such as bundling, testing, and minification. It is essential to have at least a decent grasp on how to work with Node.js and its echo system. A more detailed description of this follows in a following subsection.

As for SystemJS, it is a module bundler. Projects in JavaScript aren't written in just one file any more; sometimes, they're written in 1,000s of files. How these files relate to one another is by using a module system, and SystemJS is one of many module bundlers out there. The Angular team has chosen TypeScript as the *lingua franca* for writing Angular apps, which means we need to set up TypeScript properly in terms of compiling it and make sure TypeScript knows how to consume dependent libraries written in ES5.

Lastly, linting is about ensuring we follow best practices when it comes to writing our code, both for consistency and to avoid bugs.

Now, let's dive into these concepts in detail.

Starter web page - index.html

The purpose of this file is to be presented to the web server, which ultimately renders it into an app. It will contain some markup, but, most importantly, the `script` tags needed for our app to run.

The `index.html` also consists of a lot of `script` tags. These `script` tags are needed for your project to run.

Core files - that Angular is dependent on

A lot of browsers out there lack some capabilities that come with ES2015. To fix that, we can augment our browser with this missing functionality by adding something called a polyfill. Aside from polyfills to leverage modern JavaScript, Angular is using a whole new way of detecting changes in the app and does so by using the `zone.js` library. Lastly, the Angular teams have decided to use Rxjs for handling HTTP requests. They have even taken it one step further to integrate it into a lot of things, such as dealing with forms and routing. These three things are what make up the core functionality that we need to import for our app to work.

core-js

This file brings ES2015 capabilities to ES5 browsers. As you will be using quite a few ES2015 constructs, this is necessary for everything to work:

```
<script scr="node_modules/core-js/client/shim.min.js"></script>
```

zone.js

This file is used by Angular to handle change detection and data binding, without this library nothing would work:

```
<script scr="node_modules/zone.js/dist/zone.js"></script>
```

rxjs

RxJS is the async library that Angular uses heavily to deal with everything from HTTP requests to forms and routing.

SystemJS - our module loader

SystemJS is the library you are using to handle the loading of modules and consists of two links:

- SystemJS core files
- SystemJS configuration file

The former is needed for SystemJS to run and the latter is you instructing SystemJS what files to load and where to find your app and accompanying assets.

This points out the core SystemJS file:

```
<script src="node_modules/SystemJS/dist/system.scr.js"></script>
```

And this points out how to configure SystemJS. You need to call this
file SystemJS.config.js:

```
<script src="SystemJS.config.js"></script>
```

A look at SystemJS.config.js shows the following configuration call being made:

```
System.config({
  paths: {
  // paths serve as alias
  'npm:': 'node_modules/'
  },
  // map tells the System loader where to look for things
  map: {
    // our app is within the app folder
    'app': 'app',
    // angular bundles
    '@angular/core': 'npm:@angular/core/bundles/core.umd.js',
    '@angular/common': 'npm:@angular/common/bundles/common.umd.js',
    '@angular/compiler': 'npm:@angular/compiler/bundles/compiler.umd.js',
    '@angular/platform-browser': 'npm:@angular/platform-
browser/bundles/platform-browser.umd.js',
    '@angular/platform-browser-dynamic': 'npm:@angular/platform-browser-
dynamic/bundles/platform-browser-dynamic.umd.js',
    '@angular/http': 'npm:@angular/http/bundles/http.umd.js',
    '@angular/router': 'npm:@angular/router/bundles/router.umd.js',
    '@angular/forms': 'npm:@angular/forms/bundles/forms.umd.js',
    // other libraries
    'rxjs': 'npm:rxjs',
    'angular-in-memory-web-api': 'npm:angular-in-memory-web-api/bundles/in-
memory-web-api.umd.js'
  },
  // packages tells the System loader how to load when no filename and/or
no extension
  packages: {
    app: {
      defaultExtension: 'js',
      meta: {
        './*.js': {
          loader: 'SystemJS-angular-loader.js'
        }
      }
    },
    rxjs: {
```

```
        defaultExtension: 'js'
    }
  }
});
```

It looks quite long and daunting, but let's break the different parts down which is as follows:

- `paths`: Alias where system files are located. Noteworthy here is that we create an alias to `node_modules` by typing:

  ```
  path: { 'npm:': 'node_modules/'}
  ```

  This will serve us later when we need to mention all the libraries that our app needs to function.

- `map`: This is where we need to tell SystemJS where it can find all the parts.

  The following code snippets show the following:

  - Where to find our app, the key called app
  - Where to find the Angular files, key called `@angular/...`
  - Where to find supporting libraries, these libraries consist of angular libraries (the framework is split up in many smaller libraries) as well as the core libraries mentioned in the last section

  ```
      map : {
        app : app,  // instruct that our app can be found in the app
  directory
        '@angular/core': 'npm:@angular/core/bundles/core.umd.js'
        // supporting libraries omitted for brevity
      }
  ```

  Here, we can see our alias `npm` in use when referring to `@angular/core`, which means the following:

  ```
  'npm: @angular/core/bundles/core.umd.js'
  ```

  Is using the following full path:

  ```
  'node_modules/@angular/core/bundles/core.umd.js'
  ```

- `packages`: It is the last part of the configuration file. This instructs what files in the app folder should be loaded first, aka `main`, and also provides the `defaultExtension`.

Node.js setup - package.json

A `package.json` is a description file for a Node.js project. It consists of metadata information such as name, author, and description, but it also contains a `script` property that will allow us to run scripts that carry out work for us, such as:

- Creating a bundle
- Running tests
- Performing linting

To run one of the commands in the `script` tag, you need to type:

```
npm run <command>
```

Your app will depend on a number of libraries to build and run. Libraries listed in either `dependencies` or `devDependencies` will be downloaded using npm, by you typing `npm install`.

There is a semantic difference between what libraries should be listed in `dependencies` and `devDependencies`, respectively. Anything that will help make the app ultimately run will end up in `dependencies`, Angular libraries, as well as supporting libraries, will end up here. `devDependencies` is somewhat different, though; what you put here is more of a supportive nature. Examples are TypeScript, Linter, testing libraries, and different tools used to process CSS and create the bundle itself.

As for the angular bits in the `dependencies`, these are pure Angular dependencies denoted with `@angular`:

- `@angular/common`
- `@angular/compiler`
- `@angular/core`
- `@angular/forms`
- `@angular/http`
- `@angular/platform-browser`
- `@angular/platform-browser-dynamic`
- `@angular/router`

The remaining dependencies are the following list, which we mentioned under *Core files - that Angular is dependent on* in this section:

- `core-js`
- `reflect-metadata.js`
- `rxjs`
- `system.js`
- `zone.js`

TypeScript setup

A `tsconfig.json` is a file the TypeScript compiler will process and determine how compilation should happen.

The following are the essential settings:

```
target: 'es5',
module : 'commonjs',
emitDecoratorMetadata : true, // needed for compilation to work
experimentalDecorators : true // needed for compilation to work
```

As mentioned in the preceding code comments, `emitDecoratorMetadata` and `experimentalDecorators` need to be set to `true`, as Angular uses these features heavily.

Summary

This appendix introduced SystemJS and described how it processes files and in what order, due to it being a module loader. Thereafter, the official quickstart repo was introduced. We then looked at the different parts that SystemJS either needed or problems it needed to solve. At this point, we were ready to dive into how to use SystemJS to set up an Angular application. We also looked at what core parts the Angular framework needed the SystemJs to load and in what order. Leaving this appendix, we now have a clearer understanding of what problems SystemJS solves and how it can be made to set up Angular applications. It should be noted that most Angular applications are using Angular CLI or webpack, but this is definitely a good option that will be supported for some time.

B
Webpack with Angular

Webpack is a module bundler. It is able to bundle together different assets such as JavaScript, CSS, and HTML. The webpack is quite popular and is becoming the preferred way of setting up your app. In the world of frontend though, things come and go at a high rate. This makes it important to understand what problem needs solving, rather than the technical details of a specific bundler tool.

In this appendix, you will:

- Discover the important concepts in webpack
- Learn how to use webpack in a simple web project
- Utilize webpack to set up an Angular project

Core concepts

Essentially, webpack tries to create a graph of dependencies by crawling all the import statements in your files. Imagine you have the following code snippet:

```
//main.js
import { Lib } from './lib';
Lib.doStuff)() // lib.js

//lib.js
import { OtherLib } from './otherlib'
OtherLib.doStuff()
```

In this case, it would deduce that `main.js` is dependent on `lib.js`, which is dependent on `otherlib.js`, thereby creating a chain of dependencies.

The end result from crawling all the import statements and figuring out all dependencies is to produce a bundle that you can make part of your `index.html` and present to the browser for rendering.

Loaders

The webpack needs a loader to understand a certain file extension and operate on it. By extension we mean `.ts`, `.js`, `.html`, and so on. Why do we care? When it comes to setup, we need to ensure that the proper loaders have been set up so that a certain file extension that we care about will be processed. In webpack, when you want to handle extensions you set up rules. A rule can look like this:

```
rules: [{
  test: /\.blaha$/,
  use: 'blaha-loader'
}]
```

The `test` property is a regex where you specify what file extensions to look for.

The `loader` property is where you specify the name of your loader. The webpack comes built-in with a lot of loaders, but it's also possible to download it, should you need it.

Plugins

A plugin can fire at different steps in the build process. This means you can carry out extra work at a certain step. To use a plugin, you specify it in the `plugins` property, like so:

```
plugins: [new MyAwesomePlugin()]
```

Before we venture into an Angular webpack setup, let us first establish what we've learned so far. The webpack is able to deal with JavaScript, CSS, TypeScript, and more, and create bundles that we can include in our starter HTML file, usually called `index.html`. Furthermore, if configured through a `config` file, we can set up a number of rules. Each rule consists of a regular expression that will capture all files of a certain file ending and will point to a loader that will process the captured files. There are also things called plugins, which are able to give us further functionality at specific life cycle steps. It would, however, be nice if we put that knowledge into practice, so let's do that in the next section.

Webpack - first project

To prepare us properly for setting up an Angular project, let's first go through a simple project that showcases all the common scenarios that we will be using to set up Angular.

First off, we need to install webpack. This is accomplished by running the following command:

```
npm install webpack -g
```

After successful installation, it's time to try it out. First off, let's create a few files with the following content:

```
//index.html
<html></html>

//app.js
var math = require('./mathAdd');
console.log('expect 1 and 2 to equal 3, actual =', math(1,2));

//mathAdd.js
module.exports = function(first, second){
  return first + second;
}
```

Run the following command:

```
webpack ./app.js bundle.js
```

This will crawl all dependencies starting with app.js and create a bundle.js file from them. To use said bundle.js, add a script tag to index.html so it now looks as follows:

```
<html>
  <script src="bundle.js"></script>
</html>
```

To see your app in a browser, you need a web server that can host your files. There are many small, lightweight web servers; Python comes with one, for example. I am going to recommend one called http-server. It can easily be installed by typing the following in the Terminal:

```
npm install http-server -g
```

After it is installed, place yourself in the same directory as the `index.html` file and invoke the web server by typing the following:

```
http-server -p 5000
```

Navigate to `http://localhost:5000` in your browser and open up `devtools`; the following should be displayed:

```
expect 1 and 2 to equal 3, actual = 3
```

Congratulations, you have successfully created your first webpack bundle and you have a working app.

Improving our project - using a configuration file

It was nice and all to be able to create a bundle that easily, but it wasn't really realistic. Most webpack projects will be using a `config` file instead of invoking webpack on the command line. So let's do that: let's create a `config` file called `Webpack.config.js` and add the following code to it:

```
//webpack.config.js
module.exports =
{
  entry: "./app.js",
  output: { filename : "bundle.js" }
}
```

This essentially recreates what we wrote on the command line, that is, start with `app.js` and ensure that the resulting bundle is called `bundle.js`.

Now type `webpack` on the command line.

Fire up your app again and ensure that everything still works. Success! We have moved from the command line to the config file.

However, we don't want to have to type `webpack` in the Terminal all the time. What we want is for the bundle to be rebuilt when we change something, so let's add that functionality:

```
module.exports = {
  entry: "./app.js",
  output: { filename : "bundle.js" },
  watch: true
}
```

Note the extra property, `watch`.

Entering `webpack` in the Terminal at this point will now lead to the webpack process not actually quitting, like it did before, but still running and waiting for us to make a change.

Let's, as an example, change what the `app.js` does to the following:

```
var math = require('./mathAdd');
console.log('expect 1 and 2 to equal 3, actual =', math(1,2));
```

Save the file and note how the bundle is being rebuilt in the Terminal. That's great, but we can do even better. We can add a web server that automatically launches and relaunches our app upon changes. I am talking about something called **hot reloading**. Essentially, a change is made to the code, the bundle is recreated, and the browser reflects said change. We need to do two things for this to happen:

- Install an HTTP server utility that works well with webpack

- Enable hot reloading in the `config` file

To install the webpack HTTP server utility, we type the following:

```
npm install webpack-dev-server -g
```

Let's now update the `config` file to the following:

```
var webpack = require('webpack');

module.export = {
  entry: './app.js',
  output: { filename : 'bundle.js' },
  watch: true,
  plugins: [new Webpack.HotModuleReplacementPlugin()]
}
```

Two things have been added. Here is the first:

```
var webpack = require('Webpack');
```

Here is the second:

```
plugins: [new Webpack.HotModuleReplacementPlugin()]
```

We have added a hot reload plugin. Fire up the app using the following command:

```
webpack-dev-server
```

This now leads to the web server listening for changes; it will rebuild the bundle if a change happens, and will display said change in the web browser.

Adding more capabilities to our project

There are more interesting things we can do in a modern web app project. One such thing is to be able to use all the latest ES2015 features, as well as being able to split our bundle into more dedicated bundles, such as one for the application and one for third-party libraries. webpack supports both these things with ease.

Creating several bundles

There are multiple reasons why you would want several bundles for your application. It might be that you have several pages and you don't want each page to load a heavy bundle, but only the JavaScript that it needs. You might also want to separate third-party libraries from the app itself. Let's try to look at how we could create several bundles.

Our ideal scenario is that we want three different files, `app.js`, `init.js`, and `vendor.js`:

- `app.js`: This is where our application lives

- `init.js`: This should contain what the bundles have in common, that is, our webpack runtime

- `vendor.js`: This is where the third-party libraries we are dependent on live, such as `query` and `lodash`

To accomplish this, we need to change the configuration file to say the following:

```
module.exports = {
  entry : {
    app: "./app.js",
    vendor: ["angular"]
  },
  output: { filename : "[name].js" },
  watch: true,
  plugins: [
    new Webpack.HotModuleReplacementPlugin(),
    new Webpack.optimize.CommonsChunkPlugin("init")
  ]
}
```

Let's break that down:

```
entry: {
  app: "./app.js",
  vendor: ["angular"]
}
```

We used to have one entry here pointing to `app.js`. Now we want to have two entries, but for different things. Vendor points to an array of libraries. This means that when webpack sees `a:require('angular')`, it knows to place the `node_modules/angular` library in the `vendor.js`, that it will create.

The second piece of interest is:

```
plugins: [ new Webpack.optimize.CommonsChunkPlugin('init') ]
```

Here we are saying to take everything we have in common (the webpack runtime in this case) and place it in `init.js`.

Setting up Angular with webpack

Armed with knowledge of webpack's core concepts and how to add extra capabilities, we should now feel ready to take on bootstrapping an Angular project. First off, create the following files:

- `webpack`: When setting up webpack, it's usually a good idea to set up your config to consist of the following three files:
    - `webpack.common.js`: This is where most of the configuration will happen
    - `webpack.dev.js`: This is the `dev` environment-specific configuration
    - `webpack.prod.js`: This is the `prod` environment-specific configuration
- `package.json`: This file will list what libraries we are dependent on for Angular to be properly bootstrapped. This is listed in `devDependencies` and `depedencies`. We will also list some commands in the script that allow us to fire up the application, so it can be run on a web server. We will furthermore create commands for testing and a command for creating a production bundle.

- `tsconfig.json`: This file is meant for the TypeScript compiler. It is worth noting that we want to enable certain functionalities for the app to work, such as `emitDecoratorMetadata` and `experimentalDecorators`.

Common configuration

A brief overview of this file looks like this:

- `Entry`, the entry points of the application
- `Module.rules`, an object that specifies how certain files should be loaded, with what loader
- `Plugins`, an array of plugins that give us extra functionality during the life cycle of webpack

The `entry` session specifies that there will be three different bundles: `polyfills`, `vendor`, and `app`. Why these three bundles, you might ask? Well, to have a separate bundle for `polyfills` makes sense as it is a separate concept from the others.
The `polyfills` bundle ensures our selected browser has all the latest features from ES2015. The `vendor` bundle is where we place all the libraries that are considered helpers to our app, but not really the app itself. The `app` bundle is really where our app lives; it contains our business code.

The following code snippet shows what the configuration should look like to create the three previously-mentioned bundles:

```
entry : {
  'polyfills': './src/polyfills.ts',
  'vendor': './src/vendor.ts',
  'app': './src/main.ts'
}
```

The `module` section defines a list of rules. Just as a reminder, rules are about processing certain file extensions. Every rule consists of a `test` property that defines what file extension to look for. It also consists of the `loader` property, which points to loaders capable of processing said file extensions. For example, if the file extension is `.sass`, the loader is capable of compiling the Sass into a CSS file.

The following code snippet exemplifies how a rule can be set up to handle HTML files:

```
module : {
  rules : [
    {
      test: /\.HTML$/,
      loader: 'HTML-loader'
    }
    // other rules emitted for brevity
  ]
}
```

We can see that a regular expression tests for the `.html` extension and lets `HTML-loader` handle it. The complete rules list for our project should set up rules for handling TypeScript, assets (images), CSS, and HTML. If we have all that, we are good to go.

We also need to enhance the building process by setting up some plugins, namely:

- `ContextReplacementPlugin`
- `CommonChunksPlugin`
- `HTMLWebpackPlugin`

The job of `ContextReplacementPlugin` is to replace one context for another. But what does that even mean? The most common use case is using `require` statements that are dynamic, like so:

```
require('directory/' + name + '.js')
```

At compile time, webpack is unable to figure out what files to include. To ensure it will work at runtime, it includes everything in that directory. A common case is dealing with translation files. You might have hundreds of files in such a directory, and having all those files included will make the bundle unnecessarily big. So what you do is use said plugin and give it a filter parameter that narrows down the number of files, like so:

```
new Webpack.ContextReplacementPlugin(
  /directory\//, //when trying to resolve a file from this directory
  /(sv-SE|se).js // narrow down the search by only including files
                 that match this
)
```

The `CommonChunksPlugin` is used when you are trying to create several bundle files, like so:

```
entry : {
  'polyfills': './src/polyfills.ts',
  'vendor': './src/vendor.ts',
  'app': './src/main.ts'
}
```

To avoid that, every single bundle contains the webpack runtime and other common parts; the mentioned plugin can be used to extract the common parts. There are many ways to call this plugin; here is one:

```
plugins: [ new Webpack.optimize.CommonsChunkPlugin('init') ]
```

This will create an `init.js` file.

The webpack generates a lot of files, such as HTML and JavaScript files. You could link to all those files in your `index.html`, but that becomes quite cumbersome. A better way to handle this is to use `HTMLWebpackPlugin`, which will inject these `link` and `script` tags for you.

Without this plugin, your `index.html` would look something like this:

```
<link href="app.css"></link>
<script src="app.bundle.js"></script>
<script src="page1.bundle.js"></script>
<script src="page2.bundle.js"></script>
<script src="common.bundle.js"></script>
```

You get the idea, using this plugin is pretty much a must, at least if you want to make sure to keep `index.html` in sync with your solution and avoid unnecessary typing by having to add/alter script tags.

What we need to do to make this plugin work is to point to where the `script` and `link` tags need to be injected, like so:

```
new HtmlWebpackPlugin({
  template: 'src/index.HTML'
})
```

So far, we have covered what bundles are created, what rules need to be set up to handle all different file extensions, and lastly what plugins are needed. This is the core of the webpack setup. However, the configuration needs to differ a bit depending on whether we are dealing with a development environment or a production environment.

Dev configuration

The webpack treats your files differently in development mode from production mode. For one, your JavaScript files are all in-memory, that is, no files are actually written to the output directory, as specified here:

```
output: {
  path: helpers.root('dist')
  // other config is omitted
}
```

In development environments, we care about setting up source maps. Source maps remember what the file structure used to look like, before everything was concatenated into one or more bundles. It makes for easier debugging when the files resemble your project structure in your IDE. One way to set up source maps is to type the following:

```
devtool: 'cheap-module-eval-source-map'
```

Production configuration

In a production configuration, it's important to set up minification by using the UglifyJS plugin. It's important because we want our app to be as small as possible so it loads quickly. More of our users will probably be on a 3G connection, so we need to cater to all types of users:

```
new Webpack.optimize.UglifyJsPlugin({
  mangle: { keep_fnames : true } // keep file names
})
```

Testing

Any developer worth their salt should care about writing tests. Testing is not that hard to set up.

We need the following file to make testing work:

- `karma.conf.js`: We are using karma as a test runner. This needs a `config` file that sets up where to find the tests, whether to run our tests in a headless browser or a real one, and lots of other things.

The noteworthy `config` needed in this file is:

```
preprocessors: {
  './karma-test-shim.js': ['Webpack', 'sourcemap']
}
```

The preprocessing step is needed so that it compiles our TypeScript files into ES5 JavaScript. It will also set up proper source maps, as well as point out what files are needed from the Angular framework for our tests to run properly.

Another property worth mentioning is:

```
var WebpackConfig = require('./webpack.test');
module.exports = function(config) {
  var _config = {
    Webpack : WebpackConfig
  }

  // other config omitted
  config.set(_config);
}
```

This points to config specified in the `Webpack.test.js` file.

- `webpack.test.js`: This is just a copy of `Webpack.common.js`, normal config. However, by making it into a separate file, we have the ability to override certain configs later should we wish to.
- `karma-test-shim.js`: This file, as mentioned before, is responsible for importing all parts of the Angular framework that are needed to run, core parts of the framework, as well as dedicated parts related to testing. The full file looks as follows:

```
Error.stackTraceLimit = Infinity;

require('core-js/es6');
require('core-js/es7/reflect');
require('zone.js/dist/zone');
require('zone.js/dist/long-stack-trace-zone');
require('zone.js/dist/proxy');
require('zone.js/dist/sync-test');
require('zone.js/dist/jasmine-patch');
require('zone.js/dist/async-test');
require('zone.js/dist/fake-async-test');

var appContext = require.context('./src', true, /\.spec\.ts/);
appContext.keys().forEach(appContext);
```

```
var testing = require('@angular/core/testing');
var browser = require('@angular/platform-browser-dynamic/testing');

testing.TestBed.initTestEnvironment(
  browser.BrowserDynamicTestingModule,
  browser.platformBrowserDynamicTesting()
);
```

It is worth nothing the following line:

```
var appContext = require.context('./scr, true, /\.spec\.ts/');
```

This defines what it looks for when trying to locate what tests to run. So, let's create a test that matches this pattern, `test.spec.ts`, under the `src` directory:

```
describe('should return true', () => {
  it('true is true', () => expect(true).toBe(true) );
});
```

With all this set up correctly, you should be able to type:

npm run test

This should start up the Chrome browser. You should see the following:

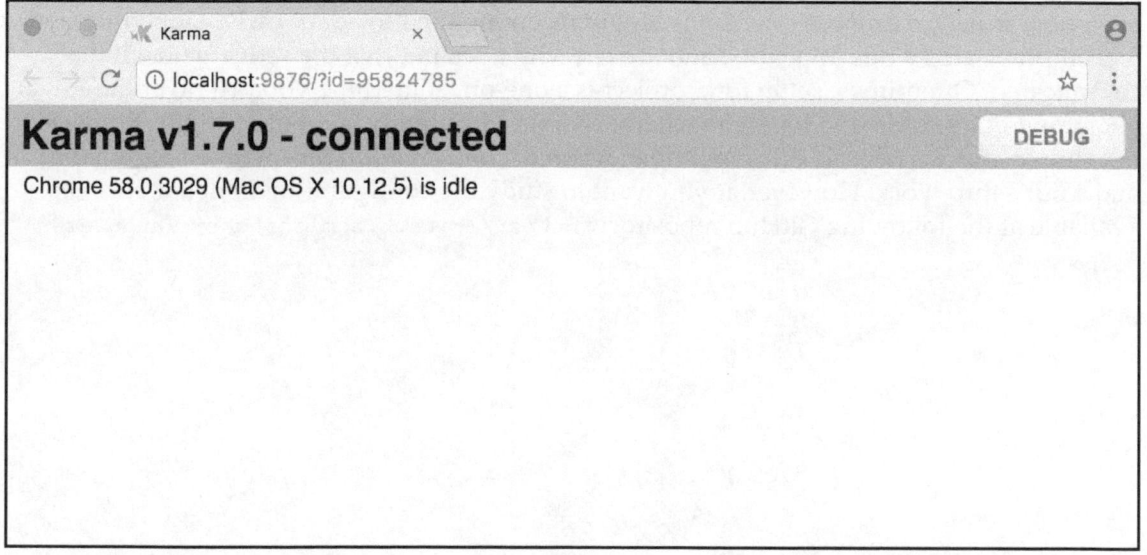

Pressing the **debug** button will show the following screen, where it clearly indicates that it is running our test and the result, which is a passing test:

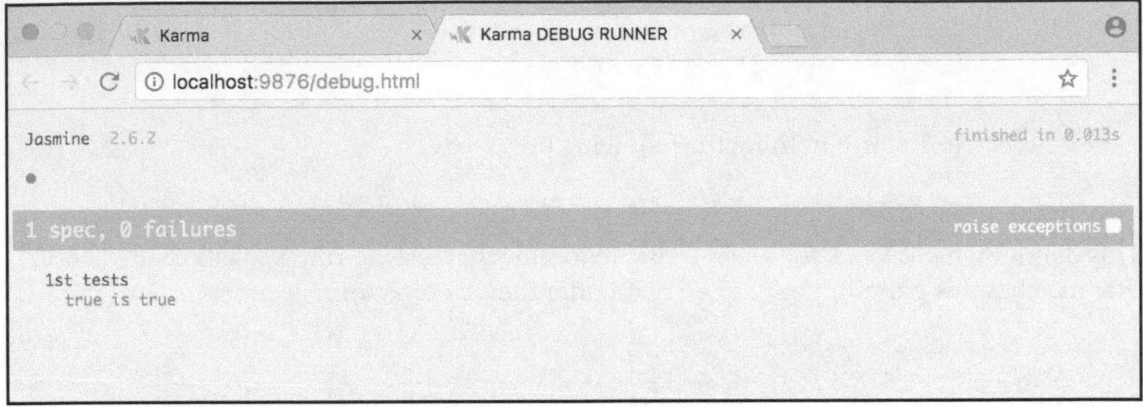

Summary

This appendix has described how webpack works in conjunction with Angular. Furthermore, we have explored the parts related to setting up an Angular application, and even how to set up unit tests, which is highly recommended to adapt early. Hopefully you feel empowered by this appendix, and are left with a feeling that the setup is not all that complicated. Oftentimes, setup for a project is a one-off, something you just do at the beginning of a project and barely touch afterwards. For brevity, a lot of configuration was not shown and we instead discussed how different configuration files worked together to make our setup work. However, if you want to study the configuration in detail, it is available at the following GitHub repository: `https://github.com/softchris/angular4-Webpack`.

Index

used, for organizing applications 73

N

named outlet 278, 279, 280
navigation, Angular Material components
  menu 333, 334, 335
ngFor directive
  advanced looping 101, 102
NgModule
  using 149
Node.js setup 413, 414
Node.js
  URL, for installing 13

O

Observable data
  serving, through HTTP 207

P

package.json 413
parameter decorator
  about 72, 73
  parameters 72
parameters
  data, filtering query parameters used 275
  detail pages, building route parameters used
    272, 273, 274, 275
  handling 271
patchValue
  about 308
  used, for updating component form model 307
percent pipe 109
pipe
  about 385
  async pipe 113
  currency pipe 106, 109
  date pipe 110
  decimal pipe 106
  i18n pipes 112
  JSON pipe 111
  lowercase pipe 106
  naming convention 142
  percent pipe 106, 109
  slice pipe 110
  testing 385

uppercase pipe 106
  used, for manipulating template bindings 105
plain vanilla CSS
  used, for creating animations 354
popups and modals, Angular Material components
  dialog 339, 340, 341
  dialog, example 341, 342
property decorators
  about 68, 69
  parameters 68
Protractor
  URL 405

Q

quickstart repository 408

R

reactive forms
  about 301
  AbstractControl 302
  component form model, updating with
    patchValue 307
  component form model, updating with setValue
    307
  controls, adding with validation rules 305
  creation, cleaning 308, 311
  custom validator, building 311
  dynamic approach 302, 303
  FormBuilder 308, 311
  programmatic approach 302, 303
  refactoring 306
  state changes, viewing 312
  turning, into dynamic form 303, 304, 305
reactive functional programming
  about 196, 197
  RxJS library, using 199, 200
reusable animation directive
  creating 365
rich composition 198
router module
  importing 262, 263
  setting up 262, 263
router service
  component, building for demonstration purposes
    265, 266, 267

CPSIA information can be obtained
at www.ICGtesting.com
Printed in the USA
LVHW01s2308210218
567519LV00003B/92/P